PROTECTING PARADISE

1. ENTRANCES.—Automobiles and motorcycles may enter and leave the park by any of the entrances, viz., Tioga Pass, Aspen Valley, Crane Flat, Merced Grove, El Portal, Wawona, and Mariposa Grove.

2. AUTOMOBILES.—The park is open to automobiles operated for pleasure, but not to those carrying passengers who are paying, either directly or indirectly, for the use of machines (excepting, however, automobiles used by park concessioners.)

Careful driving is demanded of all persons using the roads.

The Government is in no way responsible for any kind of accident.

3. MOTORCYCLES.—Motorcycles are admitted to the park under the same conditions as automobiles and are subject to the same regulations, as far as they are applicable. Automobiles and horse-drawn vehicles shall have the right of way over motorcycles.

4. ROADS.—The Tioga Road is open from July 15 to September 30, the Big Oak Flat Road from May 15 to November 1, and the Wawona Road from May 1 to November 1.

The El Portal and Valley Roads are open all the year, except occasionally during the winter, when the Valley roads may be blocked with snow for short periods. These cases are rare, however, as the roads are cleared promptly after snow storms.

On the Big Oak Flat Road between Gentry (station No. 2) and Floor of Valley (station No. 1) 4 miles, and on Wawona Road between Inspiration Point (station No. 3) and Floor of Valley (station No. 4) 2½ miles, automobiles may go east, down grade, only on the odd hours, speed not to exceed 8 miles per hour; and may go west, up grade, only on the even hours, speed not to exceed 12 miles per hour. They must travel between stations No. 1 and No. 2 on Big Oak Flat Road within the hour but in not less than 25 minutes, and between stations No. 3 and No. 4 on Wawona Road within the hour but in not less than 18 minutes.

5. SPEEDS.—Speed is li
8 miles per hour descendi
curves. On good roads wi
in nearer than 200 yards th
hour. When passing any g
crossing bridges, speed sha
per hour.

6. HORNS.—The horn w
stretches of road concealed
overhanging trees, or other
other machines, riding or d

7. LIGHTS.—All autom
tail lights, the headlights
safety in driving at night, a
sunset when automobile i
dimmed when meeting other

8. MUFFLER CUT-OU
Valley roads or while app
drawn vehicles, hotels, cam

—LEGEND—

⑥ Free Public Camp

Note.

Complaints and requ
further local infor
should be addressed
Office of the Sup
dent, Yosemite, Cali

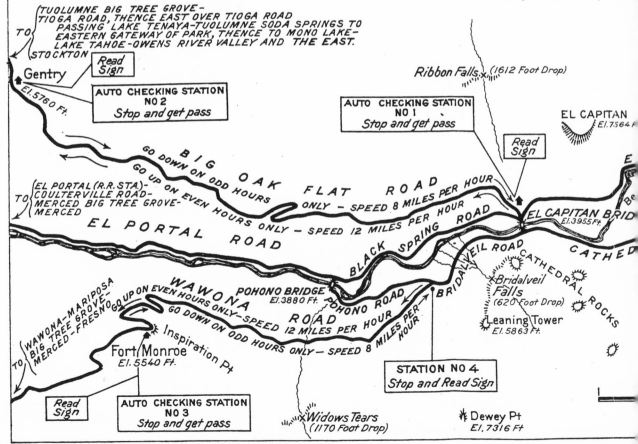

miles per hour ascending and
and when approaching sharp
stretches and when no team
y be increased to 20 miles per
ple or through the village and
ed to not exceeding 10 miles

ded on approaching curves or
nsiderable distance by slopes,
and before meeting or passing
als, or pedestrians.

t be equipped with head and
sufficient brilliancy to insure
ts must be kept lighted after
roads. Headlights must be
es or horse-drawn vehicles.

r cut-outs must be closed on
passing riding horses, horse-
king stations.

9. ACCIDENTS; STOPOVERS.—If, because of accident or stop for any reason, automobiles are unable to keep going they must be immediately parked off the road, or, where this is impossible, on the outer edge of the road. If on a one-way road, the automobile must wait where parked for the next hour schedule going in its direction of travel. If for any reason the automobile is stopped on the floor of Yosemite Valley it must be parked off on the right-hand edge of the road.

10. FINES AND PENALTIES.—Violation of any of the foregoing regulations will be punishable by revocation of automobile permit or by immediate ejectment from the park, or by a fine of not to exceed $500; or by any combination of the three, and be cause for refusal to issue new automobile permit to the owner without prior sanction in writing from the Director of the National Park Service.

11. GARAGE.—In Yosemite Valley, automobiles may be housed free of charge at Camp Curry, Yosemite Falls Camp, and other camps of this character. The garage operated by the Yosemite National Park Company is equipped for the housing of automobiles, as well as general repair work, parts, supplies, etc., at prices regulated by the Service.

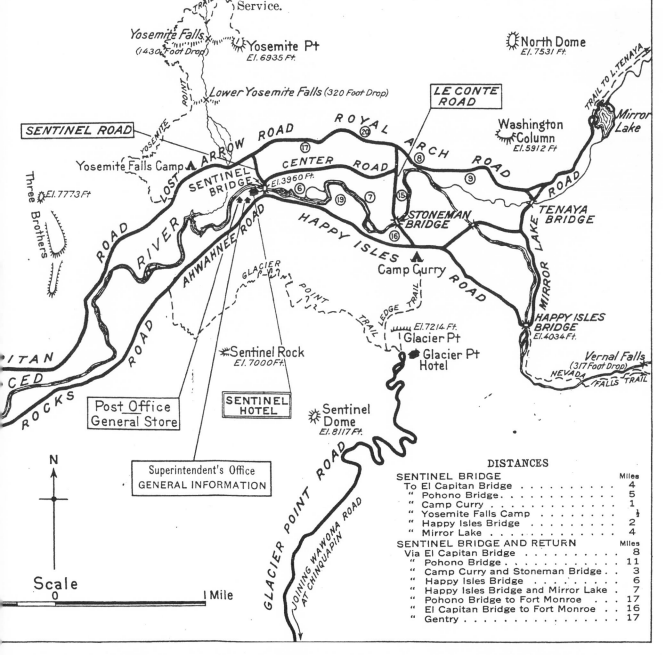

DISTANCES	
SENTINEL BRIDGE	Miles
To El Capitan Bridge	4
" Pohono Bridge	5
" Camp Curry	1
" Yosemite Falls Camp	½
" Happy Isles Bridge	2
" Mirror Lake	4
SENTINEL BRIDGE AND RETURN	Miles
Via El Capitan Bridge	8
" Pohono Bridge	11
" Camp Curry and Stoneman Bridge	3
" Happy Isles Bridge	6
" Happy Isles Bridge and Mirror Lake	7
" Pohono Bridge to Fort Monroe	17
" El Capitan Bridge to Fort Monroe	16
" Gentry	17

Scale
0   1 Mile

Other Books by Shirley Sargent

Pioneers in Petticoats, 1966
John Muir in Yosemite, 1971
Yosemite and Its Innkeepers, 1975
Yosemite's Historic Wawona, 1979
Galen Clark: Yosemite Guardian, 1981
Dear Papa. Letters Between John Muir and His Daughter Wanda, 1985
Yosemite, A National Treasure, 1988
Solomons of the Sierra: The Pioneer of the John Muir Trail, 1989
Yosemite Tomboy, 1967; revised edition 1994
Enchanted Childhoods: Growing Up In Yosemite, 1864–1945, 1993

Books edited by Shirley Sargent

Mother Lode Narratives, 1970; revised edition 1994
      by Jessie Benton Fremont
A Summer of Travel in the High Sierra, 1972
      by Joseph N. LeConte
A Western Journey With Mr. Emerson, 1980
      by James Brantley Thayer
Seeking The Elephant, 1849, 1980
      by James M. Hutchings

PROTECTING PARADISE

Yosemite Rangers
1898–1960

Shirley Sargent

Ponderosa Press
Yosemite, California

Cover design by Larry Van Dyke

Manufactured in the United States of America

Publisher's Cataloging-in-Publication
(Provided by Quality Books, Inc.)

Sargent, Shirley
    Protecting paradise : Yosemite rangers, 1898–1960 /
Shirley Sargent. — 1st ed.
      p.   cm.
    Includes bibliographical references and index.
    Preassigned LCCN: 98–66429
    ISBN: 0–9642244–1–0 (pbk)
    ISBN: 0–9642244–3–7 (hardcover)

    1. Park rangers—California—Yosemite National Park.
2. Yosemite National Park (Calif.)—History 3. United States
National Park Service—Officials and employees. I. Title

SB481.5.S37 1998   333.78′3′092
                                         QBI98–734

Ponderosa Press
P.O. Box 278
Yosemite, CA 95389

Write for free catalog

Contents

Foreword

Who has written more about Yosemite than Shirley Sargent? Her contributions range far and wide: fiction loosely based on her own enchanted childhood in Yosemite; stories of people—Muir, Hutchings, Clark, Solomons, Lukens; the "pioneers in petticoats" and famous guests; the history of concessioners; histories of Yosemite locales such as Wawona and Foresta; histories of buildings such as Camp Curry, the High Sierra Camps, and the Ahwahnee Hotel. The more widely she has written, the more widely she has come to be known and loved. Shirley's books have introduced many people to Yosemite's past. Her enthusiasm for her subject is contagious.

In this, her latest book, Shirley turns her mind to a new subject—the history of rangers in Yosemite. Her good friend Horace Albright had much earlier written a humorous book, *Oh, Ranger!"* Later, *retired ranger John Bingaman wrote Guardians of the Yosemite, A Story of the First Rangers*, which is part reminiscence, part autobiography, and part history. In the decades since Bingaman's book was published, its value has grown as a record of activity about which little has been written. The absence of other such books has made clear the need for revision and expansion of what Bingaman so ably began.

There are few diaries regarding Yosemite lives and activities. Shirley has worked hard to get around this problem by dredging up the written records of past rangers, and has encouraged retired rangers or their families to write or record their stories. She has delved into ranger family scrapbooks and photograph albums to piece together a cohesive story, always grounded in their personal experiences. And thus Shirley has become the collector, compiler, editor, and historian of the lives of Yosemite rangers over a period of more than sixty years.

What made rangers distinctive was their work in the field, with people and with the land. Rangers were people in uniform—authority figures—to whom others could turn for information and assistance. Many rangers were seasonal, often teachers working in the park during the summer months. Seasonals as well as permanent rangers had long associations with Yosemite, and carried on its traditions. Married field rangers very often worked with their wives as a team—a two-for-the-price-of-one arrangement that Shirley is the first to acknowledge and document.

Changes in the ranger force in recent years have mirrored changes in the agency at large. The beginnings of these changes are also part of Shirley's story. With this book she has certainly become an honorary ranger and an important factor in sustaining the traditions yet noting the changes in the role of National Park Service rangers in Yosemite.

Jim Snyder
Yosemite Archivist

Author's Preface

This book began as a revision of John Bingaman's *Guardians of the Yosemite: A Story of the Early Rangers,* first published in 1961 and reprinted in 1970. His book was largely autobiographical and thus narrow in its scope, but it was a trailblazer into which he put a lot of work.

Late in the 1980s, Phyllis Freeland Broyles, a daughter, wife, and mother of rangers, undertook a revision of the book, but had to give it up. I took over in 1994, and the scope of the project expanded to become the history of Yosemite rangers in general—in their own words, as often as possible. Records, letters, and extensive interviews with many retired rangers and their families provided a quantity and variety of material that had not been available earlier.

My book ends with the year 1960, because by then a policy of lateral transfers prevailed, and the relatively brief tenures of Yosemite rangers made it all but impossible to keep tabs on them. Sheila Tarvin suggested the title *Protecting Paradise,* and since it sums up the reality of rangers working in Yosemite, I gladly adopted it. She is not the only one to merit my acknowledgment. From the first I have had the support and aid of John Bingaman's second wife, Irene, which is greatly appreciated. Both Shirley Sault Randolph and her brother Jack Sault were constantly supportive, supplying pictures, stories, and tape recordings made by their father, Bert Sault. He was a Yosemite ranger—a man whom I, also, treasured.

Phyllis Broyles did a great deal of the preliminary research, plus supplying some of the ranger biographies that appear at the back of the book. Bea Freeland, her mother, also aided me as did her ex-ranger husband, Rod Broyles. Linda Eade, librarian at the Yosemite Research Library, and Jim Snyder, Park historian and the author of the foreword, were endlessly helpful. Leroy Radanovich gave me suggestions, and copied many old photos to illustrate the text.

A number of retired rangers and/or their family members told or wrote the engrossing and humorous accounts quoted in the book. Among them were Marian Albright Schenck, Tom Tucker, Ken Ashley, Jack Morehead, Elaine F. Townsley, Bob Skakel, Merlin Miller, Tom Van Bibber, John Henneberger, Fred Martischang, Phyllis and Rod Broyles, John Reymann, Doug Hubbard, and John Stratton. All of them helped me write this book. To all of them I am grateful.

A San Francisco stockbroker may seem like an odd source for Yosemite information, but Dick Otter, who spent half his childhood in Yosemite, has a passionate commitment to the Park and a wide acquaintance with it. He put me in touch with old-timers who had unique ties to Yosemite, especially to the college-boy rangers of 1914. Carol Haines, Nancy Witter Bates, and William P. Mahony, Jr. would have been unknown to me had Dick not supplied names, addresses, and backgrounds.

Butch Farrabee, now the assistant superintendent of Glacier National Park, shared his search and rescue history with me. Both Butch and John Dill read my Search and Rescue chapter and gave me constructive criticism. Sandy Sedergren Martin, Anne Adams Helms, Mary Degen Rodgers, Laura McIntyre Meyer, Ed Wade, Bob Manly, Alan Haigh, Tom Bopp, Bill Cuthbert, Duane Peterson, Helen Fowler, Mariam Woessner, Lou Becerra, and Cynthia and Dieter Goetze have all made contributions. Members of the Yosemite Collectors Group, specifically Mikki Haney, John Degen, Ray Warren, and Marilyn Guske, lent me unusual graphics. Harold May, Jr., Audrey Beck Wilson, Bart Reed, and John Wegner, Jr. also assisted. Homer Hoyt's son, Larry, gave me his father's massive collection of photographs to study before passing them on to the Yosemite Research Library. Irene Bingaman let me use pictures from John's collections, as did Doris Boothe Wanty, Clyde Boothe's daughter. Art Holmes's family lent me his log books and photographs.

Peter Browning, author, editor, and publisher, used his red pencil to the advantage of my manuscript. Among other things, he is responsible for the book's interior design. Larry Van Dyke did his usual fine job with the cover design. Typing, retyping, and more retyping was done by Sheila (where's your verb?) Bell Tarvin, who gave me the title, advice, and T.L.C.

My last acknowledgment is to fellow historian Jim Shebl, the only man I know who has actually kissed the Blarney stone, and who then used the gift of gab to persuade me to do the research and writing of the many biographies at the end of the book. That task took more than four months. Grrrr!

Anyone forgotten here is probably mentioned in the text or in a footnote, I HOPE! Bless you all.

Shirley Sargent
August 1998

This book is dedicated to the memory of John Bingaman, 1896–1984, who was not only a guardian of Yosemite but a guardian of the history of its stalwart rangers: to Ferdinand Castillo, 1918–1994, fierce guardian of Ferdinand Pass—also known as Tioga Pass—and to Carl Sharsmith, 1903–1994, staunch defender and interpreter of nature.

1 Transitions

Yosemite National Park was created by the United States Congress on September 30, 1890, and when President Harrison signed the bill on the following day it became America's third national park. Yellowstone, established in 1872, was the first, and Sequoia, six days earlier than Yosemite, the second. In effect, however, Yosemite predated even Yellowstone—since the Yosemite Grant, consisting of the "Gorge,"—Yosemite Valley—and the Mariposa Grove of Big Trees, two superb places 25 miles apart, was the premier example of land set aside for "public use, resort, and recreation . . . for all time."

Yosemite's 56.4 square miles were granted to the State of California in 1864 by Congress. The Grant was administered by less than a score of men who were on the scene, and an eight-man Board of Commissioners that visited at least twice a year. Outstanding among the former was Galen Clark, the first Yosemite Guardian and the first State ranger. The foremost commissioner was Frederick Law Olmsted of Central Park fame, whose sound ideas for the Grant's management and use, though not followed at the time, anticipated those basic to the National Park Service 51 years later.[1]

The Yosemite Grant set precedents and began organized protection, but its boundaries did not begin to encompass the Valley's watershed, the unique forests, meadows, lakes, and glacial features of the surrounding land. Loggers, hunters, a few miners, sheepmen and cattlemen and their four-footed charges continued to significantly alter the amazing landscape. Vocal and written opposition to their practices, led by naturalist John Muir and his influential friends, was so persuasive that in 1890 Congress roused itself to create Sequoia and Yosemite as national reservations. Suddenly, the

When horsemanship was in vogue.

state grant of 56.4 square miles was a small park surrounded by a much larger 1,513-square-mile national park the size of Rhode Island. Federal protection was ensured at the same time that it created conflict with the State administration.

Once a national park was created by Congress, its lands, supreme in natural wonders—whether hot springs, geysers, trees, glaciers, mountains, or lakes—had to be protected, and at least a basic trail and road system developed. Because there was no caretaker agency these developmental services were provided by the Department of the Interior, invariably short of funds and manpower, and the War Department, which had both funds and men. Beginning in May of 1891 and continuing through 1913, 150 or more cavalry troops annually rode into Yosemite National Park, usually in mid-May and stayed until late fall.[2] Headquarters at Camp A. E. Wood, near the private inholdings at Wawona, was the hub from which troopers radiated to outpost camps.[3] Whoever was commanding officer was automatically acting superintendent of the Park, in

---

1. Frederick Law Olmsted, "The 1865 Yosemite Report," *Landscape Architecture*, October 1952.
    For a comprehensive history of the Yosemite Grant, see Hank Johnston,
    The Yosemite Grant, 1864–1906 (El Portal, CA: Yosemite Association, 1995).
2. Yellowstone and Sequoia national parks also had seasonal army protection.

Posting the perimeters of the new Park was an early duty for the cavalrymen. (Ray Warren collection.)

charge of such diverse services as building, maintaining, and patrolling trails; evicting trespassers; mapping; planting fish and fighting forest fires; overseeing transportation; and, in time, operating a hospital, telephone, and electric systems.

There were several excellent officers. Over the years they directed outstanding work, particularly in mapping and trail building. In effect, the cavalrymen composed the first, and largest, body of "rangers" in Yosemite history; but their initial duty was to preserve and protect America. In a way, Yosemite was a training ground for soldiers between wars.

In the new park, the cavalry's primary responsibility was to rid the park of trespassers, especially sheep, whose dietary habits damaged high country meadows. John Muir said that "The harm they do goes to the heart." Written warnings were sent to cattle and sheep owners, but the latter, especially, were undeterred and had huge herds driven up for the free pasturage. Consequently, Wood commanded his troops to find and arrest the sheepherders, and within a few weeks of the cavalry's arrival on May 19, 1891, four indignant herders had been caught. The captain soon discovered that there was no law authorizing criminal prosecution. A warning and expulsion was all that could be done and once the troopers rode away, herders and sheep returned.

Although Captain Wood was suffering from a painful and terminal cancer of the tongue, there was nothing wrong with his brain, and he thought of an ingenious way to solve the problem. During the season of 1893, he reported to the Secretary of Interior:

> When herders are arrested, they are marched to another part of the Park for ejectment, this march consuming four or five days; and after they are ejected it takes as long to go back to their herds. In the meantime the sheep are alone, and the forest animals are liable to destroy and scatter many of them. When the owner awakens to this fact, he takes more interest in the doings of his herders and gives them orders not to enter the Park under any circumstances. So far this season no willful trespass by the sheepmen have been discovered.[4]

This practice continued until the Spanish-American War was declared on April 25, 1898. Troopers had more important priorities than what a Mariposa newsman called "the dangerous and glorious duty of sheepherding."

Sheepmen wasted no time in moving thousands of "hoofed locusts," as John Muir called them, back into the high country of Yosemite and Sequoia. J. W. Zevely of the General Land Office was dispatched from Washington, D.C., to investigate; and his advice that local civilians be hired to patrol, fight fires, and eject trespassers was followed. On June 24, he swore 11 men from Yosemite and adjacent settlements into government service as "forest

---

3. Camp Wood, now a public campground, was named for Capt. Abram E. Wood, the commanding officer from 1891 through 1893. He died in 1894.
4. Francis P. Farquhar, *History of the Sierra Nevada* (Berkeley: University of California Press, 1972), p. 205.

No matter what the season, Yosemite Valley is a paradise. (Bingaman collection.)

agents." All provided their own horses, guns, and food and were to receive $3.00 or $4.00 a day.[5]

Incredibly, within two months these agents were said to have driven nearly 190,000 sheep, 1,000 cattle, and 350 horses and their herders out of the Park. These figures had to be greatly exaggerated, since even in 1891 Captain Wood had estimated only 90,000 invaders. After years of control, and within less than 60 days, 190,000 were claimed. How anything approaching accuracy could be made from the chaos amid a milling, bleating band of sheep seems incomprehensible.

5. Under the direction of Special Agent A. W. Buick, Archie Leonard, George R. Byde, Henry A. Skelton, Charlie Leidig, and Arthur L. Thurman, all from Yosemite Valley and Wawona, were assigned to the northern part of the Park at four dollars per day. George C. MacKenzie, Joseph R. Borden, Thomas S. Carter, Darwin S. Lewis, David Lackton, and Joel L. Westfall patrolled the southern section at three dollars per day under Agent Cullum. Ten men were to receive four dollars daily, but Zevely hired eleven, causing the discrepancy. (Report of June 25, 1898 from Special Inspector Zevely to Commissioner of the General Land Office.)

The "war" with Spain was brief, and 65 cavalry men arrived back at Camp A. E. Wood on August 25. The forest agents were dismissed, but two of them were promptly rehired to assist the troopers and, once they left, provide winter guardianship. They were appointed as forest rangers, later re-designated park rangers, and paid $50 per month.

Thus Archie C. Leonard, then 52, and Charlie T. Leidig, 36, the first white boy born in Yosemite Valley, became the first park rangers. Both were able mountaineers who could handle horses, guns, fishing rods, cattle, and sheep with ease.

Sheepmen and cattlemen were not the only trespassers. Armed miners and hunters were routinely apprehended. Forest fires were another problem, and boundary markers had to be posted around the Park.

Unfortunately, Leidig carried being a "good old boy" too far, not only going hunting himself but allowing his cronies to hunt within the Park boundaries. Army Commander Harry C. Benson, a West Point graduate, complained repeatedly to the Secretary of the Interior of Leidig's disregard of authority, favoritism toward friends, and appropriation of government property.[6] He was terminated in September 1907. Despite age and ills, Leonard served until 1917. The highlight of their service, and perhaps their lives, was the three days in May 1903 when, along with an Army packer, they guided, guarded, and cooked for President Theodore Roosevelt and John Muir on their memorable camping trip.

Army jurisdiction over Yosemite National Park was continually complicated by the State-administered Yosemite Grant. Yosemite Valley and the Mariposa Grove, parks within a park, were ruled by various guardians and commissioners who, no matter how able or businesslike, were never properly funded by the California legislature. Ultimately, recession of the Grant to the U.S. Government made Yosemite a unified whole except for private inholdings.

In an attempt to eliminate many of these, Congress passed a boundary revision that lopped off about 500 square miles from Yosemite—the largest single exclusion any national park has ever suffered. "Devil's Postpile and the Mount Ritter area were withdrawn for mining claims, while much of the Park's west boundary was eliminated for timber and homestead claims." The "new boundaries conformed more to natural drainage."[7]

Before this major step was fully absorbed, the Recession Act giving the Yosemite Grant back to the U.S. Government passed in March 1905. However, formal acceptance was delayed by political battles until June 11, 1906.[8]

Before the long-fought-over recession, not even army officers were welcomed in Yosemite Valley, and there was conflict as to who should fight fires that threatened both the Grant and the surrounding Park. It was August 1, 1906 before Major Benson could move army headquarters from Wawona to Yosemite Valley. There he commandeered four and one half acres immediately west of Yosemite Creek for the new encampment. Ultimately two long, narrow barracks buildings, bath and lavatory houses, accessory structures, 156 tent frames, and a parade ground accommodated the cavalry. Separate officers' quarters were built in a rough circle between the camp and the cliff to the north. That soon was dubbed "Soapsuds Row." Before the camp was fully settled, Benson began fighting the resistance of settlers who were used to shooting wildlife and operating generally with little regard to the public good. The lack of sanitation, especially in ill-defined campgrounds, appalled Benson, who promptly closed the worst ones in the west end of the Valley and cleaned up others. He was particularly incensed at the wanton destruction of deer "in and out of season by those who carry guns for 'protection.' There is absolutely no more reason to carry guns in Yosemite National Park," he concluded scathingly, "than there is for them on Pennsylvania Avenue in Washington."[9]

6. Benson's reports were made on August 2, 1906, and on August 2 and September 3 and 20 of 1907. (Yosemite Research Library; hereinafter, YRL.) Surprisingly, Leidig served as a seasonal ranger in Yosemite in 1914 and 1915.
7. Quotations from YNP curator Jim Snyder in his letter to the author of Sept. 22, 1997.
8. Johnston, *Yosemite Grant*.
9. Biographical sketch of H. C. Benson, in YRL.

YNP Headquarters in Old Village. Both the autos are 1919 Essex touring cars bearing 1919 California license plates, one with the top up and the other with the top down. (Billy Nelson collection, courtesy of Duane Peterson.)

His intent was to make Yosemite Valley "a safe retreat for wild life instead of the 'death trap'" it had become during the state administration.

On the whole, concessionaires had had a free ride with the state administration, but that ended when the army took control. Benson enforced regulations rigorously, but sewage disposal was the biggest problem. David A. Curry had to reduce Camp Curry's capacity until an adequate disposal system was built, and the Sentinel Hotel management was warned against using the Merced River as a sewer.

Not only did the Park need protection, but visitors as well. Visitation began increasing again in 1907 after the hiatus caused by the catastrophic San Francisco earthquake and fire. A railroad to a point called El Portal, 12 miles west of Yosemite Valley, and a narrow dirt road to the Valley floor were

completed the following spring, allowing quicker and more comfortable access than by stage.

Benson could not stop trains, but with the approval of the Secretary of Interior he banned automobiles because he felt that the primitive roads were unfit for the combined use of teams and motor vehicles. For the first time Yosemite Valley was also generally accessible year round; it was no longer the seasonal park it had been.

To ensure that his law-and-order regimen continued during the winters, he appointed ex-cavalry sergeant Gabriel Sovulewski as ranger with orders to be tough and zealous. Sovulewski was, but his chief claim to fame then and later was his maintenance and expansion of the Park's trail system. He never lost his Polish accent or his regard for integrity and work. In fact, from the time he, a Polish refuge, was a handsome sergeant with a sweeping black mustache, until his retirement in 1936, he lived the American success story.

"There are six parts to remember in trail construction," he noted. "It requires strength, determination, a natural instinct for direction, love for the work, love of nature, and an ability to forget everything except the object in view, and to be able to sit in the saddle for 12 or 14 hours, or walk the same number of hours if required to find the best possible way."[10]

On the same September 1907 day that Charles Leidig was notified that he had been terminated, his successor, Andrew J. (Jack) Gaylor, was sworn in as a ranger by Major Benson. Gaylor, 51, was another ex-army man, a packer who had served in

Departure of the mail. Feb 22 - 1918.

Transporting the mail in an open-air White truck. February 22, 1918.

10. Gabriel Sovulewski to Director, NPS, Sept. 22, 1936, in biographical files, YRL.

the Philippines, Cuba, and Yosemite. Packing supplies was his primary job in the Park; but when necessary he fought fires and helped stock lakes with trout. "And in that way," he wrote for a YNP personnel form, "I became thoroughly trained and acquainted with all the trails [and] streams within Yosemite Park."

His new duties included "patrolling, planting fish, destroying carnivorous animals,[11] blasting logs and rock slides . . . & occasionally during the winters shoveling snow off buildings and bridges." In 1908 his salary was raised to $1,000 per year. Accompanying his recommendation for the raise, Major Benson commented, "Ranger Gaylor is very efficient, absolutely trustworthy, and I believe is entitled to the increase."

In a 1948 interview, feisty Elizabeth Meyer, owner of Big Meadow, a cattle ranch 11 miles west of the Valley, supplied a sidelight: "When the military came in, it was 'no cats' and all of us had to get rid of them. Then it was 'no dogs.' I used to have to put my cats under me in the seat of the buggy so they wouldn't take them out. Jack Gaylor would come out . . . he dyed his handlebar mustache black . . . reminded me of Simon Legree. . . . 'You can't have but one dog,' he would say. But I would pacify him."

Instead of soldiers, the Park would be in the hands of a small band of civilian rangers in 1914; and they would be under orders from the perpetually beleaguered Interior Department in Washington, D.C. Plans were being pushed in Washington to create a subsidiary bureau to administer all 12 national parks and 29 national monuments. Secretary of the Interior Franklin K. Lane, a Californian; his 26-year-old law clerk, Horace M. Albright, a University of California graduate; and Stephen T. Mather, still another Cal graduate, were fierce advocates of the proposal, which was winding it's tedious way through Congress.

In three major ways, the year 1913 was pivotal: the last for the army and the first in which automobiles were allowed to enter Yosemite, and passage of the Raker Act. Although 13 or so autoists had piloted their ungainly craft into the Valley between 1900 and June 1907, Benson had prohibited further excursions. Auto usage elsewhere in the nation proliferated, but in Yosemite the horse still reigned supreme.[12]

Protests were vehement and widespread. Curiously, in 1912 even John Muir, the great naturalist and inveterate walker, supported admission of automobiles into Yosemite. "All signs predict automobile victory," he wrote, "and doubtless, under certain precautionary restrictions, these useful, progressive, blunt nosed beetles will hereafter be allowed to puff their way into all the parks . . . and from the mountaineer's standpoint, with but little harm or good."[13]

In 1874 the Coulterville Road was the first stage road to enter Yosemite. After a hurry-up repair job in 1913, it was the first on which automobiles were allowed to travel. In the intervening decades, it was truly the road less traveled. None of the four pioneer routes—the Coulterville and Big Oak Flat roads opened a month apart in 1874, the Wawona Road in 1875, and the Tioga Road in 1883—followed anything much better than animal trails around boulders, across ravines, and up and down precipitous grades. Eventually tolls were abolished, bridges built, and other minor improvements made, but the roads remained primitive and barely eight feet wide until the late 1920s, when modern highways were begun and a fifth route, the All-Year Highway (140), opened. The least popular, least traveled Coulterville Road was neither replaced nor modernized to any great extent.

And so, on August 23, 1913 a few adventurous motorists and officials waited at the Merced Grove of Giant Sequoias, some 20 tortuous miles from Yosemite Valley. Park Ranger Forest S. Townsley, who had arrived by horse-drawn stage only a month earlier, had the pleasure, he said, of issuing the first permit, to J. H. Leach of Los Angeles. Besides the permit, Townsley gave Leach a long list of regulations in exchange for a $5.00 round-trip

---

11. Protection was not extended to mountain lions at that time.
12. Benson's order was given after the Interior Department approved it. See Richard G. Lillard, "The Siege and Conquest of a National Park," *American West*, January 1968.
13. Muir's picturesque opinion was in a December 1912 letter to the secretary of the American Alpine Club. (William Frederick Badè, *The Life and Letters of John Muir* (New York: Houghton Mifflin Co., vol. 2, 1924.)

ticket good for one week. "In fact," Townsley stated, "these regulations were so severe that it made it very unpleasant for people to travel . . . within the boundaries. . . . We had one-way traffic and cars had to travel on a regular train schedule. . . . If autoists were two minutes early they violated the regulations and if two minutes late, they were also in difficulty which caused no end of confusion for the few weeks in which these regulations were in force. . . . Regulations were revised later as conditions warranted."[14]

At first, speed was limited to five miles per hour downhill, nine uphill, and 10 to 12 on the rare straight stretches, and *"in no* case must it exceed 15 miles per hour." Then as now, speeding was a problem for rangers. Autoists were instructed to pull their vehicles to the side of the road and park until any equestrian traffic passed safely. "Fines or other punishments" were to be imposed if the stringent rules were broken.

Any driver unfortunate enough to arrive at the Merced Grove entrance station after 3:30 p.m. was not allowed to continue to the magic kingdom of Yosemite Valley until the following day. One of the rangers who had to placate late arrivals and collect fees, usually in coin, was newcomer Oliver R. Prien, a 32 year-old farmer, a political appointee who had been recommended by Interior Secretary Lane's brother. Prien alternated with Townsley collecting fees. At 31, Townsley was a veteran ranger, having spent 11 years at Platt National Park in Oklahoma before entering on duty (EOD) at

Yosemite in July 1913. It would be surprising if there wasn't tension, at least, between the two from the start.[15] Both had wives; but it was doubtful that either Emma Prien or Malvin Townsley, with four children, lived at the grove.

Fee collecting had to be a boring job, since only 127 automobiles checked in during the 70 or so days before snow closed the road, an average of fewer than two a day. Even with outbound vehicles, diversions and excitement were rarely more complicated than flat tires or breakdowns.

In mid-October 1913 another first was recorded when Katie-bel McGregor became the first woman driver to brave the Coulterville Road. She drove the first of four touring cars carrying 15 people from the San Francisco area.[16] However, the honor of being the first woman driver in Yosemite belonged to Lola Clark, who had piloted a Locomobile in over the Big Oak Flat Road in 1901.[17]

At day's end, a telephone call was cranked through so that headquarters could record how many, if any, vehicles had huffed and puffed their way in; how many had departed; and how much money, if any, had been collected. Yosemite finally had joined the modern world.

The third major event of 1913 did not occur until December. That was the ill-famed Raker act, authorizing the city of San Francisco to build a dam in Hetch Hetchy Valley. Once again the integrity of Yosemite was violated. The subsequent dam and reservoir still complicate ranger protection of Yosemite.

14. A one-page typescript entitled "The First Automobiles in Yosemite," by Forest S. Townsley, 1941, YRL. Among those disgusted with the additional rules was the last army commandant, Major William T. Littebrant. He told Townsley "that it was not possible for a military man to supervise and administer the rules and regulations of the national park." In saying goodbye to Townsley, Littebrant said that he hoped that the Army would never return to the national parks again.

15. A third ranger, August F. Luedke, was also hired in July 1913, but left nine months later. See John Henneberger's unpublished manuscript, "To Protect and Preserve: A History of the National Park Ranger, 1965," p. 637, in YRL.

16. Her feat was described in the *Mariposa Gazette,* Oct. 25, 1913.

17. See Hank Johnston, *Yosemite's Yesterdays,* Vol. 1 (Yosemite: Flying Spur Press, 1989.)

2 College Boy Rangers

No troops were stationed in Yosemite in 1914, but Major William T. Littebrant (irreverently dubbed *littlebrain* by David Curry) remained as the Park's acting superintendent until his departure July 10. At that time Mark Daniels, General Superintendent and Landscape Engineer for all national parks, took over. During his frequent and prolonged absences, Gabriel Sovulewski continued as acting superintendent. They supervised a small staff of maintenance men and a handful of permanent rangers: Archie Leonard, A. J. "Jack" Gaylor, Forest Townsley, and Oliver Prien, who had been promoted to acting chief ranger. In lieu of 150 cavalrymen, the 1,169-square-mile Park and its 32 concessions were in the hands of less than a quarter that many civilians.

In anticipation of the hiatus, the Department of Interior had allocated $10,000 to hire 10 temporary rangers to serve from June 1 to October 31. Seven of these were selected by Benjamin Ide Wheeler, president of the University of California at Berkeley. Actually, Wheeler's secretary, Clare M. Torrey, himself a 1913 graduate, recruited six men from the student body. The seventh was Allan Sproul, a high school senior slated to graduate from Berkeley High on May 29, two days before the job began.

"What 18-year-old with a love for the mountains and in need of a summer job wouldn't jump at such an offer?" Sproul reflected in a retrospective article written nearly 40 years later.[1]

"The job requirements were fairly simple for a group with some experience in outdoor living and having no serious inhibitions about their ability to tackle most anything," he stated. Rangers had to be in good physical shape to be "able to saddle and ride a horse and to throw a hitch on a pack animal," and to furnish these animals with their tack and feed. A rifle, pistol, axe, cooking and eating utensils, and provisions were also required. Such equipment was still common to young men who enjoyed riding and camping. U.C. Berkeley let out May 14, so the six from there took off on horseback, leading Sproul's laden mounts while he finished classes. His later trip, by train to El Portal and then on one of the new motorized stages into Yosemite Valley, was speedier.

Job training was virtually nil. The recruits were told to watch for fires; maintain telephone lines in their areas; keep cattle, sheep, dogs, cats, and guns out of the Park; and prevent damage within it. All rangers were supposed to procure uniforms, but Sproul said that none of the un-uniformed college boys was penalized for casual attire. They "wore whatever we deemed to be suitable clothing." A Park Service badge lent authority to even the most nondescript outfit. Collegians Oliver Haines, Eric Lawson, Leo Meyer, James Short, Dan Sink, Jean Witter (later a cofounder of Dean Witter), and Sproul were assigned to entrance stations on roads and trails leading into the Park: Crane Flat, Merced Grove, Soda Springs [Tuolumne Meadows], Hog Ranch (now Mather), Camp A. E. Wood, and the Mariposa Grove. Sproul and Haines rode together to the latter's cabin at the former army camp A. E. Wood.

Sproul related that "We found it convenient then (as well as often later) to have dinner at the Wawona Hotel nearby. That was an easy and nourishing introduction to life on the range." In fact, as he admitted wryly, "the 'rigors' of life as a ranger . . . in 1914 were certainly tempered by the amenities of the Wawona Hotel.

"After dinner I rode in the dark to my cabin at the entrance to the Mariposa Grove, about 6 or 7

---

1. Allan Sproul, "The 'First' Yosemite Rangers," *Yosemite Nature Notes*, April 1952. Sproul's memories supply information and human interest to the adventures of an almost-college-boy ranger. Pay of $100 per month, only $15 less than that allocated to the chief ranger, was another attraction of the job. Both Allan and his brother, Robert Gordon Sproul, later the president of the University of California at Berkeley, had grown up with Torrey.

"Fortunately," Allan Sproul wrote, "I did not realize my responsibilities, and fortunately nothing happened to the Giant Sequoias." (Courtesy of YRL.)

left his horses. His summer head-quarters was a one-room cabin recycled from the cavalry. When he went to feed his horses the next morning, they were long gone, having discovered a break in the fence that he had missed in the dark. "One of Uncle Sam's brand new shiny-faced rangers had lost his horses the first day on the job," he recorded ruefully. "I spent most of that day finding them and coaxing them back to bridle or rope.

"For the next 5 months I was the guardian of the Mariposa Grove of Giant Sequoias, the most responsible job I ever had or ever will have. Fortunately, I did not realize my responsibilities and fortunately nothing happened to the giant sequoias."

Fortunately was right. Had not Sproul been a conscientious and reliable young man, trustworthy and honorable, his lack of direction might have led the trees into danger, carved graffiti, or worse. He was a fun-loving lad, though, and within a short time he discovered happily that "My duties were not onerous: my days were pleasant." For a lean and hungry teenager, the daily highlight was noon. "I usually followed the late morning [horse-drawn] stages into the grove to keep an eye on the tourists and to pick up a lunch I did not have to cook myself. There was always plenty left at the cabin after the tourists finished, including the best pies I had ever tasted, the product of the Chinese cook [Ah You] at the Wawona Hotel. I was at the cabin pretty regularly for lunch—like a sea gull following a ferryboat."[2]

Coffee was "prepared there to supplement the

miles from Wawona by road and some less by the trail I used when I became more familiar with the lay of the land." Stumbling around in the darkness, he discerned white quartz rocks outlining a camp site and, across the road, a small corral where he

---

2. The "cabin" refers to an all-purpose shelter used as, among other things, a lunch stop. Later it was succeeded by the Mariposa Grove Museum.

hotel lunches. . . . There was a curio shop where various articles made of redwood (*Sequoia sempervirens*) were sold as souvenirs of a visit to the Mariposa Grove of Big Trees (*Sequoia gigantea*). There was a photographer [Albert 'Bert' Henry Bruce] who took individual pictures on request, and practically always took pictures of the stages going through the tunneled Wawona tree.[3] The man in charge [the concessionaire] was a skittish old customer named Ed Baxter who, in the winter, represented the district in the California State Assembly.[4] The big day for the concessionaires was the annual visit by the girls from Happy Camp, an adjunct of the not too distant Sugar Pine Lumber Company."

All play and no work didn't make Allan a completely carefree boy. "When I was not actually doing my housework or in the grove watching tourists and cadging lunch, I was riding around the limited area . . . keeping an eye out for trespassing livestock. . . . Once or twice during the night small bands of cattle had thundered by my cabin, waking me. . . . I was scared, but from under the covers I couldn't actually see these animals."

When confronted with a small band of these four-legged trespassers in the daylight, Sproul acted fearlessly. "Thinking to stampede the animals and get them started out of the Park, I fired over their heads. That is I fired over the heads of all but one which, unseen, was up the hillside from the main group. I hit him with a 30-30 bullet and dropped him cold." Sproul left the corpse at the scene of the crime and never used his rifle again.

His pistol was fired more often, for he and Ollie Haines shot at skunks through large knotholes in the latter's former cavalry cabin floor. "When we caught one under the knothole in the candle light, we shot it . . . then dragged it out through the hole and disposed of the carcass. Never one betrayed us, but looking back it seems to me we took an awful chance."

Supervision, like training, was minimal. There were only four telephone calls during Sproul's five months at the grove, and ranger Archie Leonard, then 68, stopped by but was not "very communicative. He was always pleasant, and I should say tolerant of the 'college boy rangers,' but so far as our duties were concerned there was a gulf be-

Now as in 1914, the Wawona Hotel offers meals, tennis, and genteel 19th century living. (Courtesy of YRL.)

---

3. The Wawona, or Tunnel Tree, one of the more famous trees in the world, fell unheard in the snow early in 1969.
4. Both winter and summer, Baxter represented the Washburn brothers, who ran the Wawona Hotel, the Mariposa Grove concession, and, in their prime, Yosemite politics in general. Baxter was a grandson of Fannie Bruce and J. J. Cook, another close Washburn associate. See Shirley Sargent, *Yosemite's Historic Wawona* (Yosemite: Flying Spur Press, 1979).

tween us. . . . He was too diffident, too inarticulate, too old, to share his knowledge with us."

Only once did he encounter Chief Ranger Prien, and that was on a day when Sproul was playing tennis with a pretty girl at the Wawona Hotel. "Prien suggested substituting an axe for the tennis racket and went on.

Later in the season Superintendent Mark Daniels and a party made a hurried trip through the grove, waving to me in passing. That was the only supervision I had. . . ."

On August 8, 1914, Sproul's duties increased because automobiles were finally allowed on the Wawona Road and the road to the grove. "The autos had to be checked in, the prohibition of dogs and firearms became a little more of a problem, and it was more difficult to keep track of the visitors when they came in their own cars instead of by the stage load with prescribed stopping places. Perhaps a few dried-up snow plants disappeared as a result . . . but nothing serious happened to the grove."

"I strung a rope across the road by my cabin with a hand-lettered sign hanging from it which said STOP. That kept cars from going by in the daytime without noticing me, and from going by at night when they still were not permitted in the grove. It also, sometimes, stopped the early stage, still horse-drawn, when I slept late. Since the drivers were not allowed to leave their seats, and the passengers wouldn't, the stage had to wait while I got up, pulled on my pants, and ran out to take down the rope. I can still hear such drivers as Jim Gordon or Phoenis ('Sport') Ashworth yelling for me."

Nevertheless, Sproul was sorry to see stages replaced. "Mariposa Grove is no place for a paved road," he reflected. "The horse-drawn stage, leisurely and in tune with its surroundings, used to put one in the right mood for the giant sequoias. And the drivers were picturesque and more interesting than chauffeurs. Their story of how the grove was discovered always seemed to please the people. According to them, when the Fallen Monarch crashed it made a great noise and the echo lasted 2 weeks. Some people down Mariposa way heard the echo and followed it until they came to the grove."

This picture makes teenager Allan Sproul look years older. (From 1952 *Yosemite Nature Notes*.)

By the end of October, both horse-drawn and gas-powered traffic "had pretty well stopped and when the first rains came dispelling the fire hazard, Ollie Haines and I began to pack up. . . . As we rode our horses out . . . my saddle horse was packing a load of pleasant memories, and 20 more pounds of me. . . ."

Allan Sproul's ranger days were over, but by the time he wrote this reminiscence, he was a guardian again—this time CEO of the Federal Reserve Bank of New York where, aided by a staff of 4,000, he guarded over twelve billion dollars in assets. Yet, as he said, "I had something much more precious in my care when I was the 'lone ranger' stationed at the Mariposa Grove of Giant Sequoias. . . ."

In 1915, Jean Witter, the future stockbroker, looked every inch a ranger. (Courtesy of Nancy Witter Bates.)

Soon after Sproul's instant friend, Oliver L. Haines (1891–1982), arrived at his post at Camp A. E. Wood, he wrote his family in San Diego, who preserved the letter. It is reproduced here with the permission of his daughter, Carol Haines.

June 1914

Dear Folks,

Have been trying to get time to write ever since I left Berkeley but have been too busy.

With the help of George [brother] I got hold of two horses from one Tim Carlon, a cattleman, as a loan.[5] But the rest of my outfit, principally

---

5. Tim Carlon was a politically powerful cattleman and property owner in Tuolumne County. Each summer he rented his horses and mules to the Park Service.

grub, I had to buy in a hurry. I rode to Yosemite [Valley], arriving there last Saturday [May 30]. We stayed there until Tuesday morning [June 2], when we received our orders and left for our posts. My post is at Wawona, about a mile from the settlement, at the old soldiers camp. My duties are to watch the roads, trails and see that no persons with firearms or other contraband articles enter, to register persons entering, and of course to watch out for fires and fight them if necessary. The job is somewhat lonely, but otherwise all right. I get $100 per month but have to pay my own expenses including cost of horse feed, which at my post will amount to some $20 per month. Figuring my own expenses at $30 per month outside of the extra expense of equipment to start with, I ought after this month to lay up a little money. However I didn't get my first check until sometime in July, so will have to get a little help this month. In order to get started in time I had to get some things in Merced, hardware and food, amounting to something around $20, on George's account.[6] I would like to pay him back; and before the end of the month will have to buy grain and pasture

for my horses amounting to about $15, I can get along without buying more grub until the end of the month, but my diet will be mostly bacon & beans unless I start an account at the store here.

I suppose I will be at this post more than a month, though the major said he would change us around once or twice to vary the monotony.[7] If so I hope to draw a place next time where I won't have to buy horse feed. There are five other posts, three of which have plenty of wild feed. These posts were covered last year by avalry troops: we are supposed to do the work which 2 companies did last year.

I hope you will excuse the sloppy looking letter, I haven't had time yet to fix up camp and it is pretty messy.

My address is Wawona, Ca. Hope all are well. Would like to hear some news and see some San Diego papers. Reading matter is scarce, and I have lots of time to read. Any books sent parcel post would be appreciated.

Lovingly,
Oliver[8]

---

6. Brother George Haines was an attorney in Merced.
7. Major William T. Littebrant left the Park on July 10, 1914, so Haines and Sproul remained at their original posts.
8. Oliver Lincoln Haines (1891–1982) served overseas as a cavalryman during World War I, and later became a brigadier general.

3 Politics in Paradise

From the founding of the State Grant in 1864, there have been opposing goals for Yosemite: accessibility on the one hand and preservation on the other—use verses abuse. Wilderness versus 'wildermess.' Recession of the Grant so as to effect a consolidation with Yosemite National Park solved some but not all of the problems: the basic conflict remained, creating an increasingly precarious imbalance at the present time. How to allow public access and enjoyment of the wonders without trampling, polluting, and harming the national park remains an unanswerable question.

The purpose of the act establishing the National Park service in 1916 was "to conserve the scenery and the national and historic objects and the wildlife therein and to provide for the enjoyment of same in such manner and by such means as will leave them unimpaired for the enjoyment of future generations." In the early years of the NPS, the policy was to encourage visitation, even to the extent of building a ski resort and sponsoring events such as Indian Field Days. Visitation increased and was made easier by equipment such as trailers, campers, and most recently motor homes, and so-called recreational vehicles,which followed the completion of a modern highway system and increasing affluence. Unfortunately, speed, increased litter, and other abuses went hand in hand with the ever proliferating visitor count.[1]

Rangers lives still revolve around that unresolved issue: preservation versus accessibility—yet their duties are straightforward. A ranger's job is to protect, enforce regulations, guard, and guide. A ranger naturalist's job is to interpret nature, explain its fragility, guard, and guide. Making a place accessible is the job of trail builders and road builders.

The bill creating the National Park Service was passed by Congress on August 25, 1916, but it was April of the following year before funds were appropriated. Despite the delays and frustrations, many positive steps concerning the organization of the service and duties of the rangers evolved, including the rules and regulations that would govern them and the rules that they would enforce. Predictably, Stephen T. Mather, a human dynamo, became the first director, and Horace M. Albright, assistant director. Both these Californians took a special interest in the state's four national parks: Yosemite, Sequoia, General Grant, and newly-created Lassen. Yosemite, Mather's all-time favorite, continued to receive his personal guidance—which created some political impacts and not a few problems.

For example, the fact that Oliver Prien was hired in 1913 on the recommendation of Interior Secretary Lane's brother, and within months was made chief ranger, did not sit well with other rangers. One seasonal ranger, whom Prien had hired in 1915, judged him as "a nice fellow but wasn't fitted for the job."[2] Other rangers were more outspoken, and one even accused Prien of dishonesty.[3] By late 1915 his lack of leadership and his adversarial relations with others proved so disastrous that Mather was forced to demote Prien to first class ranger and transfer him to Sequoia National Park, where his stay also was brief.[4]

Nevertheless, Prien, while chief ranger, had accomplished some needed organization of the ranger force. Grades, pay, and qualifications were

---

1. More than four million in 1996.
2. "Personal Account" by Lester S. Brown, a seasonal ranger from 1915 to 1917, September 1964, at YRL.
3. Retired ranger John Henneberger, in his 1965 manuscript, "To Protect and Preserve: A History of the National Park Rangers," pp. 91–95, elaborated on Prien's controversial actions. (Copy in YRL.)
4. Other than a mention of Prien's arrival at Sequoia on May 15, 1916, no records exist in the Sequoia-Kings Canyon National Park archives.

brought into compliance with the new Park Service (NPS) regulations. Thus the chief ranger received $1,500 a year, the two assistant chiefs got $1,350 and $1,250; Archie Leonard and Forest Townsley became first class rangers at $1,200 a year, while temporary rangers ("seasonals" or "90 day wonders") got $100 a month minus $20 for housing. This $20 was a form of rent intended for the upkeep of the often-inadequate ranger stations, tent cabins, or, after it opened in 1920, room and board at the Rangers Club, a picturesque building. It, its furnishings, and even its chinaware were financed by the independently wealthy Mather and were given to the Park for the use of unmarried seasonals, backcountry rangers in the winter months, and, sometimes, a VIP. All appointments of rangers, except for seasonals, were made by the NPS—i.e., by Mather and Albright in Washington.

Another big step toward professionalism oc-

curred in the spring of 1915, when Prien led his ten-man force to El Portal. According to the May 8th *Mariposa Gazette,* they were met by a tailor from San Francisco who fitted them with new uniforms. "They were made of German elastic cloth with a color blend of olive drab and green," the reporter stated. "They are very handsome—and breathe it softly—the cost of them is handsome too."

Phyllis Freeland Broyles, daughter of a ranger, wife of another, and mother of a third, expanded on that in 1995 by writing, "The cost of $24 was terrific for German elastique (a sort of semi-stretch wool twill that wore like iron). Sure, it was a big slice of your $100, out of which $20 had already been taken for housing—but it served as further incentive to consider making a career out of NPS—if you weren't in love with it already! Unfortunately, it was many years before the NPS got around to authorizing a uniform allowance to insure that

The Yosemite ranger force of 1915, including the three men who played musical chairs as chief ranger: Charles Bull on the white horse, Oliver Prien next to him, and Forest Townsley at far right. Between them are Jake Gaylor, Clyde Boothe, George McNabb, Charlie Leidig, Charlie Adair, and Archie Leonard. (Bingaman collection.)

The Lewis family: Bernice, "Dusty," and Carle, flanked by O. G. Taylor and John Bingaman, at the Merced Grove ranger station in 1921. (Bingaman collection.)

rangers were always neatly dressed." Employees were entitled to wear service stripes on their sleeves for each five years of service. Only Gaylor, Leonard, and Townsley qualified. Over the years, modifications to uniforms were frequent.[5]

Prien's successor was Assistant Chief Ranger Charles C. Bull, a Harvard graduate, described by Mark Daniels as "athletic, resourceful, and tactful." Hired late in 1914, Bull had only a few months in the field before he was appointed chief ranger on January 1, 1916. His tenure was even shorter than that of Prien, but for different reasons. Part of the problem was Mather who, four months later, wanted Bull to transfer to Rocky Mountain Na-

tional Park. In this case he had misjudged his man. Not only did Bull reject the offer but on May 3, 1916, resigned from the Park Service as well. Why? The next week's *Gazette* provided the reason: a position as manager of a gold mine in British Guiana was far more alluring than any NPS career. Exit the "resourceful and tactful" Bull.[6]

For the third time in two years, a chief ranger was needed in Yosemite, and this time Mather chose more carefully and wisely. He selected Forest Townsley, whose notable career and achievements are chronicled in the following chapter.

Mather's choices for Yosemite's first civilian superintendent and his assistant were excellent.

---

5. Bryce Workman's three-volume set, *Badges and Insignia, In Search of Identity,* and *Ironing out the Wrinkles* is an important and interesting source for all of the NPS changes in everything from boots to hats. All have been published since 1991 by the NPS History Collection, Harpers Ferry, West Virginia.
6. Letter to Secretary of the Interior Lane from Mark Daniels, Yosemite's acting superintendent, October 20, 1915. (YRL, Henneberger collection.)

Rangers Billy Nelson, at left, and Jim Lloyd pose in front of the original YNP Headquarters. According to Supt. Lewis, the building was "a ramshackle affair" with warped floor, poorly lighted and ventilated interior, and "infested by vermin." (NPS collection.)

Washington B "Dusty" Lewis arrived in March of 1916. He was 32, an engineering graduate of the University of Michigan with a variety of job experiences in North and South America, particularly with the U.S. Geological Survey. In addition, he was handsome, personable, and articulate. It did not hurt that his wife was also attractive and vivacious. Four years later a son Carle (Mrs. Lewis's maiden name) was born, completing the All-American family image.

During the superintendent's inspection trips in the Park, it was impossible not to acquire a layer of dust on his official car, its driver, and himself. Dust swirled up, over, behind, and into the vehicle. Before long, Lewis received the nickname "Dusty," probably in part because he constantly stressed the necessity of improving and paving the various roads. Sprinkling was a stopgap; and gravel, he stated in his annual report for 1917, "while very satisfactory when first applied, decomposes very rapidly and pulverizes into fine dust."

Lewis and assistant director Albright were close friends, as were their wives, Bernice Lewis and Grace Albright; and whenever the Albrights visited Yosemite, there were excursions, picnics, and highjinks. As Albright, known affectionately as HMA, noted in his unpublished memoirs, they were all still "footloose, fancy-free and childless" in the late 1910s and early 1920s.[7] On one languid summer day, they rode horseback to the Mariposa Grove, where they dismounted, and wandered afoot.

"As usual, 'Dusty' and I got to playing around, which almost turned into disaster," HMA recorded later. While the women were out of sight, Dusty wrapped himself in a saddle blanket and "crept up on Grace and Bernice, suddenly letting out with a wild Indian war-whoop, scaring the very devil out of them. Bernice shrieked and promptly slid into the stream. My girl instantly swung her leather bag, socking him full in the face, and was pulling out her long, venomous hat pin for a final thrust when she recognized her foe. . . . What a sight! Bernice wet and muddied, 'Dusty' nursing a red and puffy cheek, and Grace grinning like a Cheshire cat, still clutching her wicked weapon!"

On August 24, 1917, the two couples participated in the first motorized boat ride in Yosemite—a first that never made the history books. Between 1916 and 1925 the Gutleben brothers, C. T. and Phil, built almost everything new in Yosemite, including the Administration Building, the museum, the Glacier Point Hotel, the powerhouse, a new school, the toboggan slide, a zoo, and comfort stations. In 1917 C. T. invited the Albrights and Lewises, photographer Arthur Pillsbury, and two concessionaire officials to take a cruise on the Merced River in his brand spanking new steel-hulled, 10-horsepower motorboat. The Park Service representatives suspected an ulterior motive, but there were no specific regulations prohibiting boats, and it was a great day for a lark, so they set off blithely. "We drifted along at a slow pace, soaking up the magnificent sights of the towering walls above us," HMA narrated.

> Reaching a point near the base of El Capitan and Cathedral Rocks, we went ashore, lounged around on the grass, and had a huge picnic lunch. Afterwards, Gutleben edged up to Lewis and myself and popped up with a proposition. Of course, we knew he'd have one or he wouldn't have gone to the expense and trouble of hauling his boat to Yosemite. He suggested that we grant him a boating franchise in the Park. He proposed six motorboats, fifty rowboats and twenty canoes for tourists to cruise the Merced. If that wasn't enough, he stated that he'd "need a small dam" built to make possible the boat trips from El Capitan to Camp Curry road. And who do you think he wanted to build the dam on the Merced? The National Park Service, of course! Well, Lewis just hooted with laughter. I honestly believe he thought Gutleben was joking and would soon arrive at his real proposition. But I was looking directly into Gutleben's face and saw the seriousness as well as the dismay at Lewis' reaction. He meant his proposal. I didn't hesitate to turn it down on the spot—although in a reasonable, pragmatic way, telling him wartime was no time to start new ventures, no money to do anything. I added, what I had found was a universal answer when dodges had to be made,

---

7. Quotations are from Albright's unpublished reminiscences. His daughter, Marian Albright Schenck, kindly made them available.

a vague statement that Mather would have to decide a concession matter of this size. He took it all in stride at this time although boating became a real issue later on.[8]

World War I inspired far greater threats than boating. Beef was a necessity to fuel the armed services, and therefore cattlemen reasoned that there was no better place to fatten cattle than on Yosemite meadows. The Park Service lost that battle, and Lewis was forced to allow several thousand cattle to graze inside Yosemite until the war ended late in 1918. Sheepmen campaigned vigorously to introduce 50,000 "hoofed locusts" into their old haunts, and Secretary Lane caved in. Albright was ordered to keep silent; but, he said, "word leaked out and before long a lot of congressmen were call-

ing the Secretary to demand that the sheep not be allowed in. Lane felt the heat, and we won that battle."[9]

Patrolmen were needed more than ever, but enlistments and the military draft had reduced the ranger force. Superintendent Lewis noted in his yearly report for 1918 that older men, "realizing the situation . . . made an even greater effort than before to keep the ranger force going." At 33, Lewis himself had eagerly sought a commission in the Engineer Corps but was persuaded to remain in his essential position. Albright was equally thwarted when Secretary Lane said he couldn't leave while Mather was incapacitated by a nervous breakdown.

Reluctantly but zealously, Lewis continued to

Left to right: Chief Ranger Forest Townsley; Landscape Engineer Daniel Hull; Supt. W. B. Lewis; NPS Director Stephen T. Mather; Chief Naturalist Ansel Hall; Asst. Supt. Ernest Leavitt; Asst. Director Horace M. Albright; and Postmaster Fred C. "Alex" Alexander, in front of Yosemite's new post office in 1924. (Bingaman collection.)

---

8. Boating still is not allowed on the Merced, but rafting is when the river is high.
9. Horace M. Albright (as told to Robert Cahn), *The Birth of the National Park Service* (Hope Brothers, 1985) p. 58.

preside over the unprecedented development of a physical infrastructure plus protective and interpretive divisions in Yosemite. Within a decade, Yosemite was propelled from pioneer conditions, with only two miles of paved road, decrepit buildings, patchwork sanitary facilities, and inadequate power, into an entity befitting the 20th century. Now visitors could travel on a first-class all-year highway (140) that followed the Merced River Canyon through El Portal and on into Yosemite Valley.

Visitors could stay in improved campgrounds or at one of two handsome new hotels—The Ahwahnee and the Glacier Point Hotel—and enjoy, without even realizing it, up-to-date utilities and sanitation systems. A skating rink and toboggan slide had been developed by the Curry Company, as had several High Sierra Camps, gas stations, and a repair garage.

Rangers worked in comfortable, rodent-free offices, children attended a small but modern grammar school, and Park Service housing was pleasant with modern conveniences. Rustic-appearing houses were built in a separate area called Lost Arrow, near the school and within sight and sound of Yosemite Falls. They had garages and a semblance of landscaping. Later, two-story apartment buildings were added to the complex. Rangers and their families were mixed in with essential support personnel such as the chief electrician, plumbers, and the resident dentist.

While democracy was inherent, and all children—Indian, concessionaire, and Park Service mingled at school, there was a definite "town-gown" schism, with the usually better-educated Park people looking down on the more business-oriented concessionaire employees. Community activities centered around church and school, a few clubs, dancing, tennis, bridge. The part-time presence of Ansel Adams added class and good times, since he and his wife, Virginia, threw great parties.

Whereas the pioneer village (soon renamed the Old Village) was an unplanned, helter-skelter collection of flimsy frame structures, the Government Center (now called Yosemite Village) was structured in every way from terrain to architecture and convenience. At last there were substantial first-class buildings of rock and timber, housing administrative offices, a museum, and post office, plus commercial studios with living quarters for the

Assistant Director Horace M. Albright was respected and loved throughout the NPS. (Courtesy of YRL.)

Pillsburys, the Bests, the Boysens, and the Foleys. Backed by cliffs and Yosemite Falls, the widely spaced assemblage had a pleasing harmony; and all but two of those structures remain in daily use more than seventy years later.

Lewis had reason to be satisfied, but listed 12 unmet needs in his annual report for 1927, the same year in which a heart attack felled him, precipitating his departure. After his untimely death, in 1930, Yosemite's new hospital (now a clinic), a creek, and a mountain were named for him (see Chapter 5).

During the Lewis years and until 1931, Ernest P.

Leavitt was assistant superintendent in charge of office management, disbursing, purchasing, preparation of contracts, and routine functions.[10] That the Yosemite changes and building program progressed smoothly was partly due to Leavitt, who handled not only an enormous amount of detail but acted for Lewis when he was attending to governmental matters elsewhere.

Even though Lewis and Leavitt were considered outstanding leaders, Washington, meaning Mather (when he was well) and Albright, still made many of the decisions. They visited the Park several times each year and were well-acquainted with its needs, personnel, and problems. Long distance calls were limited because of the expense, but directive telegrams and letters were frequent. Mather was partial to Yosemite. Consequently it was a showplace park—the shining example to both the public and politicians of why a Park Service was important.

Mather and Albright inspired immense loyalty and dedication. As Phyllis Freeland Broyles put it, "It was a phenomenon that I still find hard to put into words: the elation, the joy, the wonder and pride of the young rangers, whether seasonal or permanent, to find themselves responsible for all this grandeur—and to be paid for the job! Those who, like my father, knew Mather—rode with him, ate with him, met with him—absorbed his reverence for the protection of nature, and it never left them."

The engineering, forestry, ranger naturalist, and protective divisions were all headed by competent men, none more visible and memorable than the chief ranger, Forest S. Townsley, a Mather man but an independent cuss.

---

10. Leavitt's Yosemite experience began in 1910 when, at the age of 25, he served as chief clerk for the Army and later continued with the Park Service, being eminently suited for his new position. Three years as assistant superintendent qualified him for successful superintendencies of Hawaii and Crater Lake national parks. His sister, Amy, married Fred Alexander, who was Yosemite's postmaster from 1920 to 1953.

4 The Chief

For nearly 30 years, Forest Sanford Townsley was called the "Chief," in recognition of his position as Yosemite's chief ranger and his authoritative stature both physically and morally. He was a big, broad-shouldered six-footer with a genial, affable expression and direct blue eyes that could turn glacial.

He was born on August 24, 1882 in Greeley Center, Nebraska, the oldest of Orpha Belle and Willis L. Townsley's four children. In 1888, Willis Townsley was appointed deputy United States Marshal with headquarters at Guthrie, soon to be the capital of the Oklahoma Territory. Because of his father's job, Forest was an eyewitness to three of the ten tumultuous land rushes when Indian land was opened to homesteaders between 1889 and 1906.

His early sense of injustice was heightened by seeing the cheaters, squatters, and land grabbers that eluded or bribed soldiers to rush in before a gunshot signalled the official opening. Along with the excitement of observing the land openings, young Forest also witnessed the eviction of the native Indians—the Cherokees, Kiowas, Comanches, and Choctaws—to lands farther and farther west. The sensitive boy acquired knowledge and appreciation of their traits, skills, and culture that he never forgot.

"I didn't have much education myself," he was to say later, "because I worked for my living before I finished the (eight) grades." However, he acquired plainsmen skills—hunting, trapping, fishing, packing, riding, and how to wield an axe, pick, and shovel. Hard work never fazed him, but he had ambitions beyond common labor. "Worked as a baker three years before I was 21," he volunteered for a Park Service questionnaire. "Owned my own bakery and store operating successfully for about four years."

Perhaps his mother taught him how to bake. More certainly it was she who taught him how to fish, for she was an avid fisherwoman. In fact, it was fish that determined the family's move to Sulphur in southern Oklahoma, where they vacationed in 1900. According to a family member, "Forest had been finned by a catfish, and a serious infection followed. The Townsleys had been told that Forest's leg would have to be amputated. They decided to try the healing springs at Sulphur, where they packed mud around the leg. It got well."[1]

Soon the family moved to Sulphur, near the fresh and mineral springs that became America's ninth national park, in 1904. In time Horace Albright labeled the 1.5-square-mile Platt National Park as "totally lacking in national park qualifications . . . established because of the parochial enthusiasm of local politicians."[2]

Travesty or not, Townsley was pleased to be hired by the Interior Department as a patrolman at Platt. He acted also as janitor, fire-maker, carrier of coal, wood, and water, and mailman, and he chased livestock. For example, during February of 1907, a total of 298 cattle and horses were evicted. Tramps, bee hunters, "and other disorderly persons" were similarly unwelcome. Forest utilized his laborer's expertise in building trails, roads, and bridges in the Park. He even helped design "a good serviceable outfit for a mounted patrol ranger . . . similar

---

1. A wealth of documentation exists in the Townsley file in the Yosemite Research Library. Material on his family is found in *Murray County, Heart of Eden,* by Opal H. Brown. (Nortex, 1977.)
2. For years the NPS worked to have Platt removed from the system. Finally, in 1976, Platt National Park and the nearby Arbuckle National Recreation Area were combined to form the Chickasaw National Recreation Area, memorializing the Chickasaw Indians, its original owners. Today, Platt is administered by a small NPS staff. Transfer there is still tantamount to exile. Albright commented disparagingly on Platt in *The Birth of the Park Service.*

Malvin Dabbs Townsley, Hazel, Virginia (seated) and her twin brother Joe, Malvin's sister, and Forest, Jr., in 1915. (Jennie Barnett collection, courtesy of Betty Zajic.)

to the regular Army uniform at that time." He had become a skilled fisherman and took advantage of the many local streams.

About 1906 he married Texas-born Malvin Dabbs. Their first child, Hazel, was born in 1907, twins Virginia and Joseph arrived in 1910, and Forest Jr. in 1913. It was a full house on a slender income and he decided to move.

Because transfers between parks were not then allowed, Forest had to resign from Platt before applying to another park for a job. Chances are that he had a promise of a job in Yosemite National Park for, in anticipation of the cavalry's departure, the Interior Department was beefing up Yosemite's tiny ranger force. Undoubtedly the support of one of Oklahoma's U.S. senators, the superintendent of Platt, and the chief clerk of the Interior Department helped too.

Asked decades later why he had chosen Yosemite, in far off California, his answer was prac-

tical. "I didn't know much about this place before I came, but I had several children, and I did know that there was a school house . . . so I said, 'There is the place for us. Lets go.'" The family arrived in Yosemite Valley in a horse-drawn stage in July of 1913. Forest found scenery, terrain, elevation, wildlife, and size in complete contrast to Platt. Yosemite was a haven and a challenge to explore, to protect, and ultimately to cherish.

Housing at first was the five-room lower floor of a former stage drivers' boarding house across the river from Camp Curry. Malvin's routine was little changed from Sulphur: cooking, cleaning, washing, and caring for the children. Only Hazel was of school age. Malvin's closest friend seems to have been Jennie Barnett, wife of stable boss Jim Barnett, with whom she took walks.

Forest was dispatched on lengthy patrols along the western and southern boundaries of the Park. Since that summer of 1913 was the last during

The Chief was a splendid horseman. (YRL collection.)

Since the season in the high country was short, Forest was assigned to other stations as well that year, following the pattern of rangers alternating between summer and winter assignments. Each job was demanding, with a different set of problems and challenges. After the college-boy rangers left, late in 1914, he was stationed at Camp A. E. Wood as an automobile checker.

During winters in Yosemite Valley, Forest's early training in trapping and taxidermy came in handy because Joseph Grinnell, director of the Museum of Vertebrate Zoology at UC Berkeley needed animal skins and skulls for study.[4] Townsley supplied specimens at $2.00 and $2.50 each and probably began stuffing and mounting animals about the same time. Some of them were exhibited in the decaying Park Service headquarters that constituted the first Yosemite museum.

Three months after W. B. Lewis was appointed superintendent, in 1916, he called Townsley to headquarters from Camp A. E. Wood. The result of their meeting appeared in the *Mariposa Gazette* on May 20.

> The appointment of Forest S. Townsley to succeed C. C. Bull, who has resigned as chief park ranger, caused much pleasure to Yosemite residents in general. Mr. Townsley is well qualified to fill the position with entire satisfaction to all.

which troops would patrol the high country, enforce laws, and administer all Yosemite affairs, it was essential that rangers should learn to know the terrain. Whereas Platt had a total of eight miles of trails at about 1,000 feet in elevation, Yosemite had hundreds of miles of pathways leading from 2,000 to over 10,000 feet.

Late that summer he alternated with Ranger Oliver Prien at manning the entrance station at the Merced Grove of Big Trees. As noted elsewhere, Townsley had the dubious honor of issuing the first automobile permit. In 1914, after the snow melted, he and his family rode "into the Tuolumne district where he was to take charge, his wife carrying their 18-month old son in the saddle with her."[3]

---

3. Townsley, as quoted in the March 1943 issue of *Westways* magazine.
4. Six years of work culminated in Grinnell and Storer's monumental *Animal Life in the Yosemite*, published in 1924. Correspondence between the authors and Townsley is preserved at the Museum of Vertebrate Zoology, UCB.

Superintendent W. B. Lewis was able, intelligent, and good-looking, although his ranger hat hid a bald spot. (Bingaman collection.)

Townsley had had the political clout to obtain the Yosemite job, but not to advance once he was there. Prien and Bull had advanced, yet neither had lasted long as chief ranger, so this time, with Mather and Albright at the helm, the appointment was made more carefully, and was based less on political considerations. Townsley was their choice on the basis of his 14 years of practical experience in both the field and the office. Here was a man they had observed, a man's man who was loyal, innovative, and good at organization. Besides, he was a good natured, likable fellow who, if resentful at being passed over twice, didn't betray it. Superintendent Lewis announced the appointment, but as with most such decisions it was made in Washington.

As chief ranger, Townsley worked directly under Lewis and Leavitt, but shouldered the responsibilities of law enforcement, fire-control, campground management, backcountry patrols, traffic control, search and rescue operations, protecting wildlife, fish planting, and public information. To do all this he supervised a disparate staff of ex-soldiers and civilians that alternated seasonally between seven and 25.

Townsley continued to ride on patrols to expand his knowledge of the Park. His detailed directives as to where to go and what to accomplish in a set period became famous, if not infamous. It may be supposed that he had decided ideas on how the force should be operated, and how a chief ranger should act. He never asked his men to undertake anything he hadn't done or couldn't do, forgetting, however, that his energy level and devotion to duty weren't easy to match. He could be tough and demanding, enough so that his men were wary of his wrath.

According to ranger Jimmy Lloyd, Townsley "was a very fine supervisor, a leader among men—thoroughly experienced in law enforcement—willing to experiment with new things—endure hardships such as snowshoe trips, which up to that time had not occurred." He realized that the old-timers who were not used to snowshoes might be inept and resistant, but he encouraged the younger rangers to accompany him on snowshoe trips which, Lloyd remembered, "were quite strenuous."

One of Townsley's immediate responsibilities was to implement a new system of controlling fire-

The Chief with "Prunes," an orphan cub that he raised in the 1920s. Taken from a postcard by A. C. Pillsbury.

1924, for instance, Lewis docked him a day's pay "for failure to file annual leave card in advance." The chief was careless about turning in receipts for car expenses, yet he sought reimbursement. On one occasion he refused to pay a $4.35 claim on uniform equipment until the superintendent became involved. In addition to a couple of dogs, during the 1920s he kept an orphaned bear cub named Prunes as a pet. Postcards of the two were sold long after Prunes was in a zoo.

Arrests were not common. Rangers made them for assault, disorderly conduct, theft, cruelty to animals, and breaking one of the numerous traffic laws. Sentences given by the U.S. Commissioner ranged from reprimands to fines to eviction from the Park to jail terms served elsewhere, and to revocation of auto permits for hours or a day or two.[5] Local residents were the chief violators of traffic laws. Occasionally Townsley shared in reward money for capturing men wanted elsewhere. For

arms. Entrance station rangers confiscated, sealed, and stored all guns carried by motorists. Upon their departure, the sealed weapons were returned. Anyone on foot or horseback with a gun had to relinquish same, and the weapons were returned by mail at the owner's expense. Approximately 1,500 guns of various sorts were collected from 33,000 visitors that year. The right to bear arms did not extend inside national parks. Naturally there were verbal and written objections, but as the word spread, violations diminished.

Soon Townsley headed a cohesive, well-organized law enforcement force, but he was also something of a maverick. He boasted a siren horn on his car that he had snagged from photographer Arthur Pillsbury. Unlike his boss, Lewis, who was always impeccably dressed in a uniform of a coat of dark green, riding breeches, leather puttees, gray or white shirt with dark green tie, shined boots and stiff brimmed Stetson, the chief was often seen with unbuttoned pockets, a scarf in lieu of a tie, and other variations of the dress code. His considerable girth rumpled shirts and trousers almost immediately.

Townsley's service record shows that his attention to regulations was less than wholehearted. In

Superintendent C. G. Thomson, who didn't always see eye-to-eye with Chief Ranger Townsley.

While stationed at Grand Canyon National Park, the Chief received a medal for his equestrian skill from King Albert of Belgium.
(Elaine Townsley collection.)

instance, Bad Axe, Michigan awarded him $250 for his arrest of a man wanted there for murder.

El Portal, 12 miles west of the Valley, was headquarters for railroad men, loggers, and some diehard miners; it was a small but tough town. Once, Ranger Jimmy Lloyd recounted, "Townsley had a gun drawn on him on the porch of the El Portal Hotel and was saved by Assistant Chief Ranger Clyde Boothe knocking the gun out of a barber's hands. He was a hot-headed Kentuckian who later shot a brakeman on the Y.V. Railroad and was sentenced to San Quentin."[6]

The Chief Ranger handled his multiple duties and still had energy to spare. His interest in Indians and their crafts, begun during his boyhood, had rekindled. Yosemite's dwindling numbers of Native Americans were hired for menial jobs in hotels and tourist camps, and Townsley felt that their worth needed recognition, encouragement, and preservation. With the cooperation of the superintendent and staff, in 1916 the Chief organized Indian Field Days. Horse races, foot races, and a tug of war were crowd attractions, but baskets and bead work were also featured. As the years passed, 50 or so local Indians and up to 100 from areas adjoining the Park participated in a parade, horse races, trick riding, basket and bead-work exhibitions, ceremonial dances, and a baby show—all of which took place in Yosemite Village and Leidig Meadow directly across the river. Cash prizes were awarded, and the prize-winning baskets were sold to spectators and collectors.

The Chief was proud of the women's participation, boasting that Leanna Tom and Lucy Telles could compete with the finest basket weavers anywhere. Additionally, he stated that "The purpose of Indian Field Days is to lead the Indians back to their original symbols and conventional designs."[7]

Mather was so impressed by Townsley's organizational and leadership abilities that he sent him to the Grand Canyon to organize the rangers there after its creation as a national park in 1919.

At the Canyon, Townsley watched two of the rangers, Clyde West and Cal Peck, using the diamond hitch in packing mules. "That's not the way we do it in Yosemite" the Chief commented, and proceeded to demonstrate the squaw hitch. West watched in silence, then strode over and "hit the pack with the heel of his palm. It slid under the mule's belly, the mule bucked all over the corral, scattering the pack's contents. "That's the way we *don't* do it," West said emphatically."[8]

The most exciting event of Townsley's temporary assignment was the visit of the King, Queen, and Crown Prince of Belgium.[9] Security was not the only aspect of the royal sojourn to worry Town-

---

5. As of June 1920, Yosemite was exclusively under Federal jurisdiction. All felonies and misdemeanors were judged by the commissioner, who imposed penalties "not exceeding $500 or imprisonment . . . not longer than six months, or both. (Superintendent's Yearly Report for 1920. The first commissioner was Chris Degnan, son of the pioneering Degnans.)
6. Letter of Nov. 28, 1979 from J. V. Lloyd to Craig Bates, in YRL.
7. Biographical article on Forest Townsley in the *Stockton Record*, Sept. 13, 1924. The most comprehensive information about Indian Field Days appears in Craig D. Bates and Martha J. Lee, *Tradition and Innovation: A Basket History of the Indians of the Yosemite-Mono Lake Area* (El Portal, CA: Yosemite Association, 1990.)
8. Bookman Michael Harrison recounted this story to the author. He heard it in 1922 when he joined the ranger force at Grand Canyon National Park.

Rangers Henry Skelton, Forest Townsley, and Billy Nelson place a plaque honoring Supt. Lewis on the mountain named for him. (Photograph by J. V. Lloyd, Hoyt collection.)

sley. "We had to scurry around to make arrangements for their reception," he recalled. "We lacked sufficient uniforms for the men. Some wore the regulation pants without regulation coats, and some the coats without the pants, but we met the king and the royal party and did them all the honor we knew how to show." Before his departure, King Albert decorated the Chief for his superior horsemanship.

Mather could not bestow medals or bonuses, but he sent the Chief a personal check with a note suggesting that he use it to visit his parents in Oklahoma.[10] Whether Townsley did or not is unknown, but he kept in close touch with his family, and various members visited him.

The Townsleys' marriage ended in divorce not long before Malvin died, in 1924. Fatherhood curbed Forest's freedom, but Hazel, his oldest, could take care of her siblings so that he could attend local dances. For a while, both he and Bert Sault liked the same girl, and Bert's bachelor friends bet him $5.00 he wouldn't dare take her out on a date.

"Well, I took her to a dance at Camp Curry," Bert told the author years later. "We had a good time, I pocketed my five bucks and about 2. a.m. walked back to the Rangers Club. I found sealed orders on my bed, and, after I read them, that five bucks didn't look so good, and neither did I. The orders were, 'Report to Merced Grove for patrol duty. Depart at 5 a.m.' Naturally, it was signed by Townsley."

"Well, Merced Grove was considered to be the Siberia of Yosemite by then. Almost no one drove in on the rutty, old Coulterville Road, and there wasn't much to do except patrol.[11] That's where my

---

9. *Stockton Record,* Sept. 13, 1924. For mention of King Albert's Yosemite visit in October 1919, see the last chapter of this book.
10. Robert Shankland, *Steve Mather of the National Parks* (New York: Albert Knopf, 1954) p. 165.
11. Only three cars came into Yosemite over the Coulterville Road in 1926. The entrance station therefore was closed. (Superintendent's Annual Report, 1927.)

The opening of the All-Year Highway in August 1926 was prelude to an invasion of what John Muir had once described as "blunt-nose mechanical beetles." (Hoyt collection.)

five bucks and I spent the next month. After that, I didn't mess with the Chief."

Both Bert and the Chief married, but neither to the woman in dispute. Bert married the local schoolteacher, and Townsley made Inez Conroy, a secretary who worked in the new Park headquarters, his bride in September of 1925.[12] He was 43 and she was 25. Their only child, John, was born in April 1927.

They lived in Chris Jorgensen's picturesque studio home. Built in 1900 near the Merced River, it had been recycled twice since the popular artist's departure in 1917. It was used as a home for single rangers until the 1920 opening of the still extant Rangers Club, financed by Mather. After that, the house was used temporarily as a museum, in which the Chief's stuffed animals and birds had a prominent part, until a permanent facility opened in 1924. Townsley and his children crowded the house, but he made an addition.[13]

An addition was made to the house at an unknown date. Its last tenants were Tom and Evelyn Tucker and their four children. They moved out in 1961; the house was intentionally burned in May

---

12. Their marriage was in San Francisco at the home of Forest's sister, Hazel Townsley Neal. She and her husband were the witnesses to the ceremony performed by the Dean of Grace Cathedral.
13. Many colorful details of the picturesque house and its outbuildings, including one that housed an acetylene gas plant, were assembled by Katherine Mather Littell for her Master's thesis in art. Two pictures of the studio, inside and out, appeared in her booklet *Chris Jorgensen: California Artist* (Sonora, CA: Fine Arts Research Publishing Co., 1988.)

1965. Inexplicably, the cabin that Jorgensen had built for his son was moved to the Pioneer History Center at Wawona under the mistaken assumption that it had been the artist's studio.

Marriage and fatherhood (again) were personal milestones, but the landmark date for Yosemite was July 31, 1926 when highway 140, the All-Year route, was opened to the public with great ceremony. No longer would Yosemite be inaccessible by automobile in the winter by the snows that blocked the still primitive Big Oak Flat and Wawona roads. Americans were already so wedded to the mobility and independence provided by automobiles that they wanted better roads and convenient gas stations. Park Service planners foresaw impact from Detroit's boxes on wheels, but no one visualized the extent of the invasion until the Memorial Day weekend of 1927.

On each day of that three-day May holiday, 3,000 or more autos entered the Valley, the great bulk of them via the new road. On the middle day, cars were backed up from the new Arch Rock checking station all the way to El Portal. Campgrounds overflowed and people camped on meadows, causing damage and a health menace. Gasoline stations ran out of gas, the store was low on staples, and people were everywhere.

It was the Chief's responsibility to implement traffic directives made by the superintendent, double the staff for each entrance station, dispatch rangers on motorcycles and horses as trouble shooters, have extra men at campgrounds and on patrols, answer a hundred complaints from the public and the concessionaire, and settle disagreements.

Not only did the Chief miss meals, but sleep as well. Only 15 extra seasonal rangers had been hired to cope with what turned out to be an 80% increase in visitations. Protecting paradise adequately was impossible. Most of the rangers were trying to cope with the overcrowding in the Valley. Other places and other needs had to be neglected. Yosemite's trial by traffic was paramount. As it still is at times!

New ideas and new faces took over in 1929. Charles Goff "Colonel" Thomson succeeded the ailing Dusty Lewis as superintendent, C. A. "Bert" Harwell became the new Park naturalist, John Wosky was named landscape architect, Jack W. Emmert and Jimmy Lloyd had new responsibilities, and more seasonal rangers were added. The old-timers were contemptuous of the seasonal 90-day-wonders, but the Park could not operate without them during summers.

The 1930s decade was paradoxical. Construction of the new Wawona, Big Oak Flat, and Tioga roads insured increased traffic at the same time that the Great Depression decreased it. In 1933, the nadir of the Depression, travel dropped to 296,000. By 1940 it exceeded 500,000, only to plummet to 119,515 in 1944 because of World War II and the attendant gas rationing. Even without crowds there were plenty of problems, and never enough money or rangers.

Although an admirer of Townsley's work, Superintendent Thomson was a stickler for rules, and the rules said that retirement came after 30 years with the NPS. Ergo, Townsley should retire on June 15, 1934. At only 52, the Chief disagreed completely, and enlisted some influential support. Consequently, Thomson was overruled, and Townsley stayed.[14]

It can be imagined that relations between the two most important men in Yosemite were strained after that, and probably not improved when in late 1936 Washington assigned Townsley to Lassen National Park as acting superintendent. An appointment like that was often the prelude to a promotion or transfer. Afterwards, if asked to accept a transfer to another park, the Chief must have refused. No wonder—he loved his job, he loved Yosemite, and he wanted nothing more than to stay there. Had he retired, he would have missed the highlight of the 1930s.[15]

On July 22, 1934, two rangers drove to Reno to escort the not yet famous First Lady of the United States into Yosemite's high country via the notori-

---

14. Ironically, Thomson's tenure ended in March 1937, when he died of a heart attack. By the 1950s, if not before, retirement was no longer mandated at any set number of years.
15. On Oct. 29, 1936, ranger Art Holmes noted: "Chief back. Everyone extending congratulations and requesting cigars."

On April 6, 1940, during her second visit to Yosemite, Eleanor Roosevelt visited the Civilian Conservation Corps camp at Wawona. From left to right: rangers Jim Skakel, John Bingaman, and John Wegner; Mrs. Roosevelt; Supt. Lawrence Merriam; Chief Ranger Forest Townsley; Secret Service agent Charles Rich, a former YNP ranger; and ranger Sam Clark. (Courtesy, Elaine F. Townsley.)

ous Lee Vining grade and pioneer Tioga Road. Eleanor Roosevelt was trying to travel incognito on vacation with her friend, former reporter Lorena Hickok, in the latter's modest convertible.[16] No Secret Service men and, after a confrontation with the press in Sacramento, no reporters, other than "Hick," who filed no stories, were present.

Like her famed Uncle Theodore, Eleanor Roosevelt was an advocate of the outdoor life. A camping trip to 9,000 foot elevation Young Lakes, six miles north of Tuolumne Meadows, had been planned and approved. Townsley had selected Billy Nelson, John Bingaman, and wildlife specialist Otto Brown, who doubled as camp cook, and others to accompany him and the women. All of

them rode horseback: pack animals carried an umbrella tent and collapsible toilet, but little else that was special. Soon the rangers realized that the First Lady was special herself. She rode well, was good company, being both interested in and appreciative of the Sierra splendor, and turned out to be an excellent camper, even taking morning swims in the lake's frigid water. After one quick dip, Hick "thought I'd never catch my breath again. It didn't bother her though. Climbing mountains, even at that altitude didn't bother her either," Hick marveled. "One morning she and the Chief Ranger climbed up to an elevation of some 13,000 feet. When they came down, I thought the Chief ranger was going to have a stroke. His face was purple.

---

16. Lorena A. Hickok's book *Eleanor Roosevelt: The Reluctant First Lady*, published by Dodd, Mead, yielded colorful details of the trip. Secret Service men were well aware of their schedule, and appeared at each state boundary to change the car's license plates to protect anonymity.

But Mrs. Roosevelt? You'd have thought she had come in from a stroll in Central Park in New York!"

Afterwards the First Lady remembered her three days of enchantment with nostalgia. Roosevelt Lake was named for her, not for her Uncle Theodore, who visited in 1903, or her husband Franklin, who was in the Park for less than a day in 1938.

Eleanor's Roosevelt's second visit to Yosemite, in April 1940, was far more official and public, featuring a tour of the Civilian Conservation Corps Camp at Wawona. This time there was some press coverage, and a Secret Service agent, Charles Rich, who had served as a Yosemite ranger in the 1920s, accompanied her.

The trip and Chief Townsley were the subjects of her "My Day" column for April 10, 1940.

> He has the kindliest face I know and the most humorous, yet the eyes look you so straight in the face that I should hate to meet him if I wished to hide anything. He gives you a sense of strength and confidence. . . .

In a 1929 letter to Townsley, Superintendent Thomson had defined his leadership qualities as a combination of "unremitting energy, foresight, and planning, and the stimulation of your own example." World War II was the supreme test of these qualities.

His perpetually understaffed force was virtually decimated by the enlistments of rangers following December 7, 1941. By mid-1943, the permanent staff had been reduced to 13! Seasonals were down to 23 from a total of 85 in 1941 and 60 in 1942. (Anyone who joined the armed forces or took a war job was furloughed, their jobs and residences being promised back upon their return.) In May of 1943, the Chief was delighted to have 70-year-old Billy Nelson come out of retirement for the duration.

Visitation also decreased dramatically once gas rationing went into effect in December 1942. Only 127,643 people visited Yosemite in 1943, the lowest total since 1922. Similarly, rescues, arrests, and fires were reduced. High school boys and men classified 4F were recruited to fight fires.

There were new problems and responsibilities. Jobs ordinarily done by maintenance men, such as clearing trails, maintaining telephone lines, cutting wood for winter, even cleaning comfort stations, had to be assumed by rangers in addition to their regular duties.

Another problem, unique to the war, was the threat of sabotage to the water system. Hetch Hetchy Reservoir, the major water supplier for San Francisco, was considered of critical importance. Round-the-clock guard duties were instituted by armed national guardsmen, and the intricate water system, including Lake Eleanor and Cherry Lake, was closed to the public. Armed rangers were assigned to night watch in utility areas. Superintendent Kittredge conferred with Townsley, then ordered tried and true ranger Bingaman to Mather Station, a few miles above Hetch Hetchy Dam, to coordinate activities of the City of San Francisco, the National Guard, and rangers in protecting the vital facilities.[17]

Though battlefields were remote, the sight of uniformed men and weapons was commonplace. There was a Signal Corp camp at Wawona, and Camp 11 (now Upper Pines) was reserved for servicemen. After July 1943, when the Ahwahnee Hotel was converted into a special Naval Hospital, sailors were abundant. Ranger and naturalist activities were made available to them, including skiing at Badger Pass and a few firefalls put on despite the fact that the spectacle had been suspended for the duration. Rangers were needed to direct and control all functions.

The Chief was a conspicuous figure in the war efforts, conscientiously purchasing a $50 Savings Bond each month, and urging the local school children to buy defense stamps. His son, John, who always referred to his father as the Chief, attended the school.

Early on he had realized that being the chief ranger's son was akin to being a minister's boy. Family and community expectations were far higher than his own. His escapades with Bob Skakel were usually clandestine, and kept that way by friendly rangers. A young, doting, and impul-

---

17. After Thomson's death, Laurence C. Merriam served as Yosemite's superintendent from 1937 to 1941. He was succeeded by Frank Kittredge, who remained until 1947.

The Chief with his dynamic and much younger second wife, Inez, and her formidable mother, Lottie Conroy, enjoying the pause that refreshes. (Courtesy, Elaine F. Townsley.)

gulf. John began high school in Mariposa not long after his parents purchased 20 acres there. Working together on the land, where horses and goats grazed, may have improved the situation, but the Chief's commitment to his job took priority.[18]

"Ranger Boss," a laudatory article by Jean Joy, appeared in the March 1943 issue of *Westways* magazine, but it must have been written at least two years earlier because no mention of World War II is in it, and the quotations of the Chief allude to a peacetime atmosphere. Nevertheless, the piece illustrated his leadership and his appreciation of the teamwork in Yosemite.

"It would be hard to beat my rangers," he told author Joy. "John Wegner, assistant chief and fire chief, has had a world of experience. Art Holmes, who works with him as assistant fire chief, has done much to eliminate fire hazards and to control the fires that start. True, we have more fires today than in the past, as there are more people in our forest, but the fires burn less acreage than formerly because they are better controlled.

"Take some of the men in charge of other divisions and look at their work," Townsley said. "Homer Hoyt supervises the office force and believe me, his job is an exacting one. Otto Brown, who heads the wild life conservation here, has splendid pictures of his activities which have been taken by Ralph Anderson, the Park photographer.

"Harry During and his staff, who look after the camp grounds, have one of the toughest jobs in the Park. They handle as many as 80,000 campers in one season. Believe me, that's some job. You can't supervise that many people and evade problems and complaints. There are always some who insist on being on the river front even if it means pitching camp in someone's lap, and those who grab three tables, make too much noise, or block the roads and

sive mother, and her formidable and often present mother, plus prolonged absences with these two major women in John's life didn't help his relations with his father.

When he had time, the Chief tried to bridge the

18. In 1936, for example, Townsley had applied for leave to coincide with John's Easter vacation, but added, "If necessary, I shall be glad to come in and help over Easter Sunday."

paths with equipment. One woman complained that the squirrels should be shot because they knocked down so many pine cones that she had to wear a cooking kettle on her head for protection."

Those who know Yosemite's chief ranger," author Joy concluded, "admire his courage and his wisdom, his love of life and sense of humor."

A few months after the article's publication, in 1943, such thoughts were uppermost in the minds of hundreds of grieving people. Not quite 61, Townsley was dead. The first announcement came when ranger's wife Eliza Danner telephoned headquarters from Tuolumne Meadows at 5:45 pm. on Wednesday, August 11.

The Chief never missed a chance to fish, even at times when trout were unlikely to rise. On that day he took advantage of a free afternoon to fish in what had been known as Townsley Lake ever since he had planted golden trout in it years earlier.

About 4 p.m., friends said, Townsley stepped back from the lake, put down his rod, sat on a rock, and collapsed. He never regained consciousness. According to the death certificate, his death was caused by an aortic aneurysm.[19]

No fewer than 15 rangers acted as pallbearers and honorary pallbearers at the Mariposa funeral parlor on August 24. It would have been Townsley's 61st birthday. Among the crowd were superintendents, assistant superintendents, and chief rangers from other national parks. Private internment was in a plot selected by John inside the Yosemite Valley Pioneer Cemetery.[20] A boulder was placed to mark the site.

The Chief was dead. Long live his influence, his law enforcement organization, his standards, and his vision. Townsley Lake, near Vogelsang Pass, memorializes not only the site of his death, but his favorite place in Yosemite, the park to which he was devoted for 30 years.

---

19. Copy obtained from the Mariposa County Hall of Records.
20. Copious and detailed documentation exists in the Yosemite Research Library on Townsley's death and the aftermath. The pallbearers were John Wegner, Buck Evans, Gus Eastman, John Bingaman, Carl Danner, Billy Nelson, Billy Merrill, Homer Hoyt, Homer Robinson, Lewis Clark, Odin "Sig" Johnson, Everett Millani, Frank Givens, Jerry Mernin, and Henry Skelton.

"Coming into Yosemite at Inspiration Point." (By cartoonist Joseph "Jo" Mora.)

5 All in a Day's Work

In the early days, rangers did not work an eight hour day, and compensation for overtime was not even envisioned. They put in whatever time was necessary to complete the job, or jobs. Nowhere is this better exemplified than in John H. Wegner's wry commentary, "All in a Day's Work."[1]

> I got phone orders at Tuolumne Meadows to pack up and come in over Sunrise Trail. Started at sunrise. Everything haywire, including cranky pack horse which kept getting off trail. Phoned in at Vernal Falls station. Ordered to hurry down, help catch two auto thieves which broke jail just after breakfast. Assigned to guard Coulterville Road. Only transportation was Chief's personal auto which I could have if I could find man who borrowed it from chief. Chief didn't know who that was. Guarded Coulterville Road until 3:00 am when ordered to valley to beat brush by the river with flashlight to locate thieves. Found one thief and captured him just before dawn. Somebody else assigned to guard him, but before I turned in, got orders to meet carload of trout fry at El Portal and help plant them in streams. Met fish O.K. but coming up El Portal Road, quad truck slipped over side of road, but was saved from going down cliff by being caught in tree. Cans of fish lashed to truck, so we saved them. Job was complicated by necessity of keeping water aerated in cans setting by roadside while we rushed more water in small bucket from stream quarter of mile away. Fish all saved. Phoned for help, and kept water in cans moving until truck dragged back on road and fish cans reloaded. Relieved of duty, with nothing to do but walk nine miles and go to bed.

Criteria for inclusion in this chapter, as in those to follow, is interest, pertinence, chronology, and quotations from participants. Unfortunately for posterity, few diaries and journals kept by rangers were preserved or have been made available to historians. One such is a terse but informative journal of eight typewritten pages kept between 1923 and the end of 1928 by Homer B. Hoyt. For more than three decades Hoyt was "Mr. Office"—in charge of the multitudinous reports and paperwork detail in the administrative office. He worked directly with the superintendent, his assistant, and the chief ranger. It was an essential position, which Hoyt filled with dogged precision until his retirement in 1959. "He has no doubt written more reports and handled more paperwork than any other ranger in the Service," John Bingaman judged.

During his early employment, however, Hoyt did a little bit of every kind of duty, as shown by his journal entries. His versatility is manifest in each cryptic, incomplete sentence, usually punctuated with dashes.

> Painted fire tools with Ranger Wegner—to Soda Springs and Devils Post Pile, Mammoth with Mr. Lewis—Overhauled Lincoln completely, blocks re-bored, new pistons—Indian Field days—handling crowds—pack trip to Pate Valley and north to Bonds Pass....

Born in Cleveland, Ohio in 1897, Hoyt worked on boats as a teenager, attended Ohio State University, and, after his parents moved to Oakland, the University of California. Along the way he acquired contrasting skills in mechanics and office work. In Yosemite his talents and education earned him an immediate niche as escort and driver for many visiting VIPs. For example, on his second day of work, May 6, 1923, he and Chief Ranger Townsley took a prominent Boston couple on a tour of the Valley. Soon Hoyt was the chauffeur for Superintendent Lewis, and for Director Mather when he was on one of his whirlwind tours of Yosemite.

---

1. Wegner's report, probably written about 1918, was reproduced by Horace M. Albright and Frank J. Taylor, *"Oh, Ranger!"* (Stanford: Stanford University Press, 1929.)

Ranger Art Holmes digs out. (Holmes collection.)

Bert Sault, at right, manned the Mariposa Grove entrance station with the company of Fred Shepherd of the Yosemite post office. (Sault collection.)

Bert Sault caulking the flume in the 1920s. (Hoyt collection.)

Chief Park Naturalist Ansel Hall using an electric jigsaw or scroll saw, probably to make a sign. (Courtesy of YRL.)

May 13, 1923 To Mariposa Grove with White [auto] first trip, Mr. Lewis and family—July 29, 1923 Mr. Mather, Myron Hunt [architect] arrive El Portal [by train] Pres Harding's visit called off [because of the President's sudden death in San Francisco]. May 13, 1924 Mr and Mrs. Walleberg, Swedish ambassador valley and to Big Trees. July

24, 1926 Crown Prince Augustus of Sweden arrived in Merced—to Big Trees and Glacier Point with party over Wawona road—hot and dusty [ranger] Walter Morse with Mather's car—secret service agents and servants.

Congressmen galore, ambassadors, writers, governors, NPS executives, businessmen—there seemed no end to the procession of VIPs. In between their visits, Hoyt

Checked [cars] at Bridal Veil to relieve Ranger

Another outdoor job for rangers was teaching people how to snowshoe and cross-country ski. It might not be much fun to meet this crowd on an icy slope. (Hoyt collection.)

Freeland—worked on pipe line putting in steel elbow—rode Dolly Gray to fire with [ranger] Westfall—Motorcycle patrol 2 weeks—Vernal Fall—boy got stuck on hillside all night on cliff—fish planting on Valley floor—Went to Half Dome with Al (Solinsky) taking down cable—fire at Bear Pits—skating at Camp 6 pond—Scraping ice pond in slush and snow. Making sleds and garbage can covers for the toboggan slide.

Occasionally, instead of escorting dignitaries, Hoyt chased crooks.

To Bridal Veil with [ranger] Rich in motorcycle [sidecar] after bootlegger Baker. [June 1924], After stolen Ford at Cascades and up Coulterville Road. Caught three convicts and got $76 reward with Green, Clark, Booth, Nelson, Chief.[2]

During slack time, especially winters, Hoyt worked in the Park Service's machine shop. Due mainly to the primitive roads, overhauls on patrol cars and motorcycles were frequent and extensive. On his January, 1925 leave without pay, he took an auto-repair course in Oakland. Probably the duty he liked best was purchasing new cars to add to the Park fleet.

---

2. According to the Superintendent's monthly report for June 1924, the escaped convicts stole the car in El Portal, ran out of gas near Cascade Fall, and began walking. One was captured by Chief Townsley, and the others were caught later the same day by Boothe, Clark, and Green. No mention was made of a reward, but it probably was from the State of California. Hoyt did not elaborate on whether the reward was shared or if each man received $76.

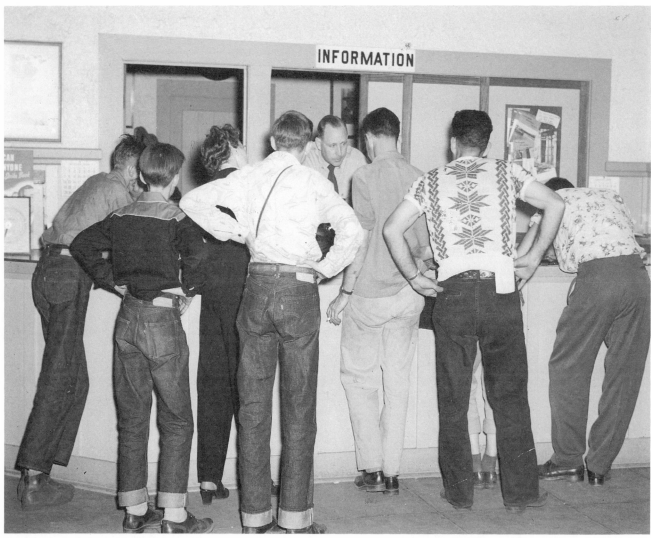

Answering visitors' endless questions was not a favorite occupation. (Bingaman collection.)

Hoyt's entries chronicled Park Service history. The illness of Superintendent Lewis in 1926, caused by heart attacks, and his departure from Yosemite in September were noted. So was Horace Albright's arrival as acting superintendent, in 1927, and his departure December 30, 1928. "Albright called East." Because of Mather's continued serious illness, he resigned, and Albright, reluctantly, became the second director of the National Park Service.[3] Recognizing that Lewis would not be able to resume work, one of Albright's early official acts was to transfer Charles G. Thomson to Yosemite as its second superintendent.

The crucial event of the 1920s was the lengthy construction and eventual opening of state route 140—the All-Year Highway. In his usual laconic style, Hoyt chronicled on July 29, 1925, "To Mariposa and Briceburg with W. B. Lewis—inspect new highway." Until then, driving to Mariposa necessitated a rugged, time-consuming trip via the Wawona and Chowchilla Mountain roads. By February of 1926, "New highway passable for the first time. Lewis and Lincoln #100 over the road in rainstorm—first car—broke clutch case."

The road was not open to the public, but official vehicles could, and did, travel it. Hoyt's June 23,

3. Albright took office on Jan. 12, 1929. Lewis died Jan. 22, 1930, and Mather on Aug. 28, 1930.

The "tunnel" was cut through the Wawona tree in the Mariposa Grove in 1881. It became one of the most photographed trees in the world. A record snowfall felled it early in 1969. In this 'first trip' of the season, in May 1923, the men have the car and the women have the tree. (Hoyt collection.)

1926 notation was almost jubilant: "Over new highway to catch train—fast trip with Mather." Finally, on August 1, 1926: "Official hi-way opening. Party went to Clark's ranch where dedication took place."

There was an almost universal thrill because at last Yosemite was linked to the world by a modern, two-lane, soon-to-be paved highway. That delight diminished, as described in the previous chapter, with the onslaught of automobiles. Hoyt noted that 1,000 automobiles drove in during the first three days of the New Year, and 6,000 over the Memorial Day holiday. "Biggest crowd ever in the valley," Hoyt commented. "Road blocked for miles." On the July Fourth weekend another 2,000 cars clogged Valley roads. Such heavy travel signified a change of jobs for Homer Hoyt, since he was needed more and more in the office on what he

labeled "headquarters duty and travel reports." In addition, Townsley put him in charge of the information desk. By November of 1927 Hoyt had taken the tests, and received permanent appointment papers. "Start of retirement deduction," he noted later.

He was no longer a gay, young bachelor as his diary entries revealed. His romance began within two months of his arrival in 1923 when he took six girls from the office to Hetch Hetchy Dam. One was telephone operator Florence Gallison, ranger Art Gallison's sister, and a member of a well-known pioneer Mariposa family. It was over a year later, however, before Hoyt mentioned a double date with Florence, himself, and ranger Bert Sault with Helen Mickle, the new school teacher. "Bert and I took the girls to a show at Pillsburys," he noted. "Started going with Florence."[4]

Another 15 months passed before the love affair heated up. "Bought ring in Oakland," Homer recorded on December 18, 1926, soon after he and Florence witnessed Helen and Bert's wedding in Oakland. On Christmas Day he gave the ring to Florence, and they began making serious plans, such as applying for government housing. On May 6, 1927 his entry described the big day with his usual imperturbability. "Drove to Fresno—got new Dodge Coupe in Fresno, got license and was married at 6 p.m. by Rev. Giffen in Fresno. Fresno Hotel."[5]

Hoyt's last entry coincided with the end of 1928, but his years and significant contributions to Yosemite, mostly as "Mr Office," were not ended for another three decades. Townsley's successor, Chief Ranger Oscar Sedergren, once growled, "You should know, Hoyt, after all you've been here a hundred years."[6]

Once the All-Year Highway was open, the automobile plague began, and Yosemite's winter isolation and quiet was ended. "The rangers spent most of their time in the winter untangling traffic," was Assistant Chief Ranger John Wegner's memory. "Every car that came in that attempted to go anywhere had to be pulled out of the snow. The rangers made it a practice of following the visitors around to keep them from getting into a jam."

At first, snow removal from the Valley to El Portal was accomplished by hooking eight to twelve horses to a 'homemade V-plow.' Later the V-plow was attached to a truck. "Shoveling snow off roofs in the old days was one of the jobs which rangers were often called upon to accomplish," Wegner continued. "Rangers used to go to work at daybreak, wore barley sacks around their feet. Clearing snow off the unsubstantial old headquarters was critical for sometimes the roof caved in, disturbing the occupants in the upper rooms even more than the bedbugs."[7]

Ranger Jack Gaylor did his share of shoveling snow, but preferred patrols. He was on one when he died with his boots on, warming himself before a camp fire at Merced Lake on April 22, 1921. He was an experienced and valuable man, and his death left a real void. Townsley thought he knew just the man to replace him, a young fellow named John Bingaman. Beginning in 1918, Bingaman had worked as a packer and guide for the Curry concession, taking parties of visitors into the high country to camp and fish. That was a job demanding competence with horses, plus tact, patience, and a genuine liking for people. He had picked up a practical knowledge of the trails, passes, lakes, meadows, and wildlife. During the winter of 1919–1920, John and his vivacious wife, Martha, had worked as winter caretakers of the Glacier Point Hotel.

Once when the telephone line was down, Townsley and ranger Charles Rich had snowshoed up to check on the Bingamans. Their welcome was doubly warm because they packed in fresh food, including a turkey.

Superintendent Lewis presumably checked with Washington before Townsley asked Bingaman to fill the vacancy left by Gaylor's death. Bingaman was flabbergasted, and said, "I'll have to talk to Martha."

"Of course." the Chief agreed, "but be here in the morning to take your oath of office."

Bingaman was. Martha and he had decided that the opportunity to continue living in Yosemite with a permanent job at $120 a month and a house, instead of a tent and seasonal work, was too good to miss.

Immediately after signing the oath of office, on June 15, 1921, John and ranger Merril Miller were ordered "to saddle up, take rations and fire hand-tools and proceed to Big Meadow," where a forest fire was threatening Park timber and the Meyer ranch. They joined the Meyer brothers, George and

---

4. Arthur C. Pillsbury had an auditorium behind his photography shop, west of the present-day post office, where he showed his Yosemite nature films. A flat-topped rock off the present pathway has "Pillsbury's Studio 1924" carved in it, marking the building's site.
5. The couple had two sons: Larry, who has donated hundreds of photographs to the Yosemite Archives and lent the author his father's journal, and Donny, who died of appendicitis at age 10. Homer died in 1962. Florence had her 98th birthday in May 1996, and died on June 8.
6. Told to the author by Merlin Miller in October 1995.
7. Wegner's memories of his 28 years as a YNP ranger were recorded prior to his departure for Sequoia-Kings Canyon in 1944, where he served as chief ranger until retiring in 1949.

Henry Skelton, Billy Nelson, and Chief. The classy touring car is a 1926 Chrysler, six-cylinder model-G phaeton. (Billy Nelson collection, courtesy of Duane Peterson.)

Horace, in clearing a fire line. "It took us three days of hard work to complete a good line," Bingaman wrote, "that stopped the 30-acre fire from spreading further."

Before the close of the 1921 season he served a short stint patrolling the Mariposa Grove, and three months stationed at Tuolumne Meadows. Martha rode along with him on local patrols, but not the intensive five- to 10-day ones. Those covered enormous amounts of terrain—one or two men who checked on trails, boundary fences, campers, fishermen, trespassers, wildlife, and fire danger.

Bingaman's experience as a guide had toughened him; his skills as handyman, wrangler, packer, and cook were utilized daily. Hardship was part of his life, but he was soon completely dedicated to the protective work, proud of and loyal to the young Park Service and to Yosemite.

"The two most important duties of a ranger" he said in retrospect, "are the saving of human life and fighting forest fires." His uniform enhanced his lean and lanky frame so that he personified the visitor's image of a ranger. Bert Sault's daughter

remarked that "John reminded me of Gary Cooper. Tall in the saddle."

In the mid 1950s, when the author was young, disdainful of rules, and parked illegally off the road at Tuolumne Meadows, John's sudden appearance on horseback was fearsome. He represented the law, and I was the lawbreaker! Fortunately, Bert Sault's daughter, Shirley, was with me and introduced me, but his admonishments and explanation of why the regulations existed made a lasting impression.

During his 34 years as a ranger, John served in every capacity from fee taker at the old Alder Creek entrance station to district ranger of every district in Yosemite, from chasing cattle out of the Park to helping escort VIPs, such as Eleanor Roosevelt. Only once was his job endangered, and then by a new rule. In 1926 the Park Service was placed under Civil Service, which required examinations. Not even Chief Townsley had more than a grammar school education, but he and other permanent rangers were safeguarded by a grandfather clause. At that time Bingaman was lured to a Southern California ranch to raise horses. Prudently he re-

The cook in the Rangers Club kitchen prepared tasty meals on large wood-burning stoves.

quested a leave of absence, but when he returned to the Park he was told he could not be a permanent again without taking the Civil Service examination. Neither he nor Ranger Carl Danner, who also lacked formal schooling, passed the test. Their consternation was great, but the Park Service closed ranks. It was still a small enough organization so that director Mather and his assistant Albright knew almost every man in each national park and monument. In March of 1928 Albright wrote Mather, defending Bingaman and Danner.

> Both of these men, in our opinion, have better qualifications for the ranger service than those who were able to make a higher grade. An examination of this kind does not bring out the ranger's special knowledge of the particular park in which he is to be employed, his tact and personality, his ability to get along well with the public and with his fellow rangers, his willingness to endure hardships and inconvenience while on patrol duty, and other qualifications and characteristics of this nature, all of which have

> been considered by us in making these appointments but which receive no consideration by the Civil Service Commission.

Mather agreed, and the two men were reinstated as permanent again at $1,620 per year less $180 for quarters, heat, and light. Danner served the Park Service until his retirement in 1949, and Bingaman until 1956. Transfers were not mandatory, and neither man sought one. Their dedication was to the Park Service as a whole, but Yosemite in particular. On leaves, however, they traveled widely, and made it a point to visit other national parks where, invariably, they encountered people who had worked in Yosemite.

Today, Bingaman Lake high on Kuna Crest commemorates John. In 1930, while a patrol ranger at Tuolumne Meadows, he decided to plant fingerlings in an unnamed, unstocked lake at an elevation of 11,200 feet. He spent several days scouting a route to the lake for pack animals loaded with 6,000 rainbow fry, which he planted carefully. "Within three years," he related proudly, "the lake had pro-

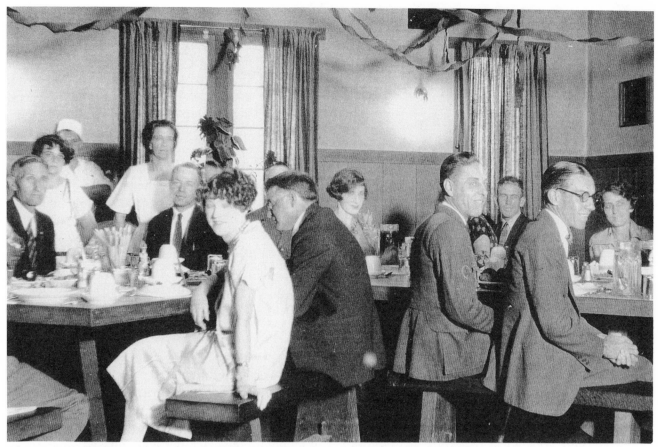

Dinner at the Rangers Club often included single women who worked in the park. Romances sometimes resulted.

duced some of the finest fishing in the area. By this plant, I established the right to call the lake Binga-man Lake and that's how it is listed on our maps."[8]

An often told anecdote about Bingaman that doesn't appear in his book is the one that retired ranger Tom Tucker loves to tell. "In 1951 Harry During, who gave us broad term instructions and expected us to use our best judgement in unex-pected circumstances, was transferred. John Binga-man became the new Wawona district ranger and I became his assistant. John had a tendency to micro-management, especially when he was going to be out of the district. (He and Martha used to go to the Valley every Thursday afternoon for bridge club). And every Thursday before he left, he would call me in and give me a list of detailed instructions. He would stand there until I read the note, which was darn near identical to the one of the proceeding

week, and then ask if I understood everything or had any questions.

"Every time that John gave me instructions, the last one always read, 'take down the flag and feed the horses.' Those words became a joke with any-one who ever worked for John. To this day Ken Ashley and I always add TDF and FTH to our let-ters. In fact, when Ken retired in 1981 from Rocky Mountain National Park, I had the pleasure of be-ing one of the keynote speakers and naturally told the TDF and FTH story. At that point, Frank Betts interrupted the ceremony by presenting Ash a handsome redwood plaque on which were burned the letters **TDF** and **FTH**. The whole place rocked."

Superintendent Lewis had maintained in his 1917 annual report that motorcycles were "no more dangerous than the automobile, and if allowed to enter it [Yosemite] it seems to me the motorcyclist

---

8. Bingaman's other monuments are his three slender books, which are mentioned in the preface to this history.

Rangers Dixon Freeland and John Wegner on their dangerous steeds in the mid-1920s. (Bingaman collection.)

lected entrance fees of $5.00 per auto, mostly paid in silver coins, and stuffed the money in canvas bags. When the bags were full, he loaded them in the sidecar of a motorcycle and took off for headquarters from the Bridalveil checking station. A visitor sped by him going the opposite direction. Morse turned around to chase the speeder, accelerated, and his front tire hit a sandy flat that slewed him sideways into a pine tree. His head was split open, and $700 in coins scattered in every direction.

A tourist informed headquarters of the wreck, and help was dispatched immediately. Morse was unconscious, but survived although he was hospitalized for two weeks before returning to work.

Rangers on hands and knees searched the scene, and ultimately found $699 in coins. After he recovered, Morse was called the 'Silver Dollar' ranger by his irreverent fellows. Superintendent Lewis had been right in predicting that the only danger posed by motorcycles was by and to the driver. It wasn't too long before the machines were phased out.

Few rangers became bored: jobs were varied, and men in Yosemite Valley, at least in the '20s, received sealed envelopes each morning. Inside were duty slips listing Fire Fighting, Desk Duty, Valley Patrol, Night Duty, etc, with check marks on those expected of each ranger. Each slip was signed by F. S. Townsley.[9]

High Country rangers had less exacting supervision, but many duties. There, as in most of the park, the 90-day-wonders, the sometimes scorned seasonal rangers, were indispensable to the operation of the Park. During the summer of 1930-31 the permanent staff or 20 rangers was increased to nearly double that number beginning in July. While he attended Stanford, Bill Myers spent summers as a 90-day-wonder, and in his spare time he wrote letters to his hometown newspaper in Michigan.[10]

himself would be the only one endangered." Three years later his report noted that while Ansel F. Hall was on a motorcycle patrol, he sustained a compound fracture of the right leg. Obviously the two-wheeled vehicles were not only allowed in Yosemite, but at least one was owned by the Park Service.

By then, according to Bingaman, Superintendent Lewis had an old White touring car for his official vehicle, and Chief Ranger Townsley bucketed around in a Dodge pickup. Even a noisy motorcycle added wheels to the Park Service's minuscule fleet.

Bert Sault's first and only experience with a motorcycle was probably in 1922. Townsley directed Sault to drive the Harley-Davidson, and gave him a crash course in operating it. Bert wobbled off, lost control, careened through the plumbing shop, and sent pipes and fittings flying before he crashed.

"Sault," Townsley thundered, "Go get your horse, and get out of here."

Around the same time, ranger Walter Morse col-

9. Art Holmes saved two handwritten duty slips from May 1922. Photostats were sent me by his daughter, Anita H. Outlaw. They are the first I have ever seen, and I believe that they are unique.
10. The following quotations were taken from a small book entitled *Back Trails*, privately printed in 1933 by H. M. Myers, Lapeer, Michigan. It is a collection of letters and a diary written between July 1929 and September 1932. This rarity was copied by its collector-owner Lou Lanzer, and sent to the author with a note saying, "I hope

A letter published in August of 1932 described an average day at Tuolumne Meadows.

> The biggest charm of the place is its isolation and feeling of freedom—doubly appreciated after being in crowded Yosemite Valley. [498,289 visitors were in Yosemite that year]. Yosemite Valley will have 7,000 campers in it [at one time] while Tuolumne will have only a scant 300. . . . There are a lot of stories circulating about the slothfulness of government employees. Maybe so . . . but if any of these yarns are directed at the National Park Service, they are grossly unfair. Strangely enough, there are days when that old $4.50 is really earned. . . .
>
> Take an average day in the life of Ye Great American Ranger. It follows a night of fitful slumber during which he was awakened twice by campers who weren't able to locate their camp after coming home in the dark. A prowling bear has awakened him several times when he tipped over the garbage can and ripped a hole in the screen door.
>
> The ranger arises at 6:30, puts on his old clothes, and goes to the barn to perform the daily chambermaid act for his horses. Breakfast is next, which he may either cook himself or get at the mess-house. Then the morning policing of the grounds around the ranger station—the sanitary detail. Orange peels, cigar butts, and candy wrappers litter the place, and the canons of the Park Service say that this must never be.
>
> Then he changes into his uniform, shines his boots and dusts off the Stetson for another day. Usually the telephone rings when he is but half dressed, or else some motorist will be tooting his horn outside, which is his gentle way of asking for information of some kind.
>
> The telephone message may be a couple of telegrams which are being phoned in from the main Western Union office. Mrs. Susan Arbuthnot will be getting a night letter from the McGillicuddies saying that they will be unable to join them on their camping party. Mr. John Woofus will have a message from "the firm" informing him that things are going splendidly,
>
> even if he isn't there. Then all the ranger has to do is hunt through a thousand acres of camp grounds for Mr. Woofus and Mrs. Arbuthnot.
>
> Returning to the station by the middle of the forenoon, he finds a flock of tourists swarming all over the porch. One lady may have lost her purse; another may be turning in an old sweater she found on the road. There may be the irate party that has had their camp broken into by bears the night before, they come up to the station expecting the ranger to settle for all damages. Another party may be complaining about "that dirty little monkey" that is all the time wading in the creek just above their camp where they want to drink the water.
>
> After acting as King Solomon, the perfect arbitrator, the ranger is then ready to start out again on some call. This time it may be a log has fallen across the road and is blocking traffic. Or perhaps a fisherman is reported catching too many fish, or fishing in a closed area. There may be a miniature forest fire getting underway as the result of a camper leaving a smoldering camp-fire. Any one of these items may easily occupy the rest of the morning, and the chances are that the bustling ranger may miss his lunch in the bargain.
>
> In the afternoon comes the daily inspection of the campgrounds, an area three miles long and dotted with 150 camps. Each camp must be individually inspected to see that it is kept tidy and that the trees aren't being mutilated by thoughtless campers. There are countless grievances that the ranger must listen to as he makes his rounds. An endless chain of gossip is continually flowing through the camps to which he politely listens.
>
> While he is making his rounds he must try to secure talent enough for the nightly camp fire programs of which he has charge. Sometimes much wheedling is necessary to overcome the unwillingness of the average person to perform in public. The ranger must be arranging the program in his mind as he makes his way about the camps. There is no time to sit down and figure anything elaborate. If it is done at all, it must be done on the run—like courtship on a tandem bicycle.

Shirley Sargent can use some of the stories." I have, with gratitude. See also chapter seven, "Search and Rescue," for Myers's delightful description of Carl Sharsmith.

Before supper time the horses must be put in the barn, bedded down, and fed. Then the usual gang who have gathered around the ranger station awaiting the return of the ranger must be taken care of. One lady may be fretting about her husband who went out fishing just a few minutes that morning and hasn't returned yet. After listening to her whining it is difficult to understand why the strayed husband would ever want to come back—but those thoughts are kept discreetly silent. A gentleman may want to send a telegram or make a long distance call. And then there is the daily fishhook-stuck-in-my-finger —and what will I do, ranger? For the moment we assume that we are practicing M.D.s and intimate as much to the tourist who has rammed the fishhook in his finger. We've never failed yet to get a hook out, although it has taken some fancy butchering at times.

When all this has been taken care of the ranger makes a belated dash for the mess-house and finds that he is five minutes late and consequently in imminent danger of starvation. After supper the campfire must be built. A couple of rehearsals for numbers on the program, a mad scramble for props and more hectic dashing about to locate a soloist who has been counted on to supply a good deal of tonight's program.

The soloist will finally appear, but with a sore throat from getting her feet wet. The song-leader will be too tired because of a long hike to do any singing. And one more program will be decidedly impromptu. The over-worked repertoire of the ranger will be gleaned for some little bit that hasn't already been used a dozen times. Perchance some Angel of Mercy in the form of an unexpected entertainer will appear and help shoulder the burden of amusing two hundred people for an hour and a half. By 9:30 the program is over and all the ranger has to do now is go to bed and grab a few hours sleep before the next day rolls around, when he can start all over again.

Now all this would be all right if it weren't for one thing. That's this remark which we hear at least a dozen times a day—"My, but I envy you your job as a ranger. What a snap you have!"

Since there are well over 300 lakes within Yosemite National Park, it wasn't uncommon for an early ranger, especially one who was a Fisherman spelled with a capital F, to be memorialized by

a lake, as Bingaman had been. Boothe, Nelson, Reymann, Skelton, and Townsley are similarly remembered. No less than three—Upper, Middle and Lower—perpetuate Jack Gaylor's name. After his premature death in 1930, popular superintendent "Dusty" Lewis merited a 12,000-foot peak between Mono and Parker passes as a memorial. His widow, Bernice, was pleased, she wrote, and her son, 10, was "thrilled" with the honor.

A good day's work was put in by three of his favorite rangers—Henry Skelton, Billy Nelson and Forest Townsley—who carried a bronze commemorative plaque up the mountain named for him. They were accompanied by Jimmy Lloyd, who photographed the scene for Mrs. Lewis and posterity.

"RIP," but not forever. In 1950 two blister-rust crewmen wrote to Superintendent Carl Russell informing him that during the previous summer they had found the marker on Kuna Peak, not Mt. Lewis. "Whether incorrectly placed through error or negligence it is a public disgrace," they said, and offered to "reseat this plaque in its proper place . . . at our B.R.C. wage."

Consternation and a flurry of inner-office memos ensued, but no other action was taken. Finally, three years later, ranger-naturalist Carl Sharsmith, who knew the mountains better than the back of his hand, was sent to investigate. Sure enough, his September 1953 memo noted, "I found said plaque on the shoulder of Kuna Peak. It was removed by me and carried back by me to Tuol. Meadows."

After that, District Ranger Walt Gammill moved fast, as another memo proves. "Cement was secured and sand, gravel and water were packed from Parker Pass to the top of Mount Lewis and the W. B. Lewis memorial plaque was set in concrete on top of a 4½-foot pile of rock on September 28, 1953."

Ironically, neither peak nor plaque was inside Yosemite National Park. Because of a boundary change, they were in Inyo National Forest. However, Lewis Creek, also named for the first superintendent, still flows out of Gallison Lake. Nearby Bernice Lake, honoring his wife, also feeds Lewis Creek, which empties into Merced Lake.

"Where can I catch fish?" has always been a common question asked of rangers. The early ones knew the answer, because during summer they

For years, more than 200 lakes were stocked with trout annually. The fingerlings were raised in the Happy Isles Fish Hatchery. The first stage on the longest trip of their lives was aboard a Four Wheel Drive truck.

were the men who stocked the streams, rivers, and some 200 lakes with rainbow, brook, brown, and golden trout. Gallison Lake, for one, commemorating ranger Art Gallison, was planted with eastern brook fingerlings, while nine-acre Adair Lake, commemorating ranger Charlie Adair, received the beautiful golden species.

Until 1951, when airplanes were utilized to plant fish in the larger lakes, it was a week's or even a month's work for rangers to complete the job, and there was nothing easy about it. After 1927, when the State Fish Hatchery opened at Happy Isles, a fish truck delivered 10-gallon cans containing roughly 1,000 fingerlings each to the high coun-

try. "In addition to the jostling of those cans . . . along the none-too-smooth roads," Jack Moody noted in his book *Yosemite Ranger on Horseback*, "the water in the cans was aerated by manually dipping and pouring water back into the cans."

Rangers met the truck at designated points, and poured the contents into five-gallon containers. These were then loaded onto mules, and sometimes onto human backs, to transport to remote and difficult-to-reach bodies of water. To keep the fingerlings alive, the water temperature had to be maintained within a few degrees of that in the hatchery. Occasionally ice was carried to add when necessary; other times stops were made at streams

The fingerlings were carried to their destination on rangers' backs—or sometimes on mules. (Hoyt collection.)

the summer was Moody's summation: "Ranger (Otto) Brown and I were planting fish almost continuously through the month of August. . . . When we planted the three McCabe Lakes it was on the fourth day. The rainbow fry rode out the trip well even though it was a long ride. Although we started from Tuolumne Meadows by five a.m., we did not get the last of the fish into the Upper McCabe lake until 2:30 in the afternoon, partly because there was no trail to follow a good part of the way. . . ."

Altogether in the fiscal year of 1928, over 800,000 fry were planted. A decade later the figure was estimated at 945,000, and that figure increased to over 100,000 annually. As the plant increased, so did the number of fishermen, and for years the daily limit remained at 25 trout! Even before plants by aircraft relieved the drudgery of planting, NPS officials were questioning the philosophy of providing such recreation in a place where scenic features, camping, backpacking, and hiking took priority and where there had been no fish before planting began.[12]

so that chilly water could be used. Between the additions and the sloshing of the water during travel, aeration kept the trout healthy until their final immersion.

When a delay of a couple of days was necessary because of the distances involved, fish could be kept alive by replacing the tops of the cans with screens and placing them at an angle in a stream so that water could circulate through them.

In 1928, Moody participated in a reverse fish plant, catching 20 golden trout from Townsley Lake to plant in the new Happy Isles Hatchery's display cases. There the specimens survived for several years, whetting fishermen's appetites as they swam lazily and safely in the tanks.[11]

That was a highlight. A more accurate picture of

Besides inquiring about activities such as fishing, visitors were curious as to what rangers did to keep busy during winters. Were they bored? Actually, rangers didn't hibernate nor were they able to catch up on their reading. Instead, as ranger Art Holmes explained to his part-time reporter-wife Dorothy, who quoted him in the Merced newspaper, "We are usually busier in winter than in summer. For, while Congress provides us money to employ some 45 extra summer rangers, during the ski and winter sports season, the 24 permanent men must do everything themselves. They must maintain the regular entrance stations on the Merced and Fresno roads, keep a 24 hour patrol on

11. Since fingerlings could be produced more economically elsewhere, the Happy Isles Fish Hatchery was closed in 1957, then used as a nature center, and eventually abandoned. In 1995 the wood and stone building was renovated and upgraded by the Yosemite Fund at a cost of $500,000, and was opened in June 1996 as a nature center. Less than a month later, July 10, 1996, an enormous rock slide damaged it and closed it again. The epic flood of January 1 and 2, 1997 further impacted the area, but repairs were made, and the nature center reopened in the fall of 1997.

12. As of 1998, the daily limit for lake fishing is five, and only barbless hooks can be used in the catch-and-release fishing in Yosemite Valley. Stocking of fish is no longer done anywhere in the Park.

roads in Yosemite Valley, maintain supervision of the Badger Pass ski area and attempt to keep accidents down by patrolling the Wawona and Badger Pass roads.

"Add to this the extra hazard of stormy or icy conditions, the limited parking and circulation facilities at Yosemite Lodge and Camp Curry ice rink, and you find that a ranger's life in winter can be a busy, cold and active one."

Another time-consuming job was the annual snow survey, made around the first of February, March, and April at several high elevation places. Core samples of snow were taken, weighed, and measured, and the resulting data yielded predictions to forecast spring runoff. These were important to agricultural and municipal water users in the San Joaquin Valley, helping to determine when the Tioga Road could be cleared and opened, as well as predicting the probable flow of the waterfalls. Winter patrol cabins were built at Merced Lake, Snow Flat, Wilmer Lake, and Buck Camp. They were stocked with food and wood to provide refuge for the snow surveyors. These men were selected partly for their skiing skill and partly for stamina. As ranger Ken Ashley wrote:

> With a foot or so of heavy new snow, the effort involved would be horrendous . . . while, on the other hand, hard packed snow resulting from a week or so of clear weather made for delightful skiing and easy measuring. Whatever the conditions there were rewards; either the satisfaction of contending with the elements and doing something that not many others could do or revelling in the magnificence of the winter scenes in Yosemite's High Country. There was also the solitude and tranquility. No one else ventured into the winter back-country in those days. There was exhilaration too—from being a couple of days away from civilization completely on your own.[13]

No wonder the assignment was coveted. In the mid-1950s, however, machinery seemed about to replace men on skis. In return for the Park Service adding Saddlebag Lake and Sawmill Flat, northeast of Tioga Pass, to their surveys, the State Division of Water Resources promised to provide an over-

If the lakes to be stocked were remote, the fingerlings had to be aerated in cold water en route. (Reymann collection.)

snow vehicle and an operator. Ashley will never forget the first experiment.

> So it was, then, that one evening late in January (probably 1955) Jim [the operator] and a flatbed with the machine chained to it showed up in the Valley. It was a relic from World War II called an M-7. These things were also called 'Weasels'. It had something a little like a jeep body mounted on a chassis with full length tracks. It had a top and was equipped with side curtains. Technology was about to take over snow gauging.

> Early the next morning Glenn Gallison, Jim and I drove up the Crane Flat Road as far as we could, unloaded the machine, cranked it up and were underway with our destination being Snow Flat where there was a well stocked cabin. The sky was overcast and it was chilly enough that rolling down the side curtains seemed like a good idea. It WASN'T a good idea as we soon discovered that

---

13. Retired ranger Ken Ashley's delightful piece "The Ultimate Snow-Gauging Trip," was written for the author in 1995.

exhaust fumes collected so we decided it was better to freeze in fresh air than to perish in somewhat warmer air.

Comfort was not on our program. The machine was without springs, the seats were hard and the sun-pitted snow made for rough going. Also rough was the engine performance. Eventually, we sputtered to a stop and Jim cleaned out the sediment bulb. We progressed another quarter mile and, the sediment bulb again being dirty, Jim deduced that there was too much dirt in the tank. No problem—we had extra gas. Jim drained the tank but soon discovered that the extra gas was also dirty. Apparently this rig had been parked since the war and we were paying for the neglect. We strained the gas through a sock and started up again. About a mile from Crane Flat we stalled again, and, with the need for clean gas being apparent, Glenn and I took off on our skis for the Ranger Station with the extra gas can. We filled the can and took turns carrying it back to Jim and the machine. As anyone familiar with 'jeep cans'

knows it is difficult to seal them completely so, before long, we both reeked of gasoline.

Gassed up with clean gas, we reached Crane Flat, topped off the tank, filled the extra can and headed up the road for Snow Flat. By now it was about 2 pm and light rain had turned into wet snow. We made it fine until we got to where the road hangs over the South Fork. The way the road cut had filled in with snow it was hard to see where the road was. In fact, as Jim drove onto what was very much a steep sidehill, Glenn and I became very uneasy. We told Jim to stop and we'd shovel a path for the uphill track. Jim didn't hear us over the engine noise and at that point the machine tipped on its side. What kept it and us from tumbling on down into the South Fork I'll never know.

Other than our personal gear the only thing that Glenn and I had contributed to this expedition were two shovels. It was a good thing! We started digging under the machine and gradually we were able to get it righted. By then it was dark, we were

Tioga Pass in the 1920s. At an altitude of almost 10,000 feet, it's as near to heaven as most motorists will get. (Courtesy YRL.)

52

The YNP fleet in 1930. Left to right: 1928 Cadillac, 1928 Dodge, 1928 Oldsmobile, 1927 Ford Model-T, and a 1928 Buick. (Hoyt collection.)

all cold, wet and tired so it was decided to return to Crane Flat. We shoveled out for a turnaround and Jim began easing it around when, suddenly, there was a loud SNAP! One of the drive chains had broken. Jim, undaunted, asked if we had a flashlight. Of course, we did. We held the light and dug out a hole for Jim to work in and, using a chain tool, he inserted a new chain link.

I should say that throughout this experience Jim was a joy to have along. He apologized for the condition of the vehicle but seemed to be able to take care of every breakdown. Of course, had we not had the machine we wouldn't have needed Jim. But having the machine, we HAD to have Jim!

We got back to Crane Flat without incident, but thoroughly wet and cold. We soon got roaring fires going in the fireplace and the wood stove and strung our clothes all over the living room to get them dried out.

Crane Flat was not fitted out with winter supplies so we had to make do with some emergency stuff we had in our packs, but, at least, we were finally warm and comfortable.

On the following "crystal clear" day, more than

16 inches of fresh snow proved even more disastrous. Ashley and Gallison alternated skiing behind and then ahead of the faltering machine so that it could follow in their tracks. "Somewhere near Smokey Jack . . . there was a horrible grinding sound, and even with the engine revving up, the machine came to a halt. Jim, with a look of despair, said, 'Fellows, we're done, I can't fix that.'"

Glenn and I looked at each other, tentatively, and then smiled and finally burst out laughing. It was as though a giant weight had been lifted from our shoulders. While we cut a long lodgepole sapling to mark the machine so plows wouldn't hit it when opening the road come spring we discussed our next move. We could press on to Snow Flat but Jim, with only snow shoes, wouldn't be able to keep up. It was also obvious that his enthusiasm for the trip departed when the gear box blew up. So we skied the 20 or so miles back to the truck and when we got to the dam called Tommy Tucker to tell him to be ready at five the next morning to go with us on the Tuolumne trip.

And so, the next morning we hiked up the Zig-Zags starting one of the most memorable trips any of us had experienced. It was the first time the trip had been done in January and the first time, as far as we knew, that anyone had traversed the Sierra on skis. Even though the State's end of the bargain had soured we went ahead with ours, skiing over to Saddlebag Lake and Sawmill Flat to measure these new courses. But the handwriting was on the wall. A year or so later the Park acquired a Tucker Snow-Cat (no relation to Tommy!) and snow gauging became mechanized. Over the years I snow gauged with Buck Evans, Duane Jacobs, John Mahoney, Dick McLaren and John Townsley as well as with Glenn and Tommy.

By the mid-1960s, technology had advanced so far that automatic sensors that could be read from an airplane were placed in remote areas of Yosemite. Conventional snow surveys by a man on skis, snowshoes, or in an all-terrain vehicle are still

Bill Reymann's bear trap was the prototype of one that is still used. (Hoyt collection.)

practiced at such places as Snow Flat, Tenaya Lake, Rafferty Meadow, Dana Meadow, and Tuolumne Meadows in the north part of the Park; and at Peregoy Meadow and Ostrander Lake in the south.[14]

A day's work on skis still provides the exhilaration, enjoyment, and physical well-being experienced by Ken Ashley and other intrepid rangers. It's just part of a winter days work!

So is the boring but essential job of manning entrance stations, answering questions, and issuing permits. One hot summer day Fred "Marty" Martischang, who was in charge of the busy Arch Rock station, overheard a commotion from the kiosk in the middle of the road. A large sign near the building proclaimed "No Accommodations Available," but the visitor had asked where he could get a room.

"Can't you read?" the exasperated ranger yelled, pointing at the sign.

"Needless to say," Marty recollected, "I hurried over to calm the visitor, and relieve the man from duty. That incident reminded me, once again, of what old-time ranger Gus Eastman told me:

"If it weren't for people asking questions, we wouldn't be needed."

Not only does an entrance-gate ranger collect fees, hand out Park maps, and answer questions, but—in the 1950s at least—he had the job of cleaning the public restrooms, removing litter, and many other odd jobs. One daily task was to record anything out of the ordinary in the daily Park Service Log. From a perusal of the South Entrance Log for the years 1956–1964, it was obvious that a station ranger's life ranged from dull to busy to harrowing. Fires, storms, robberies, hunting season, accidents to animals and autos, power outages, and complaints complicated his (no women on duty in those years) daily and nightly work. Subduing drunks was not unusual. One man, who drove his car the wrong way in the exit lane, thinking that he was in the hills above Berkeley, was detained for a couple of hours while he slept it off. No citations were issued in such cases, but car keys were confiscated until demon rum had lost its punch.

Some tourists objected strenuously to paying the $3.00 entrance fee. After a long argument, one woman handed over the cash, sputtering angrily,

14. "Forecasting the Snowmelt," by Robert V. Pavlik, in the quarterly publication of the Yosemite Associaton, Winter 1987, and text on page 89 of Yosemite's Wilderness Management Plan, 1989.

All work and no play makes even rangers dull, so party time at Arch Rock in 1938 was well attended by rangers and their wives. Most of them can be identified. Front row, left to right: Naomi and John Wosky, Chris Hauck, Henry Skelton, Caroline and Billy Nelson, Forest Townsley, and Billy Merrill. Inez Townsley, the Chief's wife, is in the second row between the Nelsons. The woman back of Henry Skelton (she's holding a child on her lap) is ranger Otto Brown's wife Ardeth, and the child their daughter Avonelle. To her right is Midge Reymann; her husband, Bill, is in back of her to the left (white shirt and dark tie). Millie Anderson, in a white dress with big buttons, stands back of Townsley, while her husband, Ralph, recorded the scene for posterity.
(Hoyt collection. Identification supplied mainly by Charlotte Ewing Wilson.)

"You are nothing but a bunch of dirty jeans!" Another female, equally reluctant to part with money, exclaimed, "I have yet to meet a ranger who is human!" A male visitor, however, topped that one, when he came to Yosemite to ski and discovered that the road to Badger Pass was blocked by a fallen tree. Indignant, he returned to the South Entrance and requested a refund.

After all the complaints, it was a thrill to hear one departing visitor say, "Best three dollars I ever spent!" Several well-known Yosemite names are contained in the log. In 1957–58, a young ranger cleaned the drains, scrubbed the restrooms, assisted motorists stranded on the icy road, and cited men hunting inside the Park. This was John Townsley, son of the Park's long time chief ranger.

Later he was Superintendent of Yellowstone National Park.

On May 26, 1956, an entry revealed that "Ferdinand J. Castillo, started today," and on June 2, 1960 Lee Shackelton (later chief of law enforcement) reported for duty. Another entry referred to a tourist who was astounded to discover that he was in Yosemite rather than at his destination, Sequoia.

Occasionally an entrance ranger had to give first aid or be on the lookout for stolen cars or apprehend drivers who had Christmas trees or manzanita branches cut inside the Park. He recorded the daily traffic volume, the weather, statistics, accidents, and other data, proving that an entrance station ranger's life is rarely routine or predictable.[15]

On the whole, rangers of both sexes have been honorable, loyal, dedicated, honest, hard-working, highly moral, law abiding, and devoted to their work. Intelligence and vision are other characteristics. Above all, however, they are human and are subject to the passions and imperfections of mankind. Over the years since 1916, Yosemite has had a few bad apples, but not many and their short-comings were minor—"midnight requisitions" (petty thefts of government property) being the most common. These people were warned quietly, and if they continued such practices were told to resign. Outright firings were rare in the Park Service, which is a close-knit community, worthy of respect and appreciation.

Hello, Tourist!

Hello! Are you puzzled, Stranger?
Just you call the nearest Ranger
Are you lost within our Park,
Have you strayed out after dark?
Just stand by and sing right out
    "Oh Ranger!"

Are you troubled, Damsel Fair?
Call that Ranger—over there—
See a bear with mean-looking eyes?
Just stand back and vocalize—
    "Oh Ranger!"

Are you stuck up on a ridge,
Or do you need a fourth at bridge?
Did your horse die, up the Pass,
Is your auto out of gas—
Do you want us to help you out?
Just look around and loudly shout—
    "OH RANGER!"

Wes Visel (1930s)

---

15. Most of the information regarding life at the South Entrance is from an article the author wrote for the February 1980 *Yosemite Sentinel*, house organ of the Yosemite Park & Curry Co.

6 Patrols

Chief Ranger Townsley, whose career began as a patrolman, was a great believer in the value of wide-ranging patrols. His orders were detailed and precise, as evidenced in the following August 1923 instructions to rangers Merrill Miller and Bert Sault.

> You will arrange to start on the morning of August 20, on the ten day's patrol trip starting from Yosemite Valley over the Vernal and Nevada Falls Trail to the junction of the Mono Meadow Trail: from there you will proceed to Moraine Meadows: From Moraine Meadows to Chiquita Pass over the Gravelly Ford Trail, returning to the Fernandez Pass Trail by a trail just to the north and west of Red Top Mountain, passing by the chain of lakes. You will leave the park at Fernandez Pass, returning again at Isberg Pass, and continue on to Merced Lake, Tuolumne Pass to Soda Springs Ranger Station, reporting to headquarters by telephone at this station for any additional orders that we may have for you. From Soda Springs you will continue around through the northern end of the park to Bond Pass, returning through Jack Main Canyon to Lake Eleanor, and from Lake Eleanor to Mather Ranger Station where you will again call headquarters for additional instructions. From Mather Ranger Station, you will patrol the western boundary of the park passing by Aspen Valley Checking Station, Crane Flat Ranger Station, Merced Grove Ranger Station, returning to Yosemite over the Coulterville Road.[1]

Whew! Such travel, virtually covering the circumference of the Park, would have wearied Paul Bunyan let alone John Muir. And then, the Chief added, "the outline of your trip, as stated above is merely an outline, of the country that I wish you to cover." There was no irony in his orders for he never asked his men to do what he couldn't or hadn't done himself.

Four more paragraphs instructed the rangers to keep "careful lookout for fires, check camping parties for unsealed firearms, report on the condition of roads, trails, lakes, and streams." Fishing conditions were always important to Townsley, and any trout caught by the patrolman relieved their bacon-and-bean diet, so they didn't mind making that report.

In addition to taking food, bedrolls, and a 7x7 tent, they packed maps, notebooks, first aid supplies, canteens, an axe, and a shovel. Their gear was packed in canvas and leather bags that were then placed on the mules and tied securely.

The chief did not allow time for leisure, let alone

Homer Hoyt on patrol in 1925. (Hoyt collection.)

---

1. Patrols were based on the cavalry approach—essentially a boundary survey.

Two well-dressed rangers on the trail. The man at the left is John Mahoney. (Bingaman collection.)

time for locating saddle and pack animals, usually mares, each morning. "Many times, mares, like all girls, wanted to go home by night," Sault commented wryly. "Now no gentleman would let a lady go home alone, so you'd find yourself afoot, if you didn't stake them."[2]

If stakes were not used, hobbles and individual bells made it easier to find stock. Some horses were so bonded to their riders that they didn't stray far even when not hobbled. Later, in many places, drift fences were put up eight to 10 miles apart so that horses wouldn't go clear back to the barns. Horses were still rented from Tim Carlon, as they had been by the college boy rangers, so a ranger would often not have the same mount from one year to the next.

Most of the rangers were tough, young, fun-loving bachelors who found humor even in onerous duties performed under rugged, sometimes dangerous conditions. For instance, ranger Charlie Adair prided himself on his excellent eyesight. One day he pointed to a cabin about a mile away, saying "See that fly on the wall?" "No," Sault admitted, putting a hand to his ear, "but I can hear him."

Townsley's orders were usually sealed, ranger Sam Clark explained, "because poaching was a major problem and the sealed orders kept us from accidently revealing our patrol area. . . . Of course, if the poachers knew our itinerary they would head for another part of the forest."

Catching the poachers who were hunting game

---

2. In the 1970s Bert Sault made a series of tape recordings to entertain an ill grandson. Copies are in the Yosemite Research Library.

illegally, campers who cut living trees, who left fires burning unchecked, or otherwise damaged park property, was only a small part of rangers' duties. Trails that needed clearing or downed telephone lines were problems they looked for and reported if they didn't have time to correct them. Patrols were essential to the protection and maintenance of Yosemite as well as educational to the patrolmen.

When John Bingaman was sent to the Mariposa Grove in June 1921, the Chief told him to go on horseback. "It was a long day's ride of approximately thirty-one miles with a full pack and saddle horse," John recalled. But during that trip he added to his geographical knowledge, noting the kind of detail not revealed by even the most diligent study of maps, which were still being refined. That, of course, was Townsley's intention.

Summer ranger Warren "Jack" Moody felt that his first ten-day patrol, in July 1927, was a field test

"To determine my competence in the back country." His "examiner" was Dixon Freeland, a three-year veteran in Yosemite, whose leadership Moody soon respected.

They set up a base camp about a mile from Merced Lake, where the roofing of a new ranger station had been halted by snow the previous fall. One of their orders was to finish the job, but patrolling came first, Moody reminisced.[3] "We rode out all of the trails that were not completely blocked with snow, up toward Isberg Pass, over Vogelsang Pass, and Tuolumne Pass and talked with hikers or fishermen on the way. We tried to get back to camp each day early enough to get some work on the roof of the cabin. . . ."

Freeland told Moody of Chief Townsley's passion for trout, so one day ". . . we laid out a good number that had been cleaned, dried out, and chilled overnight . . . double wrapped the parcel with generous thicknesses of newspaper and made

Jimmy Lloyd and Charlie Adair about 1919 while on patrol in the High Country. Adair appears to be making an entry in his daily log. (Hoyt collection.)

---

3. Quotations are from Moody's book, *Yosemite Ranger on Horseback* (Fresno: Pioneer Publishing Co., 1990.)

Sam Clark using the high-tech gear of the time. (Bingaman collection.)

ready to move on short notice. /F.S. Townsley, Chief Ranger.

During the fortnight Moody was a busy young man, riding as far south as the Mariposa Grove, as far east as Moraine Meadows, and many, many points in between and round about. The only smoke that he spotted was not in his district. While at the Chinquapin ranger station he put up a hitching rack, cleaned up the cabin, its yard, and stable, "delivered telephone messages to a man at 11-Mile-Meadow, and to some shake makers in the forest and relieved Ranger Danner at the Alder Creek Checking Station."[4] On August 2 he received telephone orders to return to Yosemite Valley. No fires, no accidents, but never a dull moment.

"What was perhaps more important to me later on," Moody commented, "was the fact that I had gotten a picture of the southern half of Yosemite Park firmly in my mind." Again Townsley would have smiled. Moody's knowledge of topography served him well in his succeeding five summers as a seasonal ranger.

Rangers on patrol were not required to wear full uniforms, but always wore badges and Stetson hats as identification. Most of them packed Smith and Wesson .45 caliber revolvers, financed by Steve Mather from his personal account. Due to Bert Sault's small stature, he carried a lighter weight .38 pistol. Tall, lanky Bingaman preferred a Colt .45. Some rangers on remote patrols carried rifles as well. Mounted patrolmen in Yosemite valley wore full uniform, but no guns. Wherever they rode, especially in campgrounds, they inspired respect and even awe from youngsters to whom they talked and whom they allowed to pet their mounts.[5]

In the fall of 1927 Dix Freeland was out on patrol with Wilfred "Billy" Merrill, a new ranger who had

arrangements at the Hikers Camp [Merced Lake] for the package to be taken to the Valley by YP&C [Yosemite Park and Curry] Company pack train." They learned later that their "apples for the teacher" had arrived at headquarters "almost as cold as ice."

Freeland's evaluation of the 90-day wonder must have been favorable, for after that trip, Moody said, "I was usually sent out on patrols such as are ordinarily made only by Permanent Rangers." A couple of days after their return to the Valley, Moody received orders:

Arrange to leave July 21st with supplies enough to last until August 1st. Your duties will be to keep a sharp lookout for fire. Call headquarters at least once a day, while patrolling the roads. Keep traffic moving and assist in every way possible, people with car trouble, accidents, etc.

When you reach Chinquapin, check and see if you have enough fire tools for five men. The country is very dry in this District now and it will be necessary to have your equipment and tools

4. The Alder Creek Checking Station was on the old Wawona Road in a horseshoe turn crossed by the present highway. The location is now designated as Mosquito Creek.
5. After a hiatus of some years, mounted patrolmen were reintroduced into Yosemite Valley in 1972, with favorable results.

I'm going to have to write you up, Shorty—jaywalking and obstructing traffic. In 1926 a determined ranger and his 1924 Studebaker confront the lawless element. (Hoyt collection.)

worked earlier for the Forest Service and for California Fish and Game. The Merced Grove cabin was their headquarters. Merrill considered himself a tough guy, and had already been dubbed "Two gun Billy" behind his back by some of the old timers.

According to Freeland's daughter, Phyllis Broyles, who heard the story several times, the two men were having dinner, seated at a table in the cabin. Merrill faced the open doorway, she said, "but Dad was seated where he couldn't see, or be seen, from the door."

Suddenly Billy, who usually had pink cheeks, turned totally pale, and put his hands up over his head. "I didn't know what was wrong, "Freeland told Phyllis, "but I figured someone had the drop on him, so I quietly slipped out the back door and grabbed a McLeod leaning against the wall."

He went around the corner and crept quietly up behind a man who had a rifle pointed at Billy, who was pleading "Don't shoot, don't shoot!"

Just as Freeland was going to hit the man over the head, the guy laughed wildly, saying "Haw,

Haw, thought I was going to shoot, didn't you? Haw, haw," and dropped his rifle.

He turned out to be the winter caretaker at the Yosemite Lumber Company camp, a mile or so north of the grove. The rangers escorted him back to it, wondering if he was really harmless. "After we got to the camp," Freeland continued, "he showed us a table in the mess hall with white sheets spread over it and World War I surgical tools neatly arranged on top.

"'Now,' he confided, with another of those peculiar guffaws, 'If you fellas ever get anything wrong with you, just come and see me, and I'll fix you up.'

"That decided us. I kept him talking while Billy slipped away to call Chief Townsley who came out and took him away."

By the 1930s most road patrols were made by cars, which had to be tough and durable to negotiate the distances, grades, curves, and largely unpaved surfaces. District 6 took in the northwest section of the Park. It contained five or more ranger stations, inholdings, three pioneer roads—the Big

61

Oak Flat, Coulterville, and Davis Cutoff routes—and both the Merced and Tuolumne Groves of giant sequoias. Although the new Tioga Road between Crane Flat and White Wolf, and the Big Oak Flat Road from Crane Flat into Yosemite Valley were under construction, travelers still had to negotiate the old roads, including the dreaded "Control Road," the final steep, four-mile one-way section descending to the Valley. Traffic was controlled to go down from Gentry checking station on the even hours, and up from the El Capitan checking station on the odd hours. The speed limit was 12 miles per hour, but drivers overwhelmed by the sheer drops and zig-zag curves rarely went that fast.

The odometer in this 1930 Model A coupe turned over 300,000 miles while Art Holmes was driving it in 1936. (Holmes collection.)

When ranger Art Holmes returned to Yosemite after five years at Lassen National Park, he was a permanent ranger. Consequently, Superintendent Thomson "put me in charge of this important district," Holmes confided in his daily diary for May 4, 1935, "so that I'll be recognized as an 'old timer' as it were without having to go through the ropes. . . .[6] " Not surprisingly, Holmes thought highly of Thomson.

His home base would be Crane Flat, in the patrol cabin where Jean Witter and John Wegner had lived. At first he spent most of his time driving, opening and equipping satellite ranger stations at Big Meadow and Merced Grove, including a handsome new cabin, and the Tuolumne Grove, Aspen Valley, and Gentry stations. All stations would house the seasonal rangers who checked cars in or out of the Park. Aspen Valley, an old ranch and at the time the site of an old logging camp, was an inholding of private land, as were White Wolf and Big Meadow. Art's job included establishing liaison with local residents, putting up flagpoles, and overseeing public campgrounds as well as those of the Bureau of Public Roads (BPR), the Morrison-Knudsen construction firm (M-K), and the Civilian Conservation Corps (CCC). Water and sanitation were attendant needs. At Tamarack Campground in August, ". . . water ok, cans and rubbish not so good." A few days later he made a map of the camps, matching campers to sites. The map was "for record purposes," he noted, "and for the psychology of inducing them to leave 'cleaner' campsites when they move out."

There was nothing routine about his duties, as his log proved. Carpentry was one of his many tasks. "Building dog house," he wrote on May 18. Dogs in a national park? Yes, at least at construction camps, where garbage attracted bears and dogs distracted same.

"Inspect Davis Cut-off (from Crane Flat to Big Meadow) pulling one tourist out of mud 1½ hr job." On May 20 Holmes kept busy "putting up tent, etc, at Tuolumne Grove Entrance Stn." "Looked over site and cause of the death of a powder-man on road construction job with Chief." "Investigating and correcting complaint of campers at Foresta

---

6. In July 1997 Bill Holmes and Anita Holmes Outlaw lent the author their father's diaries for 1928, 1930, and 1935, along with a wealth of photographs he took during those years—a treasure trove that greatly enhanced the author's knowledge. Holmes spent six weeks at the Aspen Valley checking station in 1928. He died on Jan. 1, 1997.

[adjoining Big Meadow] polluting the waters of stream." "Scratched on hand separating dogs fighting." ". . . fixing fence with Geo Meyers. Swell exercise!" All these were among the matter-of-fact entries that formed the basis of his monthly reports.

No matter what he did, driving the distances between places was rugged, but he found that riding horseback over the new Tioga Road's right of way was even harder on his posterior. "My, those first and last miles—in fact all of the day—wonderful vistas, beautiful meadows—but, oh! my, those last half dozen miles!"

Fish planting, fighting fires, and patrolling the Park boundaries during hunting season were also integral to his job. At times, finding fires was more onerous than dousing them. Take June 18 for instance: "Hiked 2½ miles cross country to fire only to find a road ran ¼ mile from the fire."

His first arrest was at the Crane Flat CCC camp. "July 2 10 am. Trial of Stanley Pitman . . . arrested Sunday and charged with disturbing the peace . . . found guilty [by the U.S. Commissioner] and sentenced to 40 days in the County jail. (Don't think I'd have arrested the kid if I'd have thought he'd get that much)."

Arrests for workmen who ran by the control points were more common. "Aug, 28. Trial of two M-K men who went thru control road after closing hour last night. Both pleaded not guilty, given suspended sentences of $15 each."

Holmes had to relieve rangers for time off, racking up more miles and repeatedly reciting the litany of "Any cats, dogs or firearms? Two dollars, please." His own days off were often abbreviated by various emergencies, making it hard to maintain a courtship. "Didn't get much sleep this night," he admitted after a dance that topped a full days work. Finally, on July 17, he managed a romantic setting at Glacier Point: dinner at the Glacier Point Hotel was followed by watching the firefall. Presumably his verbal proposal was less prosaic than the "We've fooled around long enough" that he confided to his diary. And then, "Got sent home by the night patrol." She must have said 'yes,' however, for the very next day they "saw Col and Chief re house—not very encouraging."

Storms began October 11, turning the roads into quagmires or, as Holmes phrased it, "muddy as hell." Because of the construction, bulldozers were available to scrape the gooey stuff off or to create detours, and CCC men dug out many a stuck car. Seasonal rangers were terminated by a telegram from Washington on October 31. That left Holmes the full responsibility of closing ranger stations, returning their equipment to the Valley, boarding up windows, etc. at the same time that he was driving patrol in rain or snow, supervising closure of M-K, BPR, and CCC camps as well as the public ones, and placating his bride because he was away so much. Finally, on December 10, his diary entry read in part, "PM received orders from Chief to move into Valley for winter. Arrive Valley 6 p.m. after closing up [Crane Flat] Station." A full day? Sure, but he attended the dance with his wife that same night.

Both Jack Moody and Ray Crawford were hired in 1927. Both were California teachers in their mid-

Gentry Ranger Station. In blatant violation of Park Service regulations, Ranger Hoyt offers goodies to a big bear. (Hoyt collection.)

20s with two summers worth of horse-packing and mountain-climbing background. In response to a press release stating that men with college degrees and practical knowledge of horses were needed as summer rangers, they applied.

"That's all for the written and oral parts," Clyde Boothe, assistant chief ranger, assured them one March morning in 1927. "Report to the stables at 2:00 p.m. for the rest of the interview."

Fortuitously, while lunching at Yosemite Lodge, they met another young man who had taken the horsemanship test with 10 or more applicants the previous day. It had been a circus. The program had called for catching, currying, saddling, and riding one of the two high-spirited horses named "Myrtle" and "Jim." Several men had failed to so much as mount. Forewarned, Moody recalled:

> I led Myrtle out so that I could be on the upside . . . reined her up tight with her head pulled slightly to the left. As soon as the horse quieted down so that I could get my left foot in the stirrup, I grabbed the saddle horn with my right hand and sprang and pulled myself up quickly. The reined-in movement to the left made by my horse allowed me to swing easily into the saddle. No sweat!

> Crawford had no difficulty either. Our performance was probably disappointing to the group of onlookers that had gathered to see the fun.

> Boothe mounted and led our party of three up to Mirror Lake and back at a walk, trot, gallop: jumping logs and gulches on the way. No mishaps. I enjoyed putting Myrtle through her paces on the way back and as we approached the Administration Building she was single footing nicely, throwing her feet high and fancy.

> Chief Ranger Forest S. Townsley, who was a horse fancier and a superb rider himself, came out and asked us to go with him to see Assistant Superintendent E. P. Leavitt.

> Within a few weeks we were individually notified that our temporary appointments as National Park

Rangers had been approved in Washington . . . two ninety-day wonders. . . .

By then most 90-day-wonders were hired on the basis of experience and desire documented on job application forms, and an interview by the superintendent or chief ranger. There were exceptions. For example, William Patrick Mahoney, Jr. was a P.A. (political appointee), hired because Arizona's powerful and longtime senator Carl Hayden recommended him. Sometimes P.A.s were liabilities who didn't deserve hiring; Mahoney was an asset during his summer vacations from Notre Dame—with one notable exception.

In 1936 he was assigned to the Valley District law enforcement division. "Because," he explained, "of my Irish profile and size." There were six men on the force, and "our job was two-fold: general police work, controlling traffic, patrolling camps and roads, and rescue duties, involving drowning (in the cold Merced River), lost hikers, and people stranded on the steep trails leading from the valley. . . ."[7]

None of the rangers liked working the boring midnight to 8:00 a.m. shift. Mahoney often prefaced that duty by attending the dances at Camp Curry where he had, he said, "an all-round good time."

> At three o'clock one morning, I was having difficulty staying awake in the patrol car (one of only two available) and my partner, Red Kilmartin of Fordham University was dead asleep beside me.

> I stopped at a spring, soaked my head in the icy water, and started back toward the Old Village. I fell asleep making a turn in the road and hit a pine tree head on at 30 mph. Fortunately, neither Red nor I was seriously hurt, although bloodied about the face.

> By seven o'clock that morning, everyone in the valley knew about the crash. The patrol car, a custom Dodge pickup loaded with rescue gear and other valuables was totally demolished.

> My superior, Gerry Mernin, a tough Irish cop if ever there was one, confronted me at Ranger Headquarters to ask what had happened. I simply

---

7. Mahoney's colorful memoirs are quoted from the Yosemite section of an unpublished autobiography that he wrote for his family, and shared with the author in 1995.

told him I had fallen asleep. He said something like, 'My God Bill tell them the steering column locked—or you were avoiding a deer—anything else.' I refused to change my story and was confined to quarters the next three days. I had visions of being fired, and worse, of having to pay for the patrol car.

On the fourth day, I was summoned to appear before Col. Thomson superintendent of the park. He asked me what had happened. I told him I had fallen asleep—at that point, certain the bad news was next. Instead, he said, 'Mahoney, I like the way you tell the truth. You are not going to be fired, but I have to get you the hell out of the valley. You're something of an embarrassment.' I thanked him and left a new man. The following day I was assigned to Hetch Hetchy damsite where six hundred tough construction workers were raising the dam one hundred feet. I was their cop. We got along gloriously for the next two months.

Merlin Miller, a traffic enforcement officer, but as kind and generous as he looks. He rarely gave tickets. (Courtesy Merlin Miller.)

Frank A. Kittredge was not a 90-day-wonder but a 14-year veteran of the NPS when he was transferred to Yosemite in 1941, as its fourth superintendent.[8] Two years later, in the middle of the war, he determined to make a personal investigation of the Park boundaries, so a large patrol team was organized, consisting of John Bingaman, Frank Ewing, Buck Evans, Ralph Anderson, and Ed Beatty. They started from the north side of Hetch Hetchy, spent the first night at Wilmer Lake, and rode on to Bond Pass and Huckleberry Lake the second day. About half a mile from the pass, they came upon a pastoral scene—25 fat cattle grazing placidly in a meadow.

"John," Kittredge was outraged. "How long has this been going on?"

"Not long, sir," John surveyed the trespassers with dismay and a practiced eye. "The grass hasn't been trampled down much, and there aren't many tracks in the area."

"Let's drive them out of the Park before they do any more damage." The usually desk-bound Kittredge whooped it up with the rest of the men and then watched the fence repair job. Afterwards the trip was remembered not for the savory fish caught, or the good weather, but for the sight of the superintendent playing cowboy.

Permanent rangers were the backbone of Yosemite staff, but seasonals such as Moody, Mahoney, Clyde Quick, Carey Jackson, and Arch Westfall, who returned summer after summer, were always professional, always needed, and usually welcomed.

One such outstanding seasonal was Merlin

8. Laurence C. Merriam, the third superintendent (1937–1941), succeeded C. G. Thomson.

The old-timers—Eastman, Hoyt, Danner, Nelson, and Bingaman—were still the dominant rangers in this 1945 picture, but retirement was near. The two bottom rows, left to right: Gus Eastman, Homer Hoyt, Billy Merrill, Johnny Hansen, Billy Nelson, J. Bell, Buck Evans, Carl Danner, and Don Eaton. Top row: Wolfrum Joffee, Homer Robinson, Oscar Sedergren, John Bingaman, "Sig" Johnson, and Floyd Dame.

Miller, a teacher in Fresno, who served as a patrol ranger each summer for 26 years, beginning in 1944. In mid-June 1950, Miller reported for duty and was called into the chief ranger's office. Oscar Sedergren, Townsley's successor, went directly to the point.

"There's too much speeding, and too many wrecks in this Park and I want visitors and residents alike slowed down. You have done a lot of road patrol in the last few summers. You're courteous but firm, and I want you to be Yosemite's version of a California Highway Patrolman. Let's see if we can't make the Park a safer place."[9]

His hours were to be his own, and he could pick the roads. "I'm your only boss," Sedegren concluded, "just be professional."

Not long after that, Miller ticketed a car for illegal parking that turned out to belong to Flo Sedergren. When she asked her husband to quash the citation, he refused. "I told Miller to stop lawbreakers, and I can't make exceptions."

That story quickly circulated among locals, who

---

9. Merlin Miller gave the author information in interviews, letters, and telephone calls.

already knew that Miller was not a pushover. Each June the word got around: "Miller's back, slow down." It was embarrassing for residents to have to appear before U.S. Courts Commissioner Gene Ottonello, who was a neighbor or friend to many of them.

Miller's patrol car for his new assignment was an ordinary-looking black Plymouth, but it was equipped with a golden commando engine, special brakes, and a high speed-transmission. As speeders found out, it could fly! Once Miller clocked a man at 88 m.p.h. before catching him and issuing a ticket. Another time the ranger exceeded 90 m.p.h. to stop a drunk driver. Warnings were his specialty, but anyone who fled was arrested because of the danger posed. "If they risked my life or the lives of other drivers, they always got a ticket," Miller explained.

There was one notable exception to his rule: "One night around 9:00 p.m. I saw a Mercedes going to beat hell along the Wawona Road south of Chinquapin. His tires squealed at every turn, and I thought I'd overtake him in the tunnel, but the car was halfway through before I got to the entrance. At the same time my radio came on and the dispatcher warned that there was a bad wreck at the east end of the tunnel. I hit the horn and sounded the siren to warn the speedster, slowed down myself, and pulled into the parking lot, just missing the gory body of a young man. He was beyond help, but his passenger, another Forest Service boy, needed attention. The Mercedes had pulled over too, and the driver, a woman, not a man, got out with a medical bag and, without a word to me, went to work on the severely injured youngster."

Both young men had been flung out of the vehi-cle, which tore out 30 feet of the rock wall before stopping upside down, gas and oil pouring from it. Within minutes more rangers arrived, sirens blaring, followed by the fire truck, ambulance, and water and tow trucks. While emergency crews labored, Miller took measurements of the skid marks, filled out an accident report, and assisted with traffic control. It was 2:00 a.m. before the highway was cleared, and normal traffic resumed. Suddenly Miller realized that the Mercedes and its law-breaking driver were gone. "I had been so busy, I never knew when the lady doc left the scene. Somehow it didn't matter."

Ordinarily, however, ranger Miller got his man or woman, "During one summer," Miller remembered, "I made 800 stops and each of those drivers thought he was going to get a ticket. Actually, I only made out eight citations, but talked turkey to the others."

That his words didn't always fall on deaf ears was attested to by a 1956 letter to the superintendent:

> This is to express my appreciation of the courtesy displayed by Ranger M. Miller. He stopped me for a traffic violation on June 29. The warning he issued was received more seriously because of his genuine interest in promoting safety.

Most motorists were not so appreciative. A Park Service official from the Western Regional Office tried his vocal best to have Miller tear up a speeding ticket. Another time, on the twisty old Tioga Road, where the speed limit was 35, a member of President Eisenhower's cabinet threatened to take the matter up with his boss. Unmoved, Miller said, "Tell it to the judge." He never knew how Judge Ottonello ruled, but his conscience was clear.

7 Searches and Rescues

Search if not rescue is as old as humanity. Only in the 20th century did it become a function of rangers. Indeed, S&R has been a specialized function in Yosemite only since the early 1970s. These trained men and women have access to the best equipment and, when needed, helicopters and dogs. Often grueling, dramatic rescues are effected at the cost of great physical and mental anguish to the searchers, but even now a few lost or missing people are never found.

Drowning accounted for many deaths in Yosemite's early human history. Two of the 45 graves in the Valley's pioneer cemetery are of drowning victims. One noteworthy rescue, in August 1907, was made by two boys age 17 who saved a girl, also 17, from drowning in the Merced River. Later they were awarded Carnegie Medals.[1]

Yosemite's second recorded climbing death was in June 1905, when Charles A. Bailey, an experienced climber, and a companion were attempting a climb of a cliff near El Capitan.[2] Bailey was probably not the first to fall to his death, and far from the last.

In June 1909, cavalrymen had to desert their mounts to search for a missing Englishman, last seen leaving the Mountain House at Glacier Point. Fog rolled in, obscuring his Sentinel Dome destination, and he disappeared. For four days the sol-diers used ropes, grappling irons, and a windlass in their search. According to the *San Francisco Chronicle* reporter, "every nook and cranny, every clump of bush, not only on the face of the cliffs, but on the upper levels, was diligently searched for traces of the unfortunate man." "The hazards of what they were doing," Butch Farabee commented, "was not lost on the soldiers—or the newspaper."

Once the Park Service was an organized entity,

Training exercise of Park Rangers on rescue of a visitor in the early 1920s. From the left: Townsley, Skelton, visitor, and Wegner. Above: Adair and Bingaman. (Bingaman collection.)

---

1. Charles R. "Butch" Farabee found this information in the 1907 "Report for the Carnegie Hero Fund." Park visitors Harry Maser and J. Park Jones rescued Bertha L. Pillsbury (no kin to Yosemite photographer Pillsbury). One-time Yosemite ranger Farabee, now assistant superintendent at Glacier National Park (1998), has devoted 15 years of part-time work to researching and writing a book on search and rescue in all the national parks. *Death, Daring, and Disaster* was published by Roberts Rinehart in May 1998.
2. In 1897 Bailey was the first person to ascend to what he named Sierra Point, in honor of the five-year-old Sierra Club. See Peter Browning, *Yosemite Place Names* (Lafayette, CA: Great West Books, 1988), pp. 129–30.

Drowning is one of the more common causes of accidental death in Yosemite. Here a body is retrieved in a Stokes litter after a fatal plunge over Vernal Fall. (Bingaman collection.)

rudimentary training in first aid and search and rescue was begun for rangers. Windlasses were no longer utilized, but heavy ropes were. Obviously posed pictures, taken in 1921, show Yosemite rangers at work in full uniforms except for jackets. Only the supposed victim is without a necktie!

Present-day search and rescue leader John Dill said, in 1996, "Over the last five to ten years, the death rate for real rock climbers (not including naive scramblers) has been about 1.5 to 2 per year. Three climbers died in 1996, which is above average. The death rate for all other activities together is usually around 20. (Just because a hiker tries to scramble up or down a cliff does not make him or her a rock-climber.)"

Rangers Bill Reymann and John Bingaman made

a successful rescue after dark on April 7, 1928. Billy Nelson sent Reymann, Bingaman, and three volunteers up the Ledge Trail behind Camp Curry in response to faint cries for help that were first heard around 7:00 p.m. Although the trail to Glacier Point, ascending 3,000 precipitous feet in a mile, had been much improved by the Park Service in 1918, it was hazardous even in summer—and downright dangerous when snow covered any part of it, as it did that night.[3]

Armed with flashlights, a lantern, and two ropes, the rescue party left Camp Curry at 9:30 p.m. "It was very rough going in the dark," Reymann's report read, ". . . there were several places (in the snow) where we had to help each other with ropes as footing was dangerous."

---

3. The always dangerous Ledge Trail has been closed since the 1970s because of injuries and deaths that occurred on it. The trail was partly obliterated by a rockslide from the cliff below Glacier Point in the 1980s.

None other than Ansel Adams took this photo of Chief Ranger Oscar Sedergren for a 1954 advertisement. (Courtesy Sandy Sedergren.)

About halfway up to the point, they heard women's voices, and made out the figures of two women on a ledge well below the trail. The ropes were tied together and Reymann descended 75 feet. "They were in a place covered with snow and mud," his report explained, "wet and very uncomfortable." He tied ropes around their waists, and they were hauled up safely and gratefully.

While on a spring break, the young teachers had hiked to Little Yosemite and then to Glacier Point, and planned to return to the valley by the Four Mile Trail. They had started down the Ledge Trail by mistake, slipped on the snow, and stopped themselves just short of a 200-foot drop-off. They were embarrassed at their foolishness and reluctant to give their names, because one was the daughter of Curtis D. Wilbur, then the Secretary of the Navy. Sure enough, the United Press picked up the story and it was published widely. Consequently, the rangers received letters of commendation from Secretary Wilbur, Director Mather, and Superintendent Albright.[4]

A July 1935 rescue was particularly famous because it involved a ranger-naturalist who, at 32, was spending his fifth summer at Tuolumne Meadows. Even then Carl Sharsmith showed leadership abilities and the deep reverence for and knowledge of nature that would make him a Yosemite icon.

In addition, Carl was a daring climber whose "specialty," seasonal ranger Bill Myers claimed, "was guiding parties up impossible looking peaks. Carl hauls them up with ropes, but first he must scramble up himself. There's a story current that his grandfather was a mountain goat and his great uncle a Swiss cheese."

Carl's luck ran out on July 25, 1935 while he was leading Yosemite Field Schoolers to the top of 13,114-foot Mount Lyell, Yosemite's highest peak. After that the group split, and Carl led several hardy students up nearby Mount Maclure, the Park's third highest peak. Atop its narrow 12,960-foot summit, Carl, two eyewitnesses later agreed, talked about the danger of rolling rocks, then proceeded to roll one, lost his balance, and fell.[5]

Seasonal ranger Bud Ashcraft and Field School

---

4. The author's account derives from a study of the reports written by Reymann and Bingaman the night of the rescue. They contrast sharply with Bingaman's self-serving recital on page 31 of his *Guardians of Yosemite*, written more than 30 years later. For example, Bingaman said that he, not Reymann, made the rope descent. Rose-colored memories! Both Nelson and Reymann were dead by then. Butch Farabee unearthed the reports in the National Archives.
5. The witnesses were M. D. "Tex" Bryant and J. L. Spriggs, members of the Field School. Later, others—protective of Carl and the Park Service—advanced different reasons. For details, see John Sharsmith and Allan Shields, *Climb Every Mountain, a Portrait of Carl Sharsmith* (Mariposa, CA: Jerseydale Ranch Press, 1996), pp.49–70. See also Elizabeth S. O'Neill, *Mountain Sage* (El Portal, CA: Yosemite Association, 1988).

John Bingaman (right) was a meticulous but highly respected district ranger. Tom Tucker (left) followed in his footsteps. (Bingaman collection.)

member Tex Bryant were the first to reach Carl, who had come to a precarious stop in a sitting position with his legs dangling over a sheer drop-off. Blood was streaming down his face. In lieu of a first-aid kit, Bud used the needle and thread from his animal-stuffing kit to stitch up the gash. Despite the emergency and the perilous position, Ashcraft did a neat job.

It was miraculous that Carl survived the fall and the rescue, which involved walking with support, ropes, and an improvised stretcher, and jolting across the Lyell Glacier—plus shock, probable hypothermia, and a night of pain and semi-consciousness at the base camp. The presence of his wife, Helen, and a doctor who administered a pain moderating shot, plus a stretcher carried by CCC men,

eased the long way out the following day. Miraculously, after two months of hospitalization, Carl regained his mountain-climbing agility and continued to inspire people to appreciate and care for nature until his death in October 1994.

In 1938, a vastly different kind of rescue began on a summer afternoon at Glacier Point. When Ranger Lemuel "Lon" Garrison returned to the parking area for his patrol car, he witnessed an angry confrontation between a teenaged boy and his father. It culminated when, "the youth leaped from the car and screamed that he was not going to ride with his dumb dad—he was going to walk back to Camp Fourteen." At that, Junior raced off, Dad drove off, and Garrison headed back to his station at Chinquapin.[6]

---

6. Quotations and information from Lemuel A. Garrison, *The Making of a Ranger: 40 Years with the National Parks* (Institute of the American West, 1983). Garrison was stationed in Yosemite from October 1935 to late 1939.

As was customary, he called headquarters and was ordered to return to Glacier Point to rescue a stranded hiker. A camper in Yosemite Valley had heard cries for help, and spotted the source with binoculars. Junior, (who else?) had run the wrong way, and slid down the mountainside into a small but sturdy pine that held him safely, but doubtless uncomfortably, from a 3,000-foot descent to Happy Isles.

"As I looked down," Garrison wrote in his autobiography, *The Making of a Ranger,* "I could tell from the line-up of people along the road between Camp Twelve and Happy Isles roughly where Junior would be, but I could not see him. . . ."

[Ranger] Duane Jacobs and Ross Cecil, a redheaded, local cowboy, packer, and mountaineer, drove in with the climbing ropes. We knew approximately where Junior was. The noise from Camp Twelve continued [but] Junior was losing his vocal power. It was getting dark and we simply were not going to make any exploratory trips down our 300 foot rope. We had to know exactly where he was; then we would risk our own lives getting this idiot out of the jam he was in. We didn't know who he was—we just knew we had to try to get him out, which we would do, but only after taking security protection for ourselves.

I worked down to the nearest point and got Junior's attention. 'You have to spend the night here, Junior, we will come for you in the morning as soon as it is light,' and we left him there. We slept on the Glacier Point Hotel lobby chairs, had early coffee and doughnuts with the chef, and before sunrise were back over the ledge again trying to locate Junior. The Camp Twelve roadside audience was gone.

When we located him, we selected a belay point. I volunteered to go down the rope to take the hitch on Junior, Ross and Jake both vetoed it promptly. 'You are just too damn heavy,' was their decision. 'If we've got to haul a ranger out of there we want a skinny one.'

Jake elected to take the trip over the side. I got the major belay and Ross was standby. I snubbed my belay line around a convenient white pine and away Jake went, dragging our extra rope. Our idea of lowering a line to Junior just didn't work out. The cliff appeared to be straight down, but it wasn't, and the rope simply would not slide on it. We kept Jake snubbed up, but not tightly, and in just a few minutes he hollered that he had arrived.

Junior was in a frame of mind to come out hand over hand, but Jake gave him no option. Jake tied him on the extra rope and then Ross and I kept the line snug as Junior climbed out. Before we could get him untied, Jake had taken advantage of the freedom of action and using the firm belay I had made in his line, came climbing out alone.

Success! We embraced Jake warmly! There was no audience. We loaded our gear in the pick-up to return to the valley. I called the Chief Ranger's Office. The log later showed that we had our job done by 7:00 a.m. Junior was not contrite. He looked around airily. "'Where's a good place to go fishing?' he asked. We gave him no help—just blasted him about his idiotic behavior. Lives had been risked to salvage his—was he worth it?

'You sound just like my dad,' he said."

After all that, not even the breakfast they treated him to rated a thank you. In contrast, Garrison never forgot "the surge of warm admiration I felt for (Jake) that early morning on the Glacier Point cliff."[7] In defense of the teenager, he had endured a long and frightening night during which he had to have been cold, hungry, and scared. His seeming nonchalance may have been a facade.

Reuniting lost children with distraught parents was a frequent and more satisfying kind of a rescue. One such incident was described by Garrison.

Seasonal ranger Bill Felkner, was the ranger in charge of Yosemite Valley Campground Number Seven when I parked my patrol car, a 1931 Pontiac roadster with the top down, in front of his tent one August morning in 1938. At his front table Bill introduced me to Johnnie, about three years old, last name unknown.

Roughly 40 pages of his 310-page book are devoted to the Yosemite years of his long and distinguished career.

7. Jake, who was a ranger's ranger, trained himself to do rescue work by practicing rappelling, then taught the skill to others, such as Buck Evans. (John Henneberger's letter to the author.) Jacobs rose to be superintendent of McKinley National Park in Alaska, and later served in the Regional Office in Omaha, Nebraska.

But Johnnie was starting on an ice cream cone Bill had purchased for him from the campground supply truck, which was still parked nearby. Despite his aplomb and the twinkle in his eye, Johnnie was a lost youngster. He had just been deposited with Bill by an empathetic camper who had found him crying in front of a rest room.

How could we get Johnnie and his family back together again? Probably the family was nearby or at least near a rest room. But where? There were probably two hundred cars in this unmarked area. Bill was experimenting with a new identification interview procedure and was just about to give it a try. Johnnie had mentioned Oakland to the camper who had found him, so Bill started there.

'Does your daddy live in Oakland, Johnnie?' asked Bill

There was no hesitation, 'Yes,' said Johnnie.

After a series of searching questions, answered positively by the boy, the interrogators had elicited enough information to cruise through Camp 7 in search of a black, four-door sedan with California license plates.

The ice cream cone was under control. Bill wiped Johnnie's hands and face. I drove and Johnnie stood firmly between us on the seat, with Bill's hand giving him a good anchor. The roadster with the top down was great for this kind of eyeball survey.

There were only a few official location posts in the campground and one paved loop road with many informal intervening loops It was still an 'open' camp without established campsites. Campers were free to move in wherever they found room along the sandy tracks and among the lodgepole (sic) pines. In the friendly sharing of amenities as many as three tents were often tied to the same tent peg. Whoever went home first created a disaster for the others.

I drove the car and we looped in and out and around very slowly to cover major areas, but saw nothing of a black four door sedan with the proper license plates and running board- mounted spare tire. So we returned to the ranger tent to regroup.

Another ice cream cone, and more questions from the frustrated rangers garnered a bombshell. Daddy's car was black, all right, but Mama and Daddy and Johnnie had come to Yosemite with Uncle Joe, and Uncle Joe's car was brown with a house trailer behind it. Once more, the rangers made a slow circuit of the camp with the boy anchored between them. This time they spotted the right vehicles plus some obviously agitated people. Garrison stopped the car, and Johnnie bailed out.

'Mama!' the relief in the tone of voice!

'Johnnie,' the equal relief as mother swept him into her arms. 'Where have you been?' The squashed ice cream cone abandoned, Johnnie could only point mutely to Ranger Bill Felkner. Mama, however, suddenly remembered that Johnnie had disobeyed orders about staying near the car even if he did have to go to the bathroom. She suddenly reversed her grip so that with his rear bumper in view she whacked him vigorously, but lovingly. Whack-whack-whack. 'Don't you go away from camp again!' Whack-whack. Dust flew for a minute, but suddenly all was loving joy again. This lost kid business was highly important and had top priority, but it was just normal routine.[8]

Searches for lost adults were infrequent, but far more difficult than those for children, and far less likely to result in happy endings. Even in retrospect, Sam Clark shuddered at the memory of one such grisly "rescue." Several rangers finally located the body of a missing man who had fallen from a cliff. No one volunteered to retrieve the body, so ranger Sam finally rappelled down to do it. It was bad enough to see the bloated flesh and worse to attach the harness. As Sam touched the inert figure an awful moan caused by escaping gases resounded. Afterwards, Sam told his wife, Trude, "It was so ghastly, I would have fallen myself if I hadn't been tied on to the rope."

There were two remarkable rescues within a month of each other in 1949. Both were headline news, and were vividly remembered by the participants. The first involved 19 rangers including Carl Sharsmith, blister-rust crewmen, and several zealous volunteers.[9]

---

8. According to Garrison, on July 4, 1938, there were 34 "lost" children, and 34 happy endings.

All were searching for the Thompson sisters, who were working as waitresses at Camp Curry and exploring Yosemite on their days off. On Monday, June 27, Patti, 22, a student at San Jose State and Joan, 18, a Mills College student, hitchhiked to Tenaya Lake, intending to hike back down to Mirror Lake via the Snow Creek Falls Trail. They were not novices: Patti had worked in the Park for four summers, Joan for one, and they were in good physical shape. Their tent-mates and Nic Fiore (Camp Curry's transportation agent) had been told of their plans.

They left the lake about 10 a.m., but soon missed the trail. A fisherman pointed out what he thought was the right way, so they followed the rock cairns, called ducks, until they could see the canyon far below. Patti thought she saw a trail to her right and decided, she recalled, that "If I slid that way, I would be okay." Instead, she slid straight down the granite, shredding skin from her fingers and cloth from the seat of her pedal pushers. A ledge stopped her with such force that her left heel broke.

Joan made her way down a less dangerous way, saw her sister's pain and swelling foot, and realized that it was up to her to get help. Neither girl was dressed warmly, although Joan had a large silk scarf, and Patti was wearing a light denim jacket. Joan set off alone. Patti sucked wet moss for moisture, and spent a hot, painful afternoon leaning against the granite. Toward evening, when the pain had decreased, she managed to crawl farther down to a level place, where she slept intermittently.

The next morning, "I got to the bottom of the canyon, and spent most of the day floating in the barely floatable stream. That dulled the pain, and kept me cool."

Meanwhile Joan, adrenalin running high, tried to find a way out of the forbidding gorge. After an uncomfortable night, she ate her last candy bar on Tuesday morning. That was a long day for both sisters, but they were bolstered by the thought that rangers were looking for them. Volunteers from Camp Curry were searching, but an official search was not begun until Wednesday the 29th. By then

The Thompson sisters: Joan (top left) and Patti (kneeling) at Camp Curry in 1948, before their harrowing adventure and rescue from Tenaya Canyon. (Courtesy Joan Thompson.)

Joan had scrambled up a ledge on what turned out to be the east side of Mt. Watkins, scratched, bruised, and bone-weary, and Patti was still stuck at the end of the box canyon. She tried vainly to climb out. Besides pain from her foot, her fingertips were infected and raw. Wednesday morning she napped fitfully in the shade of a boulder.

"I was awakened happily by voices, and saw three rangers (Homer Robinson, Duane Jacobs, and Jim Robertson)[10] who had been tracking us from

_____

9. Blister rust—literally blisters on the stems of pine trees—was thought to have been caused by a fungus on gooseberry bushes. For many years, crews were employed to eradicate the bushes from the Park. The men were also available to help fight fires or to search for missing persons.

In 1951, rangers attended an FBI training school. Front row, left to right: Homer Hoyt, John Mullady, Ken Ashley, J. W. Packard, John Mahoney, Buck Evans, and Stan McComas. Back row: Oscar Sedergren, Bob Sharp, Sam Clark, "Sig" Johnson, Duane Jacobs, Harry During, and Roy Ihlenfeldt. (Bingaman collection.)

Tenaya Lake. My lunch sack, and I think, Joan's yellow sweatshirt had led them to me," Patti recalled.

One ranger cleaned the infection from her fingers, her foot was stabilized, and she ate some food, but Patti's ordeal had another 24 hours to go. A ranger climbed up to summon more help, via walkie-talkie, and by night a large party of men, including Yosemite ski director Luggi Foeger, Nic Fiore, and Dr. Baysinger from Lewis Memorial hospital, arrived with medication, a stretcher, and more food.[11] The rescue could not begin until daylight, but the men kept a warming bonfire burning all night. Still, Patti said, "I doubt if anyone slept much." Her concern for Joan was great, since no one had seen her.

Even by daylight it took nine hours for the team to carry, and slide, Patti and the stretcher along

ledges and narrow, brushy pathways. "Finally, we came to the last cliff above Mirror Lake, and they had to rappel down," Patti remembered. "They dropped me 200 feet head first with Luggi Foeger rappelling beside me to keep (the stretcher) from banging against the wall. He was the only one skilled in this sort of thing, and at one time had been a guide in Austria. Of course it was scary, and I kept my eyes closed the whole time."

A crowd of people and the ambulance waited in the parking lot adjacent to Mirror Lake. Patti spied "my parents and a reporter taking a picture—I covered my face."

About the same time, partway up Mt. Watkins, Joan could see the top of Snow Creek Canyon where, she knew, was the long-lost trail to the Valley. That gave her renewed hope and strength, but by late afternoon Thursday, "I was so weak I

---

10. Robertson was a volunteer searcher.
11. When feasible, a summer doctor who could climb and accompany rescuers was hired to work at the hospital.

could not climb down or up." Her fourth night alone was the worst: she was chilled, thoroughly miserable, and more than ever worried about Patti.

"I was truly out of it the next day," she remembered. "I did find a small stream of water and that's what kept me going. I dozed in the shade of an overhanging rock, and then drank a little H2O, dozed, etc."

Joan's footprints had been spotted, giving rangers Jacobs, Glenn Gallison, and "Buck" Evans fresh direction and hope in finding her—dead or alive. By Friday morning they were about a half mile above her but had to move carefully.[12]

Carl Danner, then district ranger for Tuolumne Meadows, was the man who suspected that the sisters had gone down Tenaya Canyon, and, while investigating, located their footprints.[13]

At the same time, three college students were searching the canyon below Joan. Two of them were AWOL from jobs they stood to lose. Their search seemed futile; after several hours they stopped by a creek for a rest. One shoved his feet in the water, then yelled aloud in reaction to its chill. Miraculously, Joan, 60 feet above, heard him and tried to shout, but could only croak. "My second attempt," she remembered, "was loud enough so they looked up to see me waving. They shouted back, and I asked is my sister ok? Their resounding 'Yes' gave me enough energy to climb down to them, but first I tied my silk scarf around my torn pants to cover the large holes!"

Like Patti's experience, Joan's travail was not over, since she still had to descend 4,000 feet over rugged trailless terrain to reach the Valley. "They offered me food, but my stomach had shrunk so much I couldn't eat. They had one canteen, though, and I pretty well emptied that a little bit at a time."

Fortified by water, her rescuers, and the knowl-

Carey Jackson, Jerry Mernin, and John Wegner all ready for a search and rescue. (Hoyt collection.)

edge that Patti was safe, Joan managed to stay on her feet, albeit with frequent stops to rest. At one point, the fellows strung their belts together to help lower her over a particularly dangerous ledge. "She didn't make a sound," one said later. "She was really brave." "Actually I was scared," Joan admitted, "We all were!"

There was a crowd waiting at Mirror Lake, but neither Joan, though grimy and unkempt, nor the three clean-cut youths looked the part of rescued and rescuer. No stretcher, no uniformed rangers—people saw nothing to stare at.[14]

---

12. In 1950, Jacobs and Evans were awarded the first Meritorious Service Citation given to anyone in the NPS for the "unusually resourceful tracking, exceptional ability to traverse almost impossible terrain and sustain expenditure of extraordinary physical effort during the search."
13. Jan. 12, 1950 press memorandum issued by the YNP when Danner retired after a 26-year career in Yosemite.

Joan even gave a half-hearted wave to a boy she knew, but he didn't recognize her. They found a ranger in the parking lot who, surprised but jubilant, drove her to the hospital. Before a doctor could check her over, Joan stumbled into Patti's room. She was too dehydrated to cry, but Patti and her parents did. Joan collapsed in exhaustion, but only after she remembered to wish her mother a happy birthday. The sisters spent four days in Lewis Memorial Hospital, where curious tourists wandered in the back entrance at will and besieged them. (Once, Joan was awakened from a nap by a complete stranger taking her picture). Disgusted, Mrs. Thompson rented a housekeeping unit at Yosemite Lodge so that she and her daughters could have privacy. Joan returned to work in less than two weeks, and climbed Half Dome a week after that. As soon as Patti's foot healed, she too returned to work.[15]

In 1996 John Dill added, "People still become lost on the hike from Tenaya Lake to Snow Creek today. Many of them make the same mistake Patti and Joan did and wind up in the bottom of the Canyon, stuck, hurt, or dead."

Less than a month later, another historic rescue began. This rescue marked the first time a helicopter was used in Yosemite—and among the first in the National Park system. Heavy press coverage was further assured, since Terence Hallinan, the 12-year-old victim, was the son of Vincent Hallinan, a prominent attorney and politician in San Francisco. While returning from a pack trip with Curry packer Don Campbell, three other boys, and their chaperon, young Hallinan had been thrown from his horse and knocked unconscious. The site was far north of Yosemite Valley, in a little-traveled area near Benson Lake. Campbell had to ride 26 switch-backing miles of steep trails, varying in elevation from 4,000 feet to 10,000 feet, to telephone for help from White Wolf, then a private resort.[16]

On the way he met ranger Tom Van Bibber, who was scouting for fires. Alerted, Van Bibber rode on through a thunderstorm, stopping every fourth switchback on ascents to give his horse and pack mule a breather. Nevertheless he arrived at Benson Lake by 7 p.m. "Boy improving, reflexes slow, stayed with him all night," he scrawled in the pocket-sized log book that he used later as the basis for his monthly reports to the chief ranger, and now for this book.

After Assistant Chief Ranger Homer Robinson and a couple of packers showed up early the next morning, August 1, they carefully moved Terence, who had not regained consciousness but was showing signs of being cold, into the sun. Robinson began to set up a shortwave radio on the beach while Van Bibber and a packer scrambled up lodgepole pines to stretch a wire between two trees. Another wire was hung from the middle down to the battery-powered radio. Fishermen watched the unusual activity with curiosity. Finally the radio squawked into action, shattering the peace and quiet but establishing contact with headquarters. So that contacts would be quicker and cleaner, Chief Ranger Sedergren had established a base at White Wolf.

It was 2:30 p.m. before the ubiquitous Jake Jaccobs[17] and packer Don Campbell, who had snatched a few hours sleep, rode in with Dr. Avery Sturm, and at that moment standard operating procedure for a rescue ceased. Behind them trailed the first of the reporters, some of them encumbered with cameras and perched uncomfortably in saddles. Press coverage of a rescue, especially in such a remote area, was another first, but the prominence of the youngster's father was the stimulus.

Sturm determined that the unconscious boy had a skull fracture, needed rest and quiet, and couldn't stand the jolting or being carried out on a pack mule. Once that decision was made, headquarters

---

14. Chief Ranger Oscar Sedergren and the Thompson family thanked the boys, whose feat was also described in the press, but the Superintendent's Monthly Report, written or edited by Superintendent Frank A. Kittredge, made absolutely no mention of the volunteer searchers. It stated that the "search was one of the most hazardous and difficult searches ever carried out by the rangers in Yosemite." That, of course, was true, but dissembling.
15. Both sisters aided the author with this account. Both retain immense loyalty to Yosemite and to Camp Curry.
16. Before World War II there was a tent ranger station at Benson Lake with a telephone, but it was not replaced after the war.
17. Both Homer Robinson and Jacobs were assistant chief rangers. Jacobs was in charge of all searches and rescues, and Robinson was responsible for fire control.

was notified with the usual hums, crackles, and squawks of radio transmission. Alternative rescue plans were discussed, including the rental of a seaplane or the still-experimental helicopter.[18]

Jake walked down to the shore and told the six-man fishing party to keep fishing. "I've already caught my limit," one explained. "Never mind, " Jake said. "Catch all you can. All these people have to be fed." Subsequently, Benson Lake's supply of rainbow trout decreased rapidly.

Van Bibber was sent to Pate Valley to meet the senior Hallinans and to pick up a tent for them from a trail crew camp. Prudently he packed in enough food so that the unexpected crowd could have loaves with their fishes.

During the return trip, the darkness was splintered by Vincent Hallinan's attempts to light the trail for his horse. "I had to tell him three times, in a nice way, to turn that blankety-blank flashlight off," Van Bibber said. "He was blinding the horses and mules."

Even though it was close to 10 p.m. when they reached camp, lanterns and flashlights highlighted the confusion. "There must have been 25 to 30 people milling around," Van Bibber said. "Reporters, photographers, packers, rangers, tents, and sleeping bags were everywhere. You couldn't tell who was in charge of what. Then, of course, the parents had to see Terence. Well, I got their tent up in a hurry, and went off in the woods to sleep where it was peaceful."

Hallinan agreed to pay expenses for a helicopter, so more contacts with pilots followed. Benson Lake's elevation was near 8,000 feet, and it was surrounded by peaks of up to 10,000 feet. The only possible landing site was a small meadow, roughly 200 by 300 feet, at the north end of the lake near the beach and campsites. On top of that hazard, few rescues anywhere had been attempted by helicopter, let alone in the rugged terrain and thin atmosphere of the high Sierra.

After many phone calls from headquarters, Benson Lake was radioed that two machines were coming. One was flown from Fresno to Tuolumne Meadows, but several trial takeoffs and the difficulty in gaining altitude in the thin, turbulent air convinced the pilot that it would be impossible to lift off with the boy's extra weight.

The second helicopter, a Hiller 360, which resembled a monstrous dragonfly, was trucked to White Wolf's 8,000-foot-high meadow, where it was reassembled on August 4. Jay Deming, a former Army pilot, made two test flights, conferred with the rangers, and decided to attempt the rescue before dawn, when the air was cold and dense. He took off a 4:30 the next morning, and landed safely at Benson Lake barely 14 minutes later. Bonfires, lit by prearrangement, guided him.

After three days, Terence had finally regained consciousness, but was still groggy when he was wrapped in blankets and strapped to the passenger seat in the open cockpit. Reluctantly, Deming jettisoned extra gasoline to compensate for the youngster's 100 pounds. He took off at 5:05, climbed in slow circles until he cleared the peaks, then headed back to the meadow at White Wolf. He almost missed it, but bonfires and the resultant smoke guided him to safety.

Photographers recorded the historic event. One reporter quoted Terence as saying that "The helicopter is a nifty era," but that's unlikely, since his head hurt and he was cold, lethargic, confused, and probably scared. A waiting ambulance took him to Lewis Memorial Hospital, where Dr. Strum, who had ridden out earlier, began taking x-rays.[19]

Van Bibber missed the finale. He had ridden from Benson Lake to White Wolf late on August 3, leading five horses and mules. They were needed

---

18. A heliport and a modern helicopter are now maintained at the Crane Flat Fire Lookout for routine use in rescues, fires, and other emergencies. "In addition to the park helicopter," John Dill states, the Park Service uses "a commercial helicopter on government contract. If needed, we can use helicopters from the Navy (Lemoore Naval Air Station and Fallon Naval Air Station [NV], from the California Highway Patrol, and from commercial providers."

19. Terence Hallinan recovered completely and, like his father before him, became a lawyer and was elected to San Francisco's Board of Supervisors. In 1995 he was elected to be that city's district attorney. In an August 1995 letter to the author, Hallinan wrote, "This past summer I cut my eye and ended up in the Yosemite Clinic (formerly Lewis Memorial Hospital). As soon as I walked in, it was deja vu. I have visited Yosemite many times, and did go back to Benson, but I still wasn't able to remember what happened."

top-of-the-line mountaineering skills and desire. Many places in Yosemite . . . were beyond the capabilities of most of the Yosemite rangers in the 1950s."

Henneberger was confident that he could be an asset to the search and rescue team, but his first trial was a fiasco. On July 4, Jake Jacobs rescued him from the boring routine of the Information Desk by ordering: "Go get your climbing boots and some rope and go immediately to the base of the cliffs below Sunnyside Bench to the right of Lower Yosemite Fall. Two boys are stranded on it. There's a rotten log leaning against the cliff at the beginning of a broad ledge that leads up to just where they are. Go up and tell the boys to stay put and wait while I get a rescue party together."

Eagerly, Henneberger complied. "I had never been to this part of the Valley, but knew a lot of people got in trouble there. Jake's instructions were clear, and I climbed up the rotten log. The face of the cliff got steeper and steeper. Footholds were meager and wet and mossy from the waterfall's spray. 'Gosh' I thought, 'Yosemite climbing is tougher than I had imagined.' I had climbed some very rough routes in the Tetons, but this climbing on quite steep granite without ropes and pitons was about as hard as anything I had ever done. I decided to sit tight until the rest of the party arrived. A crowd of visitors collected below. They had heard the screaming boys but couldn't see them and thought I was the one that needed to be rescued!"

Soon he saw Jake and a man named Al, an excellent seasonal climber, starting up another log. "I had gone to the wrong rotten log," Henneberger realized sickly, having heard that Jake had little patience with foolish mistakes.

'What about John?' I heard Al say from the ledge above me. Jake's response was cool, 'We'll get him on the way down.'

Subdued, I waited on my slippery perch. Later, as

The man with glasses and a grin had been lost for 10 days in the snow. His rescuers, front row from left: Homer Robinson, Duane Jacobs, and Bill Janss; and in back, Sam Clark, Buck Evans, Bob Lint, and an unidentified man. (Hoyt collection.)

to carry the more eager reporters back to Benson. ". . . On the trail for eleven hours," he noted in his log. "Very slow going . . . reporters very annoying." While he was tying his animals to a hitching rail, photographers blinded him with flashbulbs.

As did all the key participants in the rescue, Van Bibber received lavish praise but no other compensation. His log revealed his involvement "(rode) . . . 110 miles last 4 days, 41 hours overtime." It was all in a day's, or several days', work.

Two years later, Ranger John Henneberger, 27, was transferred to Yosemite, mainly because of the climbing abilities he had acquired in the Colorado Rockies and Grand Teton National Park. He knew that "Handling Yosemite granite walls requires they passed downward with the rescued boys roped to them, Al said again 'What about John?'

'Throw him a rope,' Jake said. I caught the end of a climbing rope, tied it to a small bush on the precarious perch I had been standing on for almost an hour, and rappelled. So on my first rescue in Yosemite as a climbing ranger, I had to be rescued.

In the subsequent five years of his Yosemite tenure, Henneberger participated in many other rescues, more than atoning for his initial blunder.[20]

I spent what seemed the whole summer of '54 looking for two people who disappeared from Yosemite Valley. [Walter Gordon's search was the easier of the two.] Gordon, 26, graduate student at Cal-Berkeley, was working as a clerk at Camp Curry when, on July 20, he announced that he was going to hike the Four Mile Trail to Glacier Point. He was never seen again. Volunteers covered all the gullies and cliffs between Camp Curry and the Four Mile Trail with no results. Teams of climbing rangers began searching the bases and lower sections of Yosemite's towering and sheer cliffs.

After five days of futile search, a crop-dusting helicopter was used for low, hovering flights over the area. That was the second use of a helicopter in Yosemite. It was unsuccessful, as were bloodhounds. After ten exhausting days, the search was ended.

Within two months, climbers, rangers, and bloodhounds were needed in a search for another Cal-Berkeley graduate student, a 30-year-old Swede, Orvar von Laass, who had told his wife that he was going on a short hike in the Royal Arches vicinity. Ranger Jack Morehead and Henneberger were among the searchers. On the second day, Henneberger, aided by climbers from the Sierra Club, "spent an entire day rappelling down the 1,800 feet of smooth granite from the top to the bottom of Royal Arches, inspecting ledges and chimneys

into which von Laass might have fallen."

Both searches had been intensively covered by news people who reported on the October contacts between the Gordon and von Laass families and why they suspected foul play, possibly even murder, and urged that the FBI be called in.

Superintendent John Preston was quoted as saying that there "always is such a possibility, but foul play certainly is not a probability." Rangers discussed the case for years. "When we called off the search for Orvar," Henneberger reflected, "we sat in Chief Ranger Sedergren's office and muttered about it all." Sedergren suggested that they had both left the Park. Orvar had learned of Walter Gordon's disappearance, and did the same, so it was theorized. "But having spent considerable time on Yosemite cliffs both as a climber and rescue ranger," Henneberger said, "I knew a body can disappear awfully easily, in the gullies and many overhanging dry waterfalls where a body can fall inside a cave area . . . and never be found. The skull breaks loose one day and is found by a hiker and turned over to a ranger. About fifteen years or so later I was in Yosemite and a ranger told me about finding a skull in that general area. I came away pretty well convinced it was Walter Gordon's skull."[21]

Badger Pass had great snow in the 1930s. (Hoyt collection.)

---

20. Quotations are from John Henneberger's Dec. 19, 1995 memoir that he sent to the author. Now retired, he is working on a scholarly history of the NPS and its rangers, but took time, thank goodness, to assist me.
21. Sedergren's daughter told the author that "My dad used to say, 'I wonder what happened to Orvar'—even when he was an old man."

In a 1957 interview, given before his transfer to Olympic National Park as assistant superintendent, Sedergren commented on voluntary disappearances. "In more than 20 years we have had only about a half-dozen unsolved disappearances . . . people who wanted to drop from sight and eliminate all ties to their past. . . . We never close the books on a missing person," he added. Henneberger stated, however, that the ranger who told him about the skull appeared to be unaware of Walter Gordon's disappearance in the area of the find.[22]

Sedergren estimated that during summers "an average of six people a day get lost in the park's 1,200 square miles. . . . Some days we have five to six tots wandering from their parents. We usually find them quickly. Kids usually fare better than adults. When they're tired they lie down and go to sleep. Adults get nervous and go haywire.

"The oldest lost person," Sedergren continued, "was a man in his 70s, who left camp to mail a letter. He lost his way and wandered about 12 miles. The search lasted two days and a night. I found him myself, lying across the trail asleep."

When asked about the youngest missing child, the chief ranger cited the case of an 18-month-old girl. "Back in 1951," he recalled," this little girl walked through an entire camp unnoticed by anyone, and climbed a mile and a half into the woods. We searched all night and found her the next morning, sitting on a log. She had slept in a hollow tree and crawled out when the sun rose."

In June 1957, four-year-old Shirley Ann Miller was lost for almost three days. ". . . Park employees volunteered their time," Sedergren said. "Many helped look for almost the entire 62 hours." Shirley was found unharmed in a small meadow. Her calm announcement, "I am not lost, but the bear is lost. He went away and got lost," prompted the present name of Lost Bear Meadow.

Questioned as to the most difficult tracking job and rescue in his 13 Yosemite years, Sedergren responded without hesitation that it had been the search for the Thompson sisters, especially for Joan, in 1949. Said he, still marveling, "She climbed terrain that would be difficult for a squirrel."

The wording in the National Park Service's enabling act did not mention human life, but stated clearly that the purpose of national parks was to "conserve the scenery and the natural and historic objects and the wildlife therein. . . ." And that's exactly what ranger-naturalist Bob McIntyre did in the 1940s. A big bad bear was trashing one of the Yosemite Valley campgrounds, and McIntyre was sent to investigate. After observing the bear in action, the ranger had to agree with the irate and frightened campers that the aggressor required deportation.

Tranquilizers were new and dosage per weight still undetermined—and McIntyre overestimated the amount needed. After the shot, the bear staggered around, then dropped lifelessly to the ground.

At that, sympathies changed and some campers voiced concern for the bear—"poor fellow, he's dead." Contrite and embarrassed, McIntyre decided on resuscitation. With help from a camper, he rolled the shaggy victim onto his back, turned his head sideways and began applying pressure with his hands to the bear's chest. Resuscitating an unconscious man who might weigh around 200 pounds was not easy, but the same technique used on *Ursus americanus,* weighing up to 300 pounds, took every bit of energy McIntyre possessed. Sweat poured down his face, and his arms and hands ached, but brother bruin revived. While the bear was still groggy, the equally groggy ranger helped lift him into the bear trap to be hauled away.[23]

---

22. According to John Dill, "There is no list of missing persons, but the incident reports are certainly on file and the missing persons are entered into a national law enforcement computer system."
23. Rangers learned that jumping up and down on the rib cage of an over-tranquilized bear would reactivate it more easily. From Lemuel Garrison, *The Making of a Ranger* (Institute of the American West), p. 79.

8   Outposts and the Ladies

For years, Yosemite National Park was divided into five districts, the Valley district being the most important and receiving the most attention. The other districts were Wawona, Tuolumne Meadows, Crane Flat, and Merced Grove, later changed to Mather District. These four areas, all reached by pioneer roads, had entrance or checking stations at or near Park boundaries where rangers collected fees and disseminated information.

In 1914, the first year automobiles were allowed to travel on all the roads, the Crane Flat entrance was staffed by college-boy ranger Jean Witter who, a decade later, was one of the three founders of Dean Witter and Company. In 1914, however, he was a sophomore at Cal-Berkeley, and a seasonal ranger.

In those days, Crane Flat was not an active outpost. Not only was the Big Oak Flat Road unpaved, dusty, and deeply rutted, but autos were underpowered for its steep grades. "Consequently," Witter remarked years later, "people would try to come up the Big Oak Flat Road through the Tuolumne Grove to see the big redwoods [Sequoias] there, and the automobiles would get stuck in the deep ruts . . . caused by heavy wagons. Somebody from the Valley would have to come and pull them out. On two or three occasions, I had people sleep in my cabin because their cars were stuck. My cabin was just a shack, and they had to sleep on the floor. I had to get some meals together for them, dinner and breakfast. These people weren't prepared to go out on camping trips. They were all dressed up to stay in nice accommodations in the valley. . . . I was the cook. I wasn't very good, but we survived all right."

Witter returned in 1915 and lived in a new log patrol cabin.[1] It was roughly 25 by 32 feet with four rooms. He carved his initials inside over the doorway, and they still survive. After Witter was transferred to Wawona in 1916, new ranger John Wegner, his wife Rose, and their six-month-old baby boy lived in the cabin.[2] According to Wegner, there were one- to three-inch cracks between the logs, and bugs boring into the wood. Later the logs had to be peeled, the cracks sealed, and a 12- by 20-foot stable of poles and shakes built nearby for the horses.

There were outposts within each district, most—like Aspen Valley, Miguel Meadow, Mariposa Grove, Buck Camp, and Yosemite Creek—maintained only during summers. Daily patrols were made from them on horseback.

Outpost housing was utilitarian, either a board and screen-sided tent or a small cabin. Neither was fancy but the settings were often fantastic in beauty, and usually near a stream or lake and a trail junction. Running water came in buckets carried by the patrol ranger. A one or two-holer with a view was the nearest thing to plumbing, and garbage disposal was a deep hole in the ground—or a bear, if the hole wasn't dug deep enough. Inside, home sweet home was furnished with a table, benches, a straight chair or two, cupboards, and two stoves—an airtight for heating and a wood stove for cooking. Iron cots or bunks were the only beds. Coleman lanterns provided light and a reassuring hiss at night.

The sole modern convenience was a crank telephone, whose strident ring usually meant a call from the chief ranger's office with instructions, warnings of fire, lost hikers, or other problems.

---

1. Three identical patrol cabins were built in 1915: one at Crane Flat, another in the Merced Grove, and the third at Hog Ranch, now named Mather. Only the first exists today—in the Pioneer History Center at Wawona. See chapter 10, "A Decade of Uneasy Peace."
2. The boy was named Frances, a name he grew to hate and was able to change legally to John Jr. when he was in high school.

Calls out were business-like with only a minimum of chit-chat against a maximum of static. Many rangers had grown up in rural areas, and didn't consider the outposts primitive. Only the distance from neighbors was a bit daunting, especially to women if the ranger was fortunate enough to have a wife who would accompany him.

In fact, it was in such remote places and conditions that women showed their mettle: riding patrol, clearing trails, and cleaning up campsites alongside their husbands. The women were neither uniformed nor paid, but put in hours of work. Wives who stayed at the outposts were not free to loll in hammocks, for they answered questions from hikers and fishermen, issued campfire permits, handled telephone calls, and tried to map lightning strikes or smokes. For example, at Tuolumne Meadows in the '20s, Martha Bingaman rode patrol with John astride her own horse. In the '40s, Eliza Danner handled the telephone in emergencies as she did when Chief Townsley died and during the search and rescue of the Thompson sisters. During the 1948 Rancheria Fire, Martha Bingaman and Laura Walquist took care of many telephone calls at Mather. Evelyn Tucker, Tom's wife, gave first aid when needed.

In 1918, the persistence of Yosemite's school teacher, Clare Marie Hodges, coupled with a shortage of rangers due to World War I was responsible for her being hired as the first woman ranger in the Park Service.[3] Raised in Mariposa County, a devotee of Yosemite and horseback riding from childhood, it was only natural that she sought a job teaching the small school in Yosemite Valley from 1916 to 1919. Before long, she knew everyone in the close-knit community, yet it took courage to confront Superintendent Lewis.

"Probably you'll laugh at me," she told him, "but I want to be a ranger."

His response surprised her. "I beat you to it, young lady, it's been on my mind for some time to put women on one of these patrols—only I couldn't find the right one before."[4]

Men weren't the only ones who did stunts on the Overhanging Rock. (Pillsbury postcard, courtesy Marilyn Guske.)

Permission came from Washington, and she was issued a Stetson hat and a badge and, at 26, reported to work in May 1918. "I didn't carry a gun. Other rangers told me I should, especially when I carried money (gate receipts) from Tuolumne Meadows to the Park Headquarters. It was an overnight ride in those days, but I never had any trouble along the way."[5]

3. Six weeks later, a second woman ranger was hired, at Mount Rainier. From Polly Wells Kaufman, *National Parks and the Woman's Voice* (Albuquerque: University of New Mexico Press, 1996).
4. Ibid, p. 73.
5. As quoted by Lou Evon, *Fresno Bee*, Nov. 17, 1963.

Her job ended when the war did, but Lewis must have liked what she accomplished, because in 1923 and '24 both Beatrice and Dixon Freeland, her husband, were paid to check cars in at Bridalveil Fall, and later at the Alder Creek entrance station, twelve hours a day, seven days a week. Martha and John Bingaman were similarly employed and compensated during the next three years.

During the summers of 1926 and '27, Eva Cora McNally and her husband, Charles, officiated at Tuolumne Meadows as park rangers grade 6 at $1,620 per annum apiece. Both wore guns, but there is no record of them being used. He purchased a uniform, but Eve wore knickers and pinned her badge on a sweater.[6]

The legal window allowing couples equal salaries for equal work ended during the Depression's nadir in 1932. Although it was reintroduced in 1935, it was years before the Park Service would hire two members from the same family again.

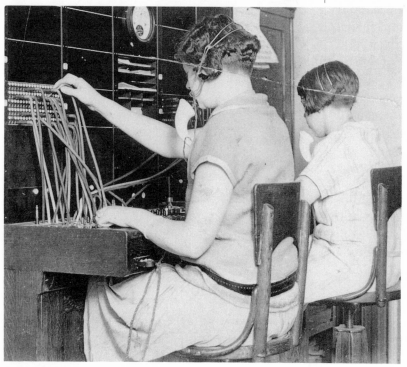

Emma Mann and Florence Hoyt kept the rangers in touch.

However, women at outposts continued to donate their time when needed. During summers at Tuolumne Meadows, beginning in 1931, Carl Sharsmith's wife, Helen, filled in for him when he was away on nature walks or rescues. A gifted botanist herself, she was perfectly capable of giving a campfire talk, hiking or backpacking alone, and writing articles for *Yosemite Nature Notes,* the monthly publication of the Yosemite Association. Sometimes she signed reports Helen K. Sharsmith, H.R.N.W.P., meaning Honorary Ranger Naturalist Without Pay.[7]

And then there was Enid R. Michael, who worked seasonally as a ranger-naturalist from 1921 until 1942. She did volunteer work for the naturalist division almost from the time she arrived in 1919 as the 38-year-old wife of Yosemite's assistant postmaster, Charles Michael. Superintendent Lewis and Chief Ranger Townsley were impressed with the numbers and variety of the plants she helped Ansel Hall collect and display on the porch of the old administration building. Ansel hired her in 1921 over the objections of Dr. Harold C. Bryant, who had begun the natural history program. "He (Bryant) did not approve of women taking part," she reminisced, "but I was there and I guess in time he concluded to make the best of an unfortunate situation."

Bryant was only the first of many men Enid managed to antagonize, mainly because she was outspoken and constantly applied pressure to become a permanent employee. Her initial supporter, Lewis, became disenchanted, and Bert Harwell, Park Naturalist from 1929 till 1940, had frequent confrontations with her."[8] Even Superintendent Thomson, who interceded for her, agreed that she had a "vivid personality."[9]

6. *Stockton Record,* 1926.
7. As did Carl, Helen earned her Ph.D at the University of California at Berkeley. After their divorce, in 1950, she served as that university's senior herbarium botanist until 1969. A plant was named for her, and she wrote the popular *Spring Wild Flowers of the Bay Area,* along with other works. She died in 1982. See Elizabeth Stone O'Neill, *Mountain Sage* (El Portal, CA: Yosemite Association, 1988.)
8. Ibid, p. 75.

Enid Michael was the first woman ranger-naturalist in Yosemite—and not always appreciated by the men. To her right stand Ansel Hall, Carl Russell, and Dr. Harold Bryant. (Courtesy YRL.)

Unlike Yosemite Valley, the entire 10,000-acre Wawona Basin, bordering the South Fork of the Merced, was homesteaded and privately owned until 1932. The trails that radiated out of Wawona were established by its principal owners, the three powerful Washburn brothers. They stocked the numerous lakes along the headwaters of the river with fingerlings so that trout would be on their hotel's menu. Early-day cattleman Robert Wellman maintained a hunting camp at the site where the cavalry later established an outpost. It was said to have been named Buck Camp because buck pri-

vates were stationed there to patrol the southern part of the Park.[10]

In 1930, Chief Ranger Townsley told ranger Jack Moody to select a site between Wawona and Moraine Meadow for a snow survey cabin that could double as a patrol station in summers. Moody picked a spot near the abandoned cavalry campsite because of its central location, creek, meadow, and to save mileage on a telephone line.[11] Buck Camp was 14 miles east of Wawona, and ideally suited for patrols. Chiquito, Fernandez, and Triple Divide passes, all leading out of the Park, were within an

---

9. It would not be right to end this chapter without at least a mention of Mary V. Hood, another woman with a "vivid personality." Her career as a collaborator—read, 'volunteer'—for YNP began in 1950 with her husband, Bill, and lasted into the 1980s.

10. Information from Jim Snyder, YNP archivist. Wellman killed the last known grizzly bear in Yosemite. The cavalry background is in Peter Browning's *Yosemite Place Names* (Lafayette, CA: Great West Books, 1988).

11. Warren Moody, *Yosemite Ranger on Horseback* (Fresno: Pioneer Publishing Company, 1990.)

easy day's ride, and no less than 19 lakes, several among the most beautiful in the Park, enriched the region.[12]

According to records, Park Service carpenters built a 14- by 28-foot two-room cabin of vertical logs at Buck Camp the following year. The $600 cost was paid by the State of California and the Merced River Irrigation District, which needed shelters for snow surveyors. A pressure box caught water from a spring that supplied cold water to the sink and, eventually, an outdoor shower. Seasonal ranger Clyde Quick added the shower for his wife, Arthayda. Grandeur in the wilds! Since then it has been seasonal home to many rangers, some of them with wives, all of whom appreciated the shower. In banner years, larkspur in its meadow tops six feet.[13]

When ranger Jim Skakel returned there for his second summer, in 1939, he packed personal gear and dynamite on his horse, and a shortwave radio on a pack horse. His towheaded son Bob, 12, rode behind him on a rented horse. They planned to catch fish and eat the provisions left the previous fall. The cabin door stood ajar, warning of trouble, and

If Enid Michael had a "vivid personality," so did her dancing instructor—"put your left foot forward and your right foot back." (Courtesy Ann Matteson.)

inside was the random devastation that only a bear can cause. Fifty years later, Bob recalled that bruin had systematically torn through the kitchen, punctured or ripped apart every can, consumed what smelled good, and discarded everything else on the floor. Then the intruder had defecated atop the mess. Flour, sugar, salt, everything was ruined except the maple syrup and the bicarbonate of soda, which the bear probably needed.[14]

"My dad had a short fuse," Bob continued, "so we shoveled out the kitchen PDQ. The bear had pretty well finished off our food supply, and Dad had been instructed not to return to the Valley for three weeks so he killed the bear when it came back

that night, and shot a deer that wandered into camp the next day. After he dressed it, Dad hung most of the meat on the clothesline. That, naturally was against every Park Service regulation, but he figured we had to eat."

A day or so later, "Jake Jacobs rode up, saw the meat, assessed its source, and refused to come in the cabin. That, unfortunately, terminated one of the few close relationship my Dad had with other rangers."

One inholder who bemused Bob was "old lady Stockton," a tiny, wizened woman, who had a homestead and two small shelters at Johnson Lake, a couple of miles northwest of Buck Camp.[15] Each

---

12. Steve Beck, author of *Yosemite Trout Fishing Guide* (Portland, OR: Frank Amato, 1995), thinks that Royal Arch Lake and Upper Chain Lakes possess "classic alpine beauty." He lauds the fishing, too.

13. The description of setting and flowers comes from "I am Only a Seasonal," a manuscript covering the summers of 1973 to 1986, written by Thomas A. (Smitty) Smith.

14. Bob Skakel made a detailed tape recording for the author regarding his Yosemite years of 1936 to 1940.

spring from 1928 until the 1940s, she arrived wearing high-buttoned shoes and riding sidesaddle on a burro, leading a heavily loaded pack string through the melting snow. "She claimed to have a gold mine," Bob said, "I can remember her coming over the hill, reciting 'Mister Ranger, mister Ranger, I heard the pack trains in the night carrying my gold off.' No one ever saw her gold mine. In Bob's opinion, "She was a bit wacky." Wawona oldtimers Albert Gordon and Norman May agreed that she was "crazy, but pleasantly crazy."[16] May related that one of her eccentric acts was carrying a rocking chair on her back up the steep trail from Wawona to the lake. When she tired, which was often, she sat the chair down and serenely rocked in it to the amazement and amusement of other hikers.

Norm May recalled, "Clara would spend the night at what we all called 'the old ranger's cabin.'" It was the Chilnualna patrol cabin, which stood near the upper Chilnualna Fall, the only cabin in the area before the one at Buck Camp was built. "A pine tree fell and pretty well crushed it, probably in the 1980s. Incidentally, Archie Leonard's son John told me Chilnualna means 'the echo of the water' no doubt referring to the booming of the water in the spring."[17]

An indelible memory of Bob Skakel's was the superlative fishing. One time he and his dad camped overnight at Moraine Meadow where, Bob found, "the only large things were mosquitos." He caught 25 small fish in half an hour. "It wasn't even a matter of casting your line. You just walked across the grass and dropped your line into a very small stream (the headwaters of the South Fork of the Merced) and—boom—you had a fish, and they were delicious!"

In 1956, Buck Camp had a woman's touch, and John Townsley's bride, Elaine Ferris Townsley, was on the business end of a shovel. "My first introduction to the cabin was the tremendous clean-up job after the bear who had lived there all winter, and, during that time, had helped himself to a large barrel of flour. My afternoons, when I couldn't be out on patrol with John, were mostly spent pinpointing particularly dangerous lightning strikes. We had a lightning storm nearly every afternoon at 3:15 on the dot. When it wasn't stormy, I never ceased to be amused by our mule, Gilbert, as he watched the humming birds enjoying the delphinium."[18]

Beside bird- and lightning-watching, John put Elaine to work with a hammer. "I helped build a new outhouse and a corral, but the cabin was already standing (barely.)" Afterward, Elaine accompanied John to many places as far afield as Hawaii National Park, Theodore Roosevelt's birthplace in New York and, finally, Yellowstone National Park, where he was superintendent and where he died, in September 1982. Elaine's favorite place was Buck Camp. "All in all," she wrote in 1996, "it was the most wonderful experience of my life with the happiest memories."

Being stationed at Buck Camp is not one of Rod Broyles's happiest memories, but it provided him with an unforgettable experience, besides several close encounters with bears. One morning in the summer of 1952 he had a telephone call from Tommy Tucker at Wawona, asking anxiously, "Are you all right! Is the cabin all right?!"

"Sure," Rod assured him, "But last night I dreamed that a mountain lion was shaking the cabin real hard."

"That wasn't a mountain lion," Tommy laughed. "That was an earthquake!" The Tehachapi-Bakersfield quake registering nearly eight points on the Richter scale was felt as far north as Yosemite.[19]

Buck Camp was quiet during the summer of

---

15. Emeterio Acosta homesteaded the land in 1890, but later it was owned by cattle raisers Stockton and Buffim. In the 1930s, teenager Norman May visited Clara Stockton's camp, and she told him that the partnership named the lake after Andrew Johnson. It was they who planted the pond lilies that now choke it. After Clara Stockton's death, the land was sold to the Park Service, and in 1958 the structures were razed.
16. Telephone interviews with the author in the fall of 1996.
17. Nov. 25, 1997 letter from Norman May to the author.
18. Letter from Elaine F. Townsley, March 10, 1995, from another, more substantial, log cabin home, this one in Vermont where she lives with her daughter, son-in-law, and their two young children, one of whom bears his great-grandfather's name of Forest.
19. "Aftershocks sent dishes flying in, and trail crew workers scrambling out, of the rickety, foundationless cabin at

1959 for seasonal ranger Bart Reed and his wife, Elnora. Sometimes ten days would go by between hikers. A telephone call from District Ranger Walt Gammill one evening changed that—it prefaced the longest and most uncomfortable day in their lives. Gammill advised that a woman had started up the South Fork from Wawona and had not returned. "Walt wanted me to leave at daylight and hike down the South Fork of the Merced River to find the woman, a matter of 14 miles by trail, but more cross country," Reed reminisced in 1997.[20]

"We did. Elnora and I had only been married for two years and she insisted on going along and I was glad for her company. She took extra clothes for the lady and I carried food and a 25-pound portable radio that wasn't very reliable."

"As soon as we reached the river, I knew we were in for it. There were enormous house-sized boulders that proved to be more than obstacles, they were a challenge." One of the "challenges" actually balanced like a seesaw. When it began to move it became a 'singing boulder.' The music however, was a chorus of rattlesnakes buzzing angrily. We were on top of a huge snake den . . . and Elnora was wearing tennis shoes!" Somehow they were able to jump off as the boulder seesawed up, and avoid the snakes.

After that, they found the terrain becoming more and more demanding and dangerous. "Elnora's ankles were cut by the thorny brush, and the radio, which wouldn't work, felt like lead. Sun beat down unmercifully. . . . The brush, mostly manzanita, was so thick we could not see the ground as we climbed over it." Between the brush, boulders, and precipitous terrain, "We would walk 20 feet and have to sit down out of sheer exhaustion. We were in worse shape than the lost hiker, I was sure, but through it all Elnora never complained. What a trooper!"

"Finally, I managed to contact Walt on the radio and he informed us that the hiker had been found hours earlier . . . just sitting alongside the river because, we heard later, she had been in a family feud!

"After what seemed like forever, we finally

"Ranger" Martha Bingaman's uniform was unorthodox. (Courtesy YRL.)

stumbled on an old fisherman's trail. It looked like an interstate highway to us."

It was easier going, but it was well past dark before they reached the Gammills's house. One more indignity awaited them. "Mrs. Gammill set out a big bowl of beans with all the trimmings and Elnora and I dove in, but we couldn't swallow. After almost an entire day in the brush, we had inhaled so much pollen that our throats were raw from irritation. We couldn't eat . . . but we didn't complain. We were safe but never forgot that amazing day."

Arthayda Quick, whose husband, Clyde, was a seasonal ranger from 1944 to 1973, loved Buck Camp. In fact, she loved Merced Lake, Harden Lake, Yosemite Creek, and Aspen Valley—all the remote outposts where Clyde was stationed. There

---

Deer Camp," Broyles added.
20. Bart Reed sent the author his recollections in November 1997.

were crises, she admitted: "... like the drowning of a guest at Merced Lake High Sierra Camp; ... the assaulting of a woman hiker in Echo Valley; trail injuries to both Clyde and myself. My best memories are the horseback patrols in the back country with our son who rode with Clyde and me... no clatter of horse shoes as on TV. We rode silently ... just looking and enjoying. We were able to see quail exploding under our feet ... an unaware family of weasels parading across the trail ... watched water ouzels in the stream, listened to the chatter of chickadees overhead, heard a bunch of does and fawns bleating as they talked softly to one another ... saw a bear run across the stream carrying our pail of stew (we hunted but never saw either one again) ... heard the scary voices of a hundred coyotes (it was probably 2 animals) ... [riding through] the blackness of the forest at night, sitting on your horse and letting him take you home when you couldn't see an inch in front of your face."

Clyde was of the pioneer Quick family in Mariposa. He owned and operated a large cattle ranch south of town and taught at Chowchilla Union High School, where he was the principal for 35 years. Above all, he was a mountaineer with a love and knowledge of Yosemite. He took pride in being a ranger who treated backcountry visitors as guests. Young men from trail and fire crews made him their mentor, and his versatility was well-known. So was his wife with the odd name of Arthayda.

In November 1994 she wrote to Gene Rose, a free-lance writer.[21] "I was the only ranger wife I knew who actually accompanied [my husband] on patrol, gave out fire permits, dispensed information, and served in Ranger capacity with my husband or in his absence, and without pay.

"Both of us loved the mountains, and the privilege of living for a while each year in them colored our lives. We literally drank them in."

There were many drawbacks and challenges to living in and protecting remote areas while raising a son and living in a tent. But the compensations, she felt, more than made up for them.

During World War II, an old danger was posed to outpost rangers: Sheep! In his autobiography, *My Life of High Adventure*, Grant Pearson described his career as a ranger and superintendent in Denali (formerly McKinley) National Park. A full chapter is devoted to his 1939–42 Yosemite experiences.[22] He loved his Alaska job, but requested transfer so as to acquire experience with crowds. In his book he wrote:

My orders came through on May 2, 1939, 'Report as a Permanent ranger at Yosemite National Park Headquarters not later than three days before Memorial Day week-end. Chief Ranger Forrest [sic] Townsley will be there to assign you to holiday crowd duty.' I'd made it.

When I arrived in Yosemite on schedule, I found Forrest Townsley filling a wide armchair in a headquarters office ... a big, stout bear of a ranger, with slightly unkempt hair and a wide smile. He stood up and stuck out a hand. 'Glad you're here, Grant! Got just the place for you. You'll like it. Arch Rock entrance gate. I need you there selling entrance permits. It'll be seven a.m. to seven p.m. over the holiday. Make it up to you later.' He gave me a broad, friendly grin, (Later I came to mistrust the innocence of that smile of his.)

Yosemite over a holiday was just exactly what I had expected. In one day, looking out the ticket window in the little shack [kiosk] at the Arch Rock gate, I saw more people drive by than had visited McKinley in an entire year.

My past caught up with me after the holidays. Because of my experience in the McKinley outback, I was assigned to the Tuolumne Meadows horse patrol, up in the high Sierra away from people. 'Be a break for you,' said Chief Ranger Townsley, smiling jovially. The job consisted of patrolling more than a hundred miles

---

21. A copy of her seven-page letter was given to Jim Snyder for the Yosemite Research Library. He was one of the young men who worked under Quick and was befriended by both the Quicks. Partly through him, the couple received the prestigious Yosemite Award from YNP in 1992. Once more Arthayda had to act in Clyde's absence, this time caused by his death in 1986.

22. This book was unknown to Yosemite historians or to the Research Library until the fall of 1996, when former Yosemite bus driver Frank Bonaventura, now working seasonally in Denali National Park, found it in an Alaska bookstore and sent it down for reference.

of trail, in a week and out a week, sometimes leading a pack horse carrying tanks of trout fingerlings to plant in the mountain streams; cleaning up campsites, hunting for occasional lost people, chopping away down timber on the trail. It wasn't as out-back a job as that at Kantishna Ranger Station, by a long shot; I saw people every day, hiking along the trail by twos, threes, and dozens. I gave out camping and fishing information. Once, back at the Tuolumne Meadows camp, a fisherman gave me some important information in return. He had come in fifteen miles from a lake tucked under the Sierra crest.

'You know you got hundreds of sheep in there?' he asked. 'Didn't think sheep were allowed to run in the park.'

'They aren't,' I said. 'Thanks.'

I got together with Carl Danner, the district ranger, and we immediately saddled up, setting out in a hurry for that high lake. When we got there the sheep had gone. But their trail was very plain indeed. I was shocked. Where those woollies had been was a path of destruction that could only be surpassed by a landslide. The grass was eaten down to the roots. Shrubs and small trees were picked clean. The ground was trodden bare. Why, even when thousands of caribou migrated through the McKinley tundra eating reindeer moss as they went, they left no such ruin behind them.

We followed the trail over the crest, and from there we spotted the herd and the dirty gray tent of the Basque sheepherders, in a pretty little hidden valley in the park. We put our horses down the slope and came up to two black bearded fellows who eyed us with a kind of dull hostility.

'Who told you to run your sheep in here?' Carl demanded

One of the Basques shrugged. 'No sabe.'

Carl looked baffled. I turned my horse away from the two and said to Carl. 'Come here a minute.' When Carl came alongside he said, 'How do you figure it? Think they really don't savvy English?'

'I've got an idea. Saw it work once on an Indian dog-breeder. We'll go back over there, and you say to me, 'What do you think we should do?' Then leave it to me.

We went back to the two Basques, and when Carl asked his question I said, 'I say we take them both in. We'll find someone who can speak their language, and then we'll find out who owns those sheep.'

We tied the two men together and got ready to march them ahead of us when the front Basque turned around and shouted, 'You can't do this! Those sheep will scatter all over the country!'

'Now,' I said, 'you're talking sense—and English. Who owns these sheep?'

'Jones, down at Mono Lake.'

'Get 'em out,' said Carl. 'Get 'em out fast, and tell your boss that we'll be calling on him with some very unpleasant news.[23]

Some time later Forrest Townsley called me in to headquarters. 'Grant,' he said, smiling in his wide, friendly fashion, 'you've been doing all right out there. Thought maybe you'd like to get back among people for a spell. I've got one of the finest assignments in the park for you. You'll love it. You're going to go on a three-week outing of the Sierra Club—two hundred people and a hundred and twenty-five horses and mules. They all have to obey park rules. You'll be in full charge.'

I was appalled. Two hundred people running about through the trees! But I managed to smile right back, and said, 'Fine, Chief. I know I have your full support in everything I do.' My stout boss looked slightly stumped, but said, 'Count on it, boy. Count on it.'

The club had set up camp in a mountain meadow in the Hetch Hetchy area.[24] When I got there and saw the costumes the members elected to wear in communing with nature, I was astonished. Women in halters and shorts, men in just shorts; some men and women wearing bright sashes, some wearing wide Mexican hats with feathers stuck in them . . . people all over the meadow,

---

23. The man got off easy—a $100 fine. The maximum was $500 plus six months in jail.
24. A late snow melt in July 1941 changed the club's itinerary to Tiltill Valley, north of Hetch Hetchy. (*Sierra Club Bulletin*, August 1942, pp. 1–13.)

prowling about looking at flowers, watching birds, taking photographs, painting pictures, fishing, wading, swimming with loud yips in the ice cold water, rock climbing on sheer upthrusts . . . I was afraid they would cut more of a swathe through the park than those sheep.

But they didn't. I think it was partly because they were really a serious group who knew what to do in the wilderness; and partly because of a measure I took in the way of delegating responsibilities. The day after I arrived I hunted up the outings leader, whom I'd met the day before—a tall, studious looking gentleman with a very tanned bald head.[25] He looked like a man of reason, though perhaps a hard one to buck in an argument. I said, 'Look here, sir. I'm sure you know that last year in Sequoia Park the club had some trouble. According to the record, the ranger was always fighting with your people about one thing or another, and arguing with the wrangler about where to graze your stock. Now, I'm not going to do any fighting like that. If anything happens that's against our park rules, I'll count on you to straighten it out. If you don't, why, I'll take *you* in to headquarters. I think we'll get along better that way, don't you?'

I had no idea whether it would work. But the Sierra Club man grinned and ran a hand over his bald head. 'Good. Wish the other ranger had done that, instead of running around like a cop on a beat too big for him. You'll have no trouble.'

And I didn't. Goes to show that when you get the people involved to do your policing for you, they'll likely do a better job of it than you can.[26] Later I came to respect the Sierra Club for another reason. All the Yosemite rangers had to have training in rock climbing, and Sierra Club instructors taught us.

Herb Ewing's experience as a back-country ranger began after World War II with his new wife and even newer son. Although born and raised in Yosemite, he didn't have a Yosemite romance. In-stead, he married Ruth B. Eleanor, a city gal who lived next door to his uncle in New Jersey. Before her 1945 marriage to Herb, a World War II pilot, she had maintained that she would live in a shack if necessary to be with the man she married, but "had never dreamed I would have to prove it."

Actually, the first place they lived in at Tuolumne Meadows wasn't a shack, but two ad-joining 12-foot by 14-foot tents. Herb was ecstatic at obtaining a job as a Yosemite ranger in the giant footsteps of his trail-building grandfather, Gabriel Sovulewski, and father Frank Ewing, whose nota-ble Park Service career lasted from 1916 until 1950. "Herb's salary was to be $2,200 per annum," Ruth reported to *Good Housekeeping* readers in 1956.[27]

> (I thought I had heard it wrong the first time too, but it was $2,200, minus deductions and uniform expenses—and an annum still sliced into 365 equal parts.) Naturally, at this point, I expressed what I thought was reasonable concern over ways and means. Just how, I wanted my husband to explain, did one feed a family, including a newborn son, for a whole year on a ranger's pay?

> 'You don't have so many expenses in the mountains, was his lame reply.' There'll be no movies to spend money on, no monthly utility bills to pay, no keeping up with the Joneses, no big entertainment bills. . . .'

> 'You paint a very enticing picture,' I said sarcastically. 'No beauty parlor, no dress shop, no fun, no nothing.'

> My easy going six-footer just said, 'Don't worry, honey. You're going to love it.'

Ruth didn't love tent living with an outhouse, where the altitude of 8,600 feet made her dizzy at first, and she hated heating water on a wood-burn-ing stove, "for Bobby's formula, for diapers, for sterilizing, for bathing, cooking, and for more dia-pers." Bending over a hot stove was bad enough, carrying water (until Herb piped it to the tent) was worse, and the lack of familiar noises—trains,

---

25. Dick Leonard was the Outing leader that year, but the description fits Will Colby, the previous (1901–1937) leader.
26. Pearson didn't mention them, but Superintendent Merriam dispatched rangers Homer Hoyt, Jack Reigelhuth, and Buck Evans to help manage the crowd.
27. "The Ranger and I" appeared in the October 1956 issue of *Good Housekeeping*. Quotations from it are used with permission of the magazine's 1995 editor.

Midge Haigh Reymann was small, but she ran her husband Bill and son John. (Reymann collection.)

important outpost because of its proximity to the Merced Lake High Sierra Camp, established in 1916, and for being the hub of several heavily traveled trails. Best of all, as far as Ruth was concerned, it boasted the snug log cabin Freeland and Moody had roofed in 1927. "It had a kitchen with a wood stove and hot and cold running water (hot while the stove is burning), a combination living-dining room with fireplace, and a bedroom which doubles as a food cooler. And," Ruth enthused, "we have a homemade shower outside the cabin, where we bathe by candlelight when we can spare the [stove-heated] hot water." Nightlife, provided by nature, was wild, and about once a week she changed from denim pants to a denim riding skirt and went out for dinner at the High Sierra camp, "our only social activity in the summer."

Ruth still enjoyed beauty shops, spiked heels, dancing, and the like, but she bragged "I can now throw a saddle a third of my own weight over a horse and cinch it up. I can pack a mule and often do, throwing a squaw hitch that would be a credit to a professional mule skinner, and I can run the station when Herb is away."

Another ranger's wife-turned-author was Margaret Becker Merrill, whose book *Bears in My Kitchen* was published by McGraw-Hill in 1956. She had a coauthor who, presumably, heightened the drama she supplied. Certainly one of them did. After publication, the action-studded narrative was scoffed at by Yosemite's ranger fraternity because Mrs. Merrill "borrowed" events that happened to other rangers and their wives and attributed them to her "heroic" husband and herself.[28]

Ranger Tom Van Bibber had no wife to assist him while he was stationed at Yosemite Creek Campground in 1949 and '50. Although he lived there in a tent, he was responsible for the small campgrounds at Smoky Jack, White Wolf, Harden Lake, Porcupine Creek, and Porcupine Flat. All were unimproved and were reached by the old Tioga Road, but only Yosemite Creek, White Wolf, and Porcupine Creek exist today. Thanks to a scrawled log book Van Bibber used as a basis for his

planes, autos, sirens—was worrisome. However, by the end of the summer "I got the knack of ironing his uniform shirts on the rough kitchen table, using a kerosene iron. And even at that high altitude, I learned how to bake what passed for a cake. At least the squirrels thought so. . . ." She loved "seeing my blond, fair-skinned Bobby get tan and healthy in the bright mountain light. . . . And to know that for Herb, there was work to do and satisfaction from doing it."

The Ewings spent several summers at 7,200-foot-elevation Merced Lake Ranger Station, an

28. Martha and John Bingaman and Helen and Bert Sault were my principal informants. My own study of the incidents recounted in the book confirmed their opinions.

monthly reports, lively details of the two summers are incorporated into this book.

Until 1961, when the last link of the new Tioga Road opened, the old road snaked down the west side of Yosemite Creek grade to a log bridge, ran along a level stretch east of the creek, and climbed tortuously back up a precipitous 21-percent grade. It was so steep, Van Bibber remembered. "that the only car that could buzz right up was the Model A Ford. My '35 pickup couldn't make it without getting stuck, an embarrassing plight for a ranger." Vapor locks, traffic jams, and frayed tempers were common experiences in summer. So was camping, either forced because of car trouble or made intentionally for the camping fun and fishing.

While training to be an Air Force pilot near Tonopah, Nevada, Tom flew a B-24 over Yosemite, and afterward he drove over to explore it while on leave. The mountains thrilled him—his favorite place was Yosemite Creek where it flowed down to create Upper Yosemite Fall. After a year's experience flying in the Philippines, a malaria-plagued place he detested, he was discharged and headed for Yosemite, where he joined the ranger force in 1947.

Not only did Van Bibber answer a zillion questions from motorists and complaints from campers, but he made extensive patrols on Bucky, a big buckskin gelding, and in the Ford pickup. His normal patrol range was from the top of El Capitan to North Dome, then north to May Lake and Ten Lakes, west to Pate Valley, south to Harden Lake, and on to Gin Flat and back to Yosemite Creek. By car, he drove northeast out to the May Lake junction and west to Crane Flat. On both the narrow road and narrower trails, there were trees and rocks to move and sometimes refuse to clean up.

There was a lot of physical work to his job, but his days were never monotonous. On June 24, 1949, for example, he recorded, "Opened the station, repaired the tent frames and platforms, put up tents." The one building with windows was his habitat. An extra tent was used by gravelly-voiced

district ranger Sam Clark, his affable boss, or by other rangers. After putting up the tents, Van Bibber repaired and cleared out the corrals, checked telephone lines, hoisted Old Glory, and he was in business. His settling-in chores were interrupted by motorists and campers registering and requesting information.

His station and a few campsites stood on the flat backed by a rock ridge west of the creek. Most of the camp sites were sandwiched in between the creek and road on the east side. Over a busy weekend, Van Bibber said that there could be as many as 150 camps, separated from one another by boulders, lodgepole pines, or a blanket hanging over a rope.[29]

There were more happy campers than unhappy ones, but the latter groused about the weather, their neighbors, loud car radios, bear, deer, mosquitos, poor fishing, and the lack of toilet paper in the shingled outhouses. One incident Van Bibber and probably the onlookers never forgot was the day an obese woman plunked her 300-plus pounds down in the one-holer near his tent, and because of her bulk and the still damp June earth, the little building sank down several inches so that the door would not open. After great confusion, some hysterics on her part, and ill-concealed amusement on the part of the other campers who gravitated to the scene, the outhouse had to be tipped over on its side to extricate her. That incident was not recorded in Van Bibber's log, but stuck in his memory.

Many other vignettes of camp life were recorded, however, such as: "Had a wild crowd sailing garbage can covers around and throwing rocks in the creek to annoy fishermen. Straightened them out good." Invariably the holiday most anticipated by visitors, and dreaded by rangers, was the Fourth of July. "Roads jammed all day on all grades from May Lake (trail junction)," Van Bibber commented in 1950, "1½ miles of cars stalled on Y [Yosemite] C [Creek] grade at 11:30 a.m. Cleared with some difficulty."

---

29. The camp expanded to the west side of the creek after that area was used as a construction camp for the Tioga Road from 1957 to 1960. In 1996, 75 large, numbered campsites remain in what still is a popular, peaceful place even though reached only by trail or by one of the two remaining passable sections of the original Tioga Road, potholes and all.

Between 7 and 10 p.m that same day, he patrolled ten miles on horseback before falling into bed. At 2 a.m., he was roused by an almost incoherent Chinese woman who somehow managed to convey that her husband had been bitten in his sleep by a rattlesnake. Van Bibber pulled clothes over his long underwear, grabbed his flashlight, and accompanied the upset woman back to her campsite. There another woman, seemingly a second wife, also speaking in Chinese, also incoherent, and the victim himself showed him the puncture wound on his thigh. After a flashlight investigation the ranger realized that the visitor had turned over in his sleep onto his fishing tackle and had been caught by his own hook!

After putting up the tents, Van Bibber repaired and cleaned the corrals, hoisted the flag, and Yosemite Creek campground was open for the summer. (Courtesy Tom Van Bibber.)

Since Van Bibber couldn't speak Chinese, and their understanding of English was further limited by high emotion, it took him several minutes to explain the ludicrous situation. "No damage," he summed up for his log, "just excited."

Compared to Yosemite Creek, Crane Flat, at the junction of the old Tioga and new Big Oak Flat roads, had become a metropolis, although it was still considered an outpost during the 1950s. For the first three summers, Ken "Ash" Ashley and his wife Ethel were assigned there. She, he recorded in 1995, was indispensable to its smooth functioning.

"Getting a station out of winter 'mothballs' and ready for action required a lot of work," Ash wrote the author. "Sweeping, shoveling snow, washing windows and picking up debris, not to mention arranging furnishings, stowing dishes and cooking utensils, hanging curtains and hanging up clothes. A special touch that Ethel added was a colorful window box of petunias. And, of course, there were our two small children to care for and the house to keep."

That was paramount, but Ethel always made time to welcome seasonal rangers, and maintenance people who lived in the "tent city" nearby. Their wives "were grateful for Ethel's tips and friendliness. She showed them how to kindle a fire, use a Coleman lantern, store food so as not to attract bears, bake bread in a wood stove, identify the more common wild flowers and where to go for hikes or picnics. She organized potlucks, visits to other stations and morning coffees.

"Yosemite had a barber, but when located at an outpost station it wasn't always convenient to drive to the Valley for a haircut so Ethel learned to cut hair and did it very well," Ash wrote proudly. "One summer this came in handy in an unexpected way."

It was the summer that the office of the Secretary of Interior "got into the employment act by appointing park rangers politically. . . . At Crane Flat we ended up with three of these young fellows. They were good boys, but green as grass and without a clue as to what rangering was all about."

When they showed up all had hair much too long for a man in uniform and I told them before they could go to work they'd have to have their hair cut. Going back to the Valley seemed burdensome so I told them I was sure my wife would be glad to give them a hair cut. Their apprehension was obvious but there wasn't much choice so, one by one, Ethel barbered them. The boys had all kinds

94

Both Eliza and Carl Danner ran the Tuolumne Meadows district for years. (Hoyt collection.)

visitor need—it would probably be illegal now—but we sold gas out of the government pumps, collected the money, issued a receipt and the next time one of us was in the Valley with a government car we used the money to buy replacement gas at the Chevron Station.

Well, Ethel didn't feel comfortable about this group but she didn't have much choice so sold them the gas and they paid and left. She did memorize their license number and noted that they headed down the Big Oak Flat Road toward Manteca. She reported the incident to the Ranger Office in the Valley. It turned out they had just received a report of four escapees from the brig at the Naval Station near Henderson, Nevada and the license number of their car matched. A call to the Sheriff of Stanislaus County resulted in the group being captured near Groveland.

of advice, suggestions and instructions about how they wanted the job done but Ethel followed my instruction. Crew cut! So we got them off to a good start.

Even though wives didn't wear uniforms or receive pay they "were as valuable to the Park Service and the public as if they had been on the payroll," Ashley stated. He gave a chilling example of the hazards.

One evening in early October, when Ethel was alone at the station, four young men in a car stopped, just having come down from Tioga Pass. One of them knocked on the door and asked if they could get some gas. This wasn't uncommon. Lee Vining, on the east side of the Pass, offered gas but, after Labor day, the stations at Tuolumne Meadows and Crane Flat closed for the season.

We had a simple arrangement to contend with this

Compensations at Crane Flat, the Ashleys felt, far outweighed the dangers and inconveniences. "In spring seeing the meadow come alive as the snow receded, frequent observations of the great grey owl; the peace and tranquility of the late evenings, broken by sounds of night creatures, the most thrilling of which were the coyotes. They seemed to have a chorus. In the fall the gradual decrease in traffic until quiet and solitude again descended over Crane Flat. . . ."

Once snow had closed both roads, the Ashleys happily moved back to the Valley with its barbershop, school, chapel, organizations, and other amenities. They always anticipated outpost life, however, and now recall it with nostalgia, as do many other retired rangers and wives.

9 Disasters

Natural events such as earthquakes, fires, landslides, and floods, are perceived by people as disasters. Certainly their aftermaths can be disastrous, as Yosemite's rangers learned early on. The clean-up process ranges from disagreeable to dangerous, enervating to exhausting. Fighting a fire and cleaning up after it are arduous jobs. For years, manpower, equipment, training, and understanding of the ecological role fire played were woefully lacking.

The most important of the few duties given the college-boy rangers in 1914 was not so much suppressing conflagrations as keeping then from spreading. "During the three summers I was there [1914–1916]," Jean Witter reminisced, in his oral history for the Bancroft Library, "the chief ranger gathered the rangers together on two or three occasions to fight fires. . . . In each instance, the fire had been started by lightning hitting the top of a tree. The tree top would [burn] then fall to the ground and the fire would start."

Wielding a shovel, an axe, or a rake, he would "clear an area so the fire couldn't jump, or [he would] start a back-fire so that a big fire couldn't go on." Witter emphasized that the "fires I speak of were not caused by visitors, who were few, but by lightning."

When interviewed in 1944, Assistant Chief Ranger John H. Wegner referred to the 1913–20 period as "the old days, [when] often, one man went to a fire and he stayed with it until it was out regardless of its size. "Sometimes," he said, "one man would be on a 300-acre fire."[1] What equipment existed was primitive. A small trailer, some hose, and hand tools—rakes, axes, and shovels—were all in bad shape. "Shovels, for instance, had had their points worn and broken so badly," he recalled, "that they had to be cut off to a straight edge." Lack of a central storage place was still another drawback. Rakes were kept in the warehouse, other tools elsewhere.

Of all people, the usually deskbound Superintendent Lewis used his ingenuity rather than tools to put out a lightning-caused blaze sometime in the 1920s. He was checking the smoking remains of a forest fire before releasing the weary men to go home when he spotted flames up in an old tree trunk. "It was too high to reach with a wet sack or dirt thrown by a shovel, or by water thrown from a bucket. . . . The tree was too large to be cut down without help, and Lewis hesitated to call back his already exhausted rangers. He scratched his head, and puzzled over the engineering problem of snuffing out that small blaze. Then he and the remaining ranger scouted for a spring. Finding one, they made a lot of mud balls and carried them in their hats to a point near the blazing tree.

"Both had been baseball players in their younger days, and as Lewis afterward said, 'The old soup-bones were still in fair shape.' Cheering each other's pitching, they heaved mud balls until the last 'strike' smacked out the last flickering blaze."[2]

In June 1921, controlling a man-caused forest fire near Big Meadow, west of Yosemite Valley, was ranger John Bingaman's first duty after signing the oath of office. For three tiring days he, fellow ranger Merrill Miller, and ranchers Horace and George Meyer worked to clear a fire line around 30 acres of burning timber. There was no fire camp, but Elizabeth Meyer, widow of the homesteader, kept her sons and the rangers supplied with food and drinking water.

Despite a prolonged drought, there were no major fires in the 1920s. Lewis noted that "forest fires were practically unknown." In his annual re-

---

1. Before Wegner left for Sequoia-Kings in 1944, Elizabeth Godfrey interviewed him regarding his 28 years as a Yosemite ranger and recorded this account.
2. Horace M. Albright and Frank J. Taylor, *Oh, Ranger!* (Berkeley: University of California Press, 1929).

Careless campers were a hazard, but so was lightning. (Courtesy Ray Warren.)

acquired a Graham-Dodge truck and converted it into a fire truck equipped with a tank. Fire prevention was spearheaded by Wegner, who helped prepare a protection plan, attended fire schools and, in 1931, became the Park's fire chief. After Wegner transferred to Sequoia-Kings as chief ranger in 1944, Homer Robinson succeeded him. Both were able and zealous advocates of prevention as well as protection. Art Holmes was Robinson's indispensable assistant in the 1950s.

Promptly at noon on weekdays, the wail of a fire siren sounded throughout the upper end of the Valley. Tourists often asked why, since no other signs of unusual activity followed the klaxon call. "Testing the siren," was the answer. Today, it is tested each Wednesday at noon.

September was always dreaded because of its dryness and the frequency of lightning strikes. September of 1948 was no exception. Fires outside Yosemite had sent a pall of smoke over the Sierra, making it difficult for fire lookouts to spot local blazes. As he fed the horses on the morning of the 10th, John Bingaman, then the Mather district ranger, was filled with foreboding. He smelled smoke, but could see nothing other than the overcast. Most of the seasonals had left for various colleges, so he had only two men left as a fire crew: the

port for 1927, he said that only nine acres had burned. Those and structure fires kept men alert. Once cold weather set in, winter chimney fires were common.[3]

Major change began about 1926 when the Park

---

3. For some unknown reason, chimneys were not cleaned out annually. Instead they were allowed to burn out even though that was frightening and sometimes dangerous. (Phyllis Freeland Broyles, in a September 1995 interview with the author.)

experienced Clarence "Spud" Wal-quist, and young, inexperienced Rod Broyles.[4] Broyles was the first to report for duty.

"Better not take that [patrol] ride today," Bingaman said. "Stick around. I have a feeling we'll be fighting fire soon."[5]

Less than eleven miles east, a man-caused fire was raging in Pate Valley, its smoke indistinguishable from the pall overhead. For 24 hours a trail crew had tried to confine it to the south bank of the Tuolumne River, but wind-blown flames had jumped to the north side and raced to Rancheria Mountain. Ironically there was a telephone line but it was inoperable due to a lack of sufficient maintenance funds. "For want of a nail. . . ."[6]

Finally a lookout spotted the smoke and broadcast the alarm. By 10:30 a.m. Walquist and Broyles, laden with equipment including a short-wave ra-dio, were on the way—the first of an eventual 447 fire fighters. For nearly three hellish weeks they helped build fire lines. In retrospect, Broyles said, "I remember leading a crew 12–14 hours a day, and then at night I would be used as a scout to bring back the latest information on where the fire lines actually were! It seemed that almost every afternoon about 3 or 4 o'clock the wind would blow up and wipe out the work we had done.[7]

"Several times," he continued, "we were cut off and not able to get back. . . . Once, the only food we

Billowing smoke is a fearful sight. (Courtesy YRL.)

had was raisins, and we took our canteens, put the raisins in, cooked it over a fire and had raisin soup, our only food for a day and a half!"

Eventually they were able to make their way to what was dubbed "Omaha Beach," where Tiltill

---

4. At 39, Walquist was a veteran of several seasons in Yosemite, with lots of savvy, Broyles said later. He was a member of the original Sons of the Pioneers singers.
5. Bingaman described the fire on pages 29 and 30 of his *Guardians of the Yosemite.*
6. "Had congressional funds been allocated for maintenance work, telephone lines between outposts like Pate Valley and Hetch Hetchy would have been working," author Bernard de Voto wrote caustically in the February 1949 issue of *Harper's Magazine.* It took 24 hours instead of two minutes to get word to park headquarters that a fire had broken out.
7. Rod Broyles, who rose from a seasonal to superintendent of Pinnacles National Monument in his Park Service career, taped memories of his part in the Rancheria fire. By the time he was released from fire fighting, he had to get special permission to register late at Colorado State University. Ironically, one of the reasons that he wanted to work in Yosemite was to get experience in fighting fires.

After fighting fires, running the entrance station was easy for ranger Rod Broyles. (Courtesy Rod Broyles.)

Creek empties into the north side of Hetch Hetchy Reservoir. Two boats owned by the City of San Francisco had been commandeered to carry men and supplies from the dam to the beach. The headquarters fire camp was near the dam, and eight other fire camps were set up around the fire. Savage winds, heat, and low humidity compounded the problem of keeping the flames from spreading.

Even though men had been recruited from such diverse places as the nearby recreational Camp Mather, the Yosemite Valley post office, and Fort Ord, more manpower was desperately needed. Already the burned area exceeded that of any other fire in Yosemite's recorded history to that time, and confinement, let alone control, was not in sight.

One of the last-ditch containment measures plotted by Chief Ranger Oscar Sedergren and Superintendent Carl Russell was implemented by rangers Herb Ewing and Ken Ashley. Ash was on a crew clearing lines "to keep the fire from going up Pate Valley to Harden Lake," when he was summoned to meet Sedergren at the then private resort of White Wolf.

I hopped on an empty mule in a pack string that was headed up the trail . . . never dreaming of the unlikely assignment I would be handed that hot September day.

Herb and I were to drive to Stockton to pick up a bus that had been chartered and take it around the Skid Row district where we were to recruit fire-fighters, sober or not.

I didn't know a thing about Stockton and Herb didn't know much, but we found the bus depot and claimed the charter. Soon the driver swung into a littered street lined with rundown stores and bars. Derelicts were everywhere—standing in doorways, sitting on the curb and, yes, even lying in the gutters.

We had devised a message and we delivered it through a megaphone—fire-fighters needed in Yosemite, so much an hour, there would be no booze, if you don't have suitable footwear we'll buy it and charge it to you. Bring a jacket. It didn't take long to fill the bus and then we headed for a Sears store and those needing boots were allowed off.

While I signed up those left on the bus, Herb took a purchase order and the half dozen or so men needing boots into the store and got them fitted out. The boots were tagged with the men's names and Herb had the driver lock them up in the luggage compartment for safekeeping until we got back to Yosemite. We did this to avoid having to buy those boots ourselves in case they walked off with the new owner!

We then flipped a coin. I lost and had to accompany the bus back to the Park while Herb drove the car back.

. . . Imagine a hot bus loaded with 30 unwashed bodies! But, except for a couple of hung-over guys that got sick on the winding Big Oak Flat Road, it was really a neat trip. They were full of questions; some were familiar with Yosemite. Others had never heard of the place. They were excited and

99

apprehensive. I did my best to reassure them that the danger would be minimal and that they'd be treated well.

We unloaded our bus at White Wolf in time for supper and then bedded them down until morning when they'd be on their way to Pate Valley and the Rancheria Fire.

As far as I know this was the first and last time that we recruited in this manner.[8] More than half of the group stuck it out until they were released in late September, and some of them vowed to build on this experience and turn their lives around.

Summer afternoon thunderstorms and their legacy of lightning fires were nearly daily occurrences in the high country. Patrol ranger Tom Van Bibber documented several while he was stationed at Yosemite Creek in 1949 and '50. "Spotted fire top of hill ½ mile due west," he noted in his log on August 13, 1949. "Changed packs & rode up arriving at 4:15. Fire small . . . 50 x 50 feet. Worked fire down to few smoldering spots by 9 p.m. Next morning a fire crew arrived to help." Van Bibber "carried water with mule till 10:00," when he spotted another fire north of Eagle Peak, and taking all but one man, rode toward it. "Arriving Eagle Peak fire 3:00 p.m. with 3 men. Very hot, 1 acre & hauled water with mule for mop up. Returned to Yosemite Creek 12:00 p.m."

In early August 1950, it took him and a 13-man crew to control a more severe fire near Pate Valley. "Reinforcements led by Buck Evans arrived at 5:00 a.m. the morning of 22," but the pump Van Bibber was "desperately in need of" didn't arrive by pack train until afternoon. "Extremely poor cooperation from outside," he scrawled angrily. "Very poor efficiency all over. I was thoroughly disgusted the way higher ranks took the fire away from me and my 13 men after we held it and controlled it alone." Two

Fighting fires with water carried on pack animals was all too common. (Courtesy YRL.)

charges of dynamite set off by the other fire crew "nearly killed two of my men. Close call."

By the 1970s a "let burn" policy in certain areas, especially near or above treeline, was beginning to be implemented. When blazes posed little or no danger to people or structures, and had the potential of burning thickets of dead and/or down trees, they were allowed to burn with minimal supervision. Visitors complained of smoke and what appeared to be negligence, so public education was begun to explain that "the long-term benefits [of fires] outweighed the short-term disadvantages." Such fires are called "prescribed natural fires," whereas "prescribed burns" are ignited by man. Wegner, Townsley, and other early rangers would have been aghast.

Ray Warren began his service as a seasonal in 1952, working on trails and later as a fire crew foreman under Dick McLaren at Chinquapin. He admired McLaren and, in writing about him, revealed some of the varied activities of fire fighting. "It was fairly common to see Dick in a direct assistant role when fires were active, [supplying]

---

8. Even in the late 1960s, however, commandeering men at roadblocks to fight fires was done in emergencies.

hands-on assistance; i.e., fire-control line, hose and water operations, tree falling, mopping up. . . . Even routine duties required operating in a hazardous environment. Patrolling steep and narrow back roads, flying recon and fire spotting by helicopter, moving fire engines on highways and back roads, even helping cut and split the large volume of firewood needed for heating, cooking, and hot water (no electrical power in the area at that time) were part of the job"[9]

Wildland fires were seasonal, Warren pointed out, but "structure fires and hazard were year-long and just as, or more, dangerous . . . as they involved special equipment, toxic smoke and other interior dangers." Money and manpower were also lacking in the winter.

McLaren was just one of a dedicated band of rangers who responded time and again to fires, usually in inaccessible places. Harry During, Buck Evans, John Bingaman, Homer Robinson, Art Holmes, Jerry Mernin, and a handful of others showed particular expertise. Tom Tucker was no slouch either. As a forestry division employee in 1936, and Yosemite ranger until 1962, he acquired such a good reputation as a fire-experienced person that young rangers wanted to train under him. Ruefully, he said that "the only problem was [that] the Mather district, where I was district ranger from 1958 through 1961 took in about half the Park then, and had about 300 fires during that time, so no one wanted to trade me jobs. Sometimes I would have over 500 people on a fire, utilizing every possible method of transportation to get to the fires— men on horseback, walking, flying helicopters, and on a boat crossing Hetch Hetchy Reservoir. Mather Ranger Station was frequently the staging area for major fires in the district. Each fire was like fighting a battle, and each required a campaign."[10]

The fire Tom recalled as the most memorable in his career took place in the fall of 1953, when he relieved Herb Ewing on a fire near Liberty Cap that threatened Little Yosemite Valley. Thirty lightning blazes were burning in Yosemite, and thus fire fighters had been recruited from other places. Among them were a hotshot crew of Indians from the Santo Domingo Pueblo in New Mexico. They were battling the misnamed Half Dome fire when Tucker took over. Their English was limited, he said, and "they communicated with each other in their native language, which sounded like a lot of clicking noises made with their tongues augmented by grunts and other sounds. At times, they were touchy about being addressed directly by anyone other than their assigned liaison officer who, in this case, was Jim Eden, an NPS superintendent of a national monument in the Southwest.

"There were 50 Indians, mostly in their 20s, but led by Mesa Bird, a striking figure with a commanding air of dignity and a shock of white hair captured by a cloth headband. All of them wore headbands, all were working professionals needing little direction from me. In fact they taught me one thing I'd never seen, and never practiced. No water was available, so we conducted what is known as 'Dry Mop Up,' a technique where you mix dirt in with live coals until they cool down. The Indians hastened this tedious process in a surprising but practical way. Sometimes, they would communicate with their strange clicking language and several would come running over to urinate on the hot coals, supplying water to assist putting out the fire.

"I should add that this was done with the utmost seriousness, and, needless to say, this was a long time before women were employed as fire fighters on the fire line."

The incident that awed Tucker occurred several days later, after the stubborn fire was officially declared out. "By that last night, we had gained a lot of respect for each other and we had a real fine companionable meal at our last camp in Little Yosemite. Several NPS staff from other parks, the Indians and I were sitting around a bonfire when a big, full Harvest moon began to rise over the canyon walls to the east. Because the air was still smoky, the moon had an orange glow and was absolutely spectacular.

"From their belongings, the Indians brought forth some gallon cans and pieces of rubber inner tube and stretched the rubber over the cans. A couple of the young men beat on these makeshift

---

9. Ray Warren wrote his one-page report on Dick McLaren's fire suppression abilities in March 1992.
10. Tom Tucker recorded Yosemite memories for the author in December 1995 and March 1997.

tom-toms, and a rhythmic throbbing permeated the night air. The others began to chant and circle the campfire in a slow dance. The very hair on the back of my neck began to stand up as they celebrated.

"They were celebrating the winning of a battle, a victory. Picture this bright orange moon shining around us in the serene beauty of Little Yosemite and the quiet night except for the wailing and the chanting and the beating of the drums. The other white men and I felt privileged to see this ceremony, to hear, feel, and experience it.

"Suddenly Mesa Bird appeared in front of me, and by smiling and beckoning made me to understand that he wanted me to join the dancers. Well, I felt a little self-conscious and foolish, but the fire camp boss, said, 'They are according you a high honor,' so I got to my feet and joined the shuffling dancers, circling the bonfire. I have never forgotten that experience, the beauty and the ancient ritual, and the great solemnity of the men. It was awesome, then, and even now I am tremendously moved by it."[11]

Whereas lack of water contributes to wildfires, an overabundance of water brings floods. Both are considered disasters by people, natural events—often made more dire by human intervention. During Yosemite's five major floods in the 20th century, natural housecleaning has significantly altered the Merced River Canyon below Yosemite Valley.

Each time the Merced River, named *El Rio de*

During the 1937 flood the old "Pavilion," where movies were shown, was moved down stream by the overflowing Merced River. (Courtesy YRL.)

---

11. In 1954 Tucker was assigned to fight a 20,000-acre fire in a national monument near Tucson, Arizona. When a crew of Indians arrived, one of them smiled and waved. Tom recognized Mesa Bird. Indians are still called upon to fight fires. A group of them served ably on the Ackerson Complex fire in Yosemite in 1996, winning the respect of Tom's son, ranger Jim Tucker.

Harry During using a dispatch base station.
(Hoyt collection.)

Nuestra Señora de la Merced (The River of Our Lady of Mercy) by the Moraga expedition in 1806, has been merciless. Torrential warm rain, often in December, melts the snowpack, and the resulting run-off pours into Yosemite Valley. The swollen Merced overflows and creates a seething lake, and the water churns westward down the canyon. It rips out great chunks of earth, uproots trees, moves huge boulders, and tears out trails, roads, picnic tables, tent frames, vehicles, structures, and utilities from both above and below ground.

All this happens within hours, yet the resulting devastation is only gradually revealed as the flood waters slowly recede. In 1997, damage to the infrastructure at higher elevations, such as at Tenaya Lake and Tuolumne Meadows, could not be completely ascertained, even by observers in low-flying helicopters or on skis, until the snow melted.

Park Service officials, weather experts, and the media speculate about the "100-year flood." Take your pick of the floods that occurred in 1937, 1950, 1955, 1964, 1980, and the spectacular one that ushered in 1997. Inasmuch as this book's scope ends with 1960, the floods of 1937 and 1955 are featured, mainly because eyewitness reports from rangers or their children are available, and each flood in turn appeared to be the hundred-year flood. Both were exceeded in most ways by the flood of 1997.

On December 9, 1937 warm rain began falling and, within two days, almost 11 inches had poured down. At Happy Isles the gauging station measured the Merced at a depth of 10.40 feet, and 19.10 feet was recorded at Pohono Bridge at the west end of the Valley. A record breaking 8,400 cubic feet per second was measured as the water thundered on down the Merced. (It was relatively simple then to set a new record, because the gauging systems were not installed until 1916 and 1917.)[12]

Ranger's son Bob Skakel "couldn't believe what I saw" when he first viewed the lake-like expanse of water from his attic bedroom on December 11, 1937. He ran to wake his father, who couldn't believe what he heard, and said "My God!" in an awed voice when he did look out.

Superintendent Lawrence Merriam, Sr., who had succeeded C. G. Thomson, was issuing orders to his staff by telephone, and to his wife and sons in person. Their home, known as the Superintendent's house or Residence #1, was close to the Merced and also backed up to Yosemite Creek, which had already swept away the back porch. The two-story house was marooned by water. "You'll have to wade," Merriam told his family, "but carry some essentials and get out of here."

High-schooler Larry Jr. remembered the forced evacuation as a "great lark" for him and his younger brother. They stayed at the Rangers Club, where they were privy to all the excitement, yet were warm and dry. Later, when the water was waist high, his father and a couple of other rangers had to row a boat to Residence #1 and enter the waterlogged downstairs to move furnishings and other lares and penates to the second floor.[13]

Before nature had completed its massive house-

---

12. Between January 1 and 3, 1997, the Merced River rose to a depth of 13.24 feet at the Happy Isles gauging station and to a phenomenal 24.60 feet at Pohono Bridge.
13. Bob Skakel and Larry Merriam, Jr. provided detailed accounts of the 1937 flood in the author's

cleaning, more than $300,000 in property damage had been done, and the general store's warehouse had been swept clear of all its contents, paper and canned, which were strewn far down the Valley. Even further down, near The Cascades, most of the frame buildings used as dorms and a dining hall by the Civilian Conservation Corps had been swept into the river. Long stretches of roadbed for both automobiles and trains were washed out all the way down the Merced River Canyon.[14]

Later there were three other floods, with the worst occurring in November 1950. This time damage to roads, trails, buildings, and utilities totaled $430,000! But that was exceeded by the lalapalooza that began on December 23, five years later, resulting in $767,000 damage to Park facilities.

"At the height of the [1955] flood," John Bingaman recorded in his *Guardians of the Yosemite*, there were fifty-two inches of water in the Yosemite Store building. . . . Sentinel bridge registered sixteen feet, a dangerous flood stage. The All Year Highway (140) was closed by slides and washouts, and damage was done to the [other] major roads in and out of the Park. All travel both ways was stopped until December 28th."

Lessons had been learned from each of the previous floods, and a plan of operation was implemented by Superintendent John Preston once the water at Sentinel Bridge measured 9.1 feet. Employees were evacuated from quarters in the flood plain, including Preston's Residence #1, and, when possible, "furniture and belongings moved to a second floor or attic. House trailers were towed to higher ground near the church bowl, stock was removed from the general store and its warehouse and pumps were taken out of pumping stations." None of these preparations was completely successful, since it was dark, raining incessantly, and "the flood waters rose too rapidly during the night to accomplish complete removals."[15] The main

John Henneberger officiated at Arch Rock Ranger Station come rain or shine. (Courtesy John Henneberger.)

sewer line broke, but the water supply was switched to a spring used in emergencies.

Christmas was a flood casualty, including cancellation of the famed Bracebridge Dinner at the Ahwahnee Hotel. During the 1937 flood the dinner was held, even though few guests were able to attend. Residents were welcomed for a $1.00 per person! In 1955, however, both sittings were canceled, although residents helped eat the already prepared feast, again at a nominal price. As usual, the superintendent's house was isolated and inundated by water, as was the Yosemite Chapel. Afterwards, as usual, Park Service officials urged relocation of structures so that they would be out of reach of high water, and, also as usual, funds weren't available and nothing was done. In 1965, however, the Chapel was rehabilitated and its foundations raised more than five feet to make the

---

Enchanted Childhoods (Yosemite: Ponderosa Press, 1993).

14. The Yosemite Valley Railroad operated between Merced and El Portal from 1907 to 1945, when it was abandoned—in part because of its vulnerability to floods.

15. Information and quotations are from the superintendent's "Summary and Highlights of the 1955 Flood," issued soon after the event.

building safe from water. (Not even that height was enough: on January 2, 1997 three feet of flood water inside the Chapel did a great deal of damage to the interior).

Arch Rock Ranger Station, crowded in on a narrow flat between the cliffs and the river, is another invariable flood victim. In 1955, John Henneberger was not only an eyewitness but a terse chronicler of the 133 harrowing hours in which 18 inches of rain fell and the flat was covered with water and silt.

"River rising fast, rate about one foot per hour," he recorded at 7:00 a.m. on Thursday, December 22. . . . Many rocks on road. Culverts plugged." By 9:00 the Merced River was at the bottom of the retaining wall separating the public rest rooms, dorm, and house from the road and kiosk. "Old timers said it wouldn't be as bad as 1937 and 1950, but the Arch Rock 1950 ranger log indicated that the 1955 water was rising faster than either, so I concluded it would flood and moved my family to Mariposa." Actually the road remained open 14 hours longer, before it was officially closed. Henneberger suspected that "the Curry Company prevailed upon the Supt. to keep it open because of the Bracebridge Dinner crowd coming in." Henneberger and fellow ranger Ed Parsegan kept the station open all night the 22nd, and befriended employees who drove that far but couldn't go up or down because of slides and high water. Finally, half an hour past midnight, "Chief Ranger [Sedergren] phoned. Said to close the road. By then, it had pretty well closed itself," Henneberger noted. At 2 p.m., "Started putting up furniture higher in house and getting ready to move out." Five hours after that, "Water coming into house." Brother ingenuity was working overtime too, and Henneberger reacted by cutting a hole "in the hall to drain the water through the basement. "That saved my furniture." At 8:00 a.m., "Water a foot deep in the men's restroom," and nearly that high against his front door. Power was still on, but the telephone line was out. Half an hour after that, "Left station in Govt pickup for El Portal. Broke up part of a rock slide above Windy Point and was able to squeeze by putting a few dents on pickup."

At El Portal, where the river had crested half an hour earlier, Henneberger assessed the damage to the service station and ate breakfast. At 10:30 he and Parsegan headed back to Arch Rock. They didn't get very far in their truck. Crane Creek had not only undermined the bridge but had removed 150 feet of the roadbed as well. Undeterred, the two rangers continued on foot through hard but lessening rain, over and around many new slides, and two hours later reached the waterlogged station. "Power still on. Had lunch, changed clothes," and at 1:00 p.m. he started for the Valley in his personal car to report conditions to the chief ranger. "Drove the car to short bit below Steamboat [Bay]. . . ."[16] After that he was afoot and wading in water often to his knees from Steamboat to The Cascades. "Pavement breaking up in many places near old Coulterville Road Junction." [That happened again in 1997.]

"Water on the road in most places, but only up to the knees or less." Whenever water reached his waist he had to climb above the roadbed. Despite the rain and impediments, Henneberger reached Pohono Bridge by 2:30. But "most of the approach road on the northside out." The telephone at Bridalveil Fall parking lot was out, too, so he continued slogging along, impressed by the way "the whole lower part of the Valley was pulsating with the sound from Bridalveil Fall, and its lake-like appearance."

His next stop was at the sewage plant, across the road from Bridalveil, and there he encountered four rangers "giving first aid to an accident victim." She had driven into a sinkhole near Grouse Creek on the Wawona Road the previous night. No one found her, principally because no ranger patrolled during that frightening night.

"Crane Flat entrance station and the one at South Entrance had closed down at 5:00 p.m.," Henneberger claimed in 1997, "because no overtime was authorized . . . so much for old-time ranger superiority. . . . Didn't seem like they measured up to the 'giving of oneself' as a ranger should. They waited for the overtime authorization. . . . We all looked forward to fires, rescues, and

---

16. Steamboat Bay is a deep, normally quiet stretch of the Merced River where "great pieces of granite appear like the prows of large ships." Peter Browning, *Yosemite Place Names* (Lafayette, CA: Great West Books, 1988).

emergencies in those days to make extra money. A couple of big overtime pay checks meant down payments on new cars."

To Henneberger's credit, he had not even considered quitting work at 5:00 p.m. on the 22nd or at any time after that. The needs were great and he tried to cope. Nevertheless, when he finally walked into headquarters to give his first hand account of conditions and heard that overtime had been authorized, he was delighted. "Afterwards old-time rangers put in for the most overtime," he recorded. "Superintendent was furious." Henneberger continued to work until after 10 p.m. that night, then had a bath and a good night's sleep in the Rangers Club, his first rest in three days.

On Christmas Eve day he participated with rangers Buck Evans and John Mahoney and two Curry Company men in clearing the road enough so that an expectant mother could be taken from El Portal to the hospital in the Valley, where Dr. Sturm was waiting. Just before noon, the log reveals, "brought woman to Crane Creek and took her across washout to cars." Others took over from there. "Picked up Parsegan at Parkline and returned to Arch Rock. River down below rock wall. Started cleaning up."

On Christmas day itself, "First blue sky—but still raining intermittently." At noon the two rangers set up a roadblock at Pohono Bridge, which they manned during the night. The road "will be closed 24 hours a day to visitors. Will be opened by key to authorized use." From midnight on, Henneberger and Parsegan manned the roadblock, explaining to the few motorists that the road was too dangerous to travel. It was weeks before repair work was competed and normal traffic resumed to El Portal.

Before their first graveyard shift began they managed a bit of festivity, recorded thus. "Parsegan at Christmas dinner at the Ahwahnee with girl friend. Henneberger with Sturms." It wasn't until December 30 that Henneberger picked up his wife

and children in Mariposa and brought them home to the cleaned house, with reboarded walls, rewaxed floor, and all in good repair. By then his overtime pay of $173 exceeded his regular pay of $167 for two weeks.

However, Henneberger was so disenchanted with the NPS performance and "Homesteading attitude and anti-visitor attitude" during and before the flood that he solicited and accepted a transfer to Olympic National Park as a GS-7 district ranger. Until the actual day of his mid-January departure, however, he was engaged in clean-up. For example, on January 6 "(Ken) Ashley, (Ed) Parsegan, Henneberger picked up picnic tables from El Capitan Bridge to Stoneman Bridge." On the 11th, he made a final entry in his log. "Crane Creek washout down to grade. Still muddy. State going to concrete weak side of bridge and [continue to] use present bridge [State] cleaning up from Briceburg grade. [Highway] 140 still closed."[17]

Besides floods and fires, nature has provided a variety of other disasters such as drought, earthquakes, slides, needleminer and bark beetle infestations, and blister rust disease. Both drought and hoof-and-mouth disease blighted California in 1924, causing "a frenzy of fear" and "uncontrolled publicity" according to the Superintendent's Annual Report for that year. John Wegner was assigned as liaison officer for Yosemite in "control of activities in and adjacent to the park." One of his sad and difficult responsibilities was finding experienced hunters to shoot Yosemite's stricken deer. They were trapped and trucked to one of five different emergency camps. Many were saved, but 1,100 had to be killed. Storms, beginning in September, ended the drought, and in 1925 the deer population began recovering. Amazingly, the Annual Report for 1926 stated that "while estimates of the deer in the park cannot be at best more than a rough guess, it is confidently believed that during the summer months, the number reached as high as 50,000."[18]

---

17. Route 140 wasn't reopened to Park visitors until January 18, and then only with traffic control. "It required months of work to restore the road to acceptable standards," stated Superintendent Preston in his official report on the flood. In 1997, because damage was even more extensive, it was five months before normal two-way traffic was allowed.

18. Even today a realistic estimate of the deer population is impossible to make, but wildlife biologists are confident that 50,000 is much too high, then or now.

As far back as in 1869, John Muir had noted "ghost forests" of dead, needleless, but still standing lodgepole pines. In time, entomologists realized that the blight was caused by tiny needlemining caterpillars that nature turns into moths after they destroy forests. Periodically, eradication campaigns have been waged by men using poison sprays. Conservationists challenged that practice. Should the Park Service, charged with protecting nature, use chemicals that destroy it? Should blister rust crews eliminate all gooseberry and currant bushes that host diseased rust spores because they could infest and eventually kill white bark pines? The controversy continues.

Still another sort of disaster, often influenced by weather, are airplane crashes. John Wegner witnessed what could have been—but fortunately wasn't—the first airplane wreck in Yosemite Valley, in May of 1919. He happened to be at the top of Yosemite Falls when Lt. J. S. Krull was ready to take off from the meadow below the chapel, where he had landed safely on the 27th. From his grandstand view, Wegner watched with fascination as Krull attempted to lift off from the narrow uneven ground between the river and the cliff in his 150-horsepower Curtiss biplane. Taking off proved impossible, and eventually the plane had to be shipped out in pieces. Rangers were involved to the extent of guarding the aircraft from small boys and souvenir seekers.

In the early 1920s Clarence Washburn had a 3,000-foot airstrip cleared in the upper end of Wawona meadow (a nine-hole golf course was at the opposite end). Afternoon winds, however, made takeoffs tricky.

On December 8, 1925 two army pilots landed the first airplanes on the rough field. A year later, a plane crashed while attempting to land, and there were two fatalities. But that didn't discourage Frank Gallison. In 1927, after the strip was lengthened to 5,000 feet, he began daily summer flights from Merced in an Eagle Rock airplane. He carried the mail, a supply of the *San Francisco Chronicle,* a few light-weight supplies, and occasionally a daring guest for the hotel.

Rangers were stationed in the huge Wawona basin after it was acquired by the NPS in 1932. Governmental support was promised for a first-class airport, but funding wasn't available. Nevertheless, for five years a curious trade-off existed between Yosemite Superintendent Thomson, a golf addict, and concessionaire Don Tressider, who loved flying and kept his plane at Wawona. Their mutual support ended with Thomson's death in 1937. World War II ended the airfield, except for emergency landings.

Several airplanes crashed in the Wawona vicinity. The worst was in March 1938, when a small TWA airliner with six passengers and three crew members went down in a storm. Despite an intensive search by 400 men on foot and more than 50 planes, covering an area of 88 square miles, the wreckage was not found until June. The plane had crashed in the snow roughly 200 feet below the summit of a 9,000-foot peak 12 miles east of Wawona and not far from Buck Camp.

According to John Bingaman, it took rangers 16 arduous hours to carry the bodies out on mules. Two months later, Bingaman and local resident Gladys Gordon escorted the mother of two of the passengers who

Several people were killed when this Luscombe Model 8A crashed at Wawona. (Courtesy YRL.)

died in the crash to the site, where she placed a small plaque. Years later, Jim Snyder tried to find the marker but couldn't. On another occasion he relocated what he described as "a mess of rubber and metal just across Givens Creek on the Buck Camp-Moraine Meadow trail." It was the remains of a P-38 Lightning that had also gone down in the late 1930s. "I carted one of the machine guns out to Buck Camp ranger station," he said. "Eventually it was transferred to Pearl Harbor as part of the museum collection there."[19]

After the original discovery, Bingaman and seasonal ranger Jack Bell guarded the remains of the plane and the pilot until an army major arrived to remove the valuable military equipment. Since then, airplanes and even a helicopter have crashed at other places in Yosemite, usually during storms and usually in the high country. Although it may take years, what wreckage isn't removed by rangers will eventually be hidden or obscured by natural growth.[20]

Nature continues to bestow beauty upon Yosemite, and also provides what people refer to as disasters—and the conditions for human-created unnatural disasters.

In 1952 snow was considered a disaster, but not at Badger Pass. (Hoyt collection.)

---

19. June 16, 1996 letter from Jim Snyder to the author.
20. Shirley Sargent, *Yosemite's Historic Wawona* (Yosemite: Flying Spur Press, 1979). Superintendent's Monthly Reports, 1938–1940. Contemporary newspaper articles.

10 A Decade of Uneasy Peace

Aside from the major flood of 1955, and the highest number of fires in a single year to that time—79 in 1953—the 1950s were years of uneasy progress in Yosemite. They were marked by major changes, some of them controversial. Construction of the last link of the Tioga Road, replacing the 21 miles of narrow, steep, outdated pioneer road, stirred animosity and violent opposition. Outraged environmentalists, led by Ansel Adams, actually stopped work temporarily as they tried in vain to halt blasting of the glacial polish near Tenaya Lake. At the same time the Sierra Club's long-time support of the NPS was also blasted, and an adversarial relationship ensued.

Seven years before the Tioga Road's completion, travel to Yosemite had exceeded the one million mark for the first time. Entrance fees were raised to $3.00 per car, but most of that sum was sent to NPS headquarters in Washington for distribution to poorer parks. Acquisition of private land inside Yosemite National Park by an aggressive condemnation program bought organized opposition.[1] An ambitious program of building was carried on by the Park Service and the chief concessionaires.

In 1956 the new Yosemite Lodge was opened; it was the first important building in the Park since the construction of the Ahwahnee during 1925–26. A sorely needed general store, called the Merchandise Center, and a huge new warehouse, followed three years later. All were funded, built, and operated by the Yosemite Park and Curry Co. In 1958, the Degnan-Donohoe delicatessen restaurant was opened under the auspices of the pioneering Degnan family, a much smaller concessionaire. Even now its distinctive A-frame structure of concrete and glass is an architectural landmark in Yosemite Valley. Unfortunately its construction was such an expense that the company went bankrupt, but was allowed to continue operating so that the government could continue receive revenue.

Rangers were essential to all these events. They manned the entrance stations, answered questions, collected fees, and did scut-work such as spraying for mosquitoes at Tuolumne Meadows to ensure a fairly insect-free site for a barbecue after the ribbon-cutting of the new Tioga Road. (Even the most hostile environmentalist broke bread at the celebration, which climaxed 30 years of road building.) Engineers from both the Bureau of Public Roads and the YNP staff had observed each curve and berm. The latter surveyed the site of a construction camp just west of the public campground at Yosemite Creek. Other specialists had negotiated land acquisitions and overseen the new buildings as they took shape. Rangers performed duties that were far different from the public's romanticized view of heroic figures on horseback, but one and all they were protecting Yosemite in a variety of ways.

The highlight of the 1950s was the introduction of Mission 66, the Park Services's billion-dollar plan to rectify neglect and improve all parks. During World War II, the parks had deteriorated due to lack of maintenance, manpower, and appropriations. Since the war's end, many new parks, monuments, and historic sites had been added to the system, but not supplied with funds to properly protect and upgrade them. Mission 66 was the dynamic, carefully planned, wide-ranging program designed not only to meet current needs but to foresee future ones. Better training, housing, and salaries were provided, to the benefit of rangers. Completion of Mission 66's multitudinous goals

---

1. Chuck Cushman is the disgruntled and dispossessed son of Dwight Cushman, a Wawona inholder; Chuck spent the summers of 1958 and '59 as a ranger-naturalist. After Dwight's cabin was taken and burned by the Park Service, Chuck bought a place of his own, and when that too was threatened by condemnation, he founded a national group of inholders to oppose unfair taking and extreme environmental legislation. It has become a powerful movement, based in Washington, D.C., with membership exceeding 16,000.

Doug Hubbard began his NPS career when he was 19. (Courtesy YRL.)

was to coincide with the 50th anniversary of the Park Service, in August 1966. Planning, publicizing, and implementing dominated both the 1950s and 1960s.[2]

One of the earliest, and oddest, benefits of Mission 66 to Yosemite was the rescue and restoration of the historic covered bridge across the South Fork of the Merced. Built in 1857 by Galen Clark and covered by the Vermont-raised Washburn brothers in 1875, it carried all traffic until the modern Wawona Road opened in 1931. By 1955 the bridge was so weakened that the flood waters of December left it barely standing. "Saving it was the

beginning of what was known as Doug's Berry Farm among the park staff," admitted Douglass H. Hubbard, Yosemite's chief naturalist from 1956 to 1966.[3] Superintendent Preston was sympathetic, funds were made available, and Doug was off and running.

"First I was able to find a bridge builder among the poison oak of the Mariposa foothills. No construction job daunted Glenn Gordo, grandson of a pioneering Portuguese couple. Gordo and his workmen shored up the bridge's sagging middle, used pieces of heavy pipe, and with a bulldozer-powered winch rolled it smoothly ashore. After months of intensive work, during which the deteriorating timbers, siding, and roof were replaced, the process was reversed and the bridge rolled back to its original position."

Meanwhile, back at the drawing board, Hubbard had consulted the staff, former superintendent and avid historian Carl Russell, and old-timers to make an inventory of Yosemite's abandoned buildings with historic origins. If some of them could be moved to Wawona, he reasoned, the covered bridge could be the focal point of a pioneer center. Already the old Washburn barn and wagon shop stood near the bridge's south end in its original location. Historic structures could be resettled on the north end. The Mission 66 program drafted by NPS planners had received a special audience and approval from President Eisenhower himself.[4] One of its aims was to disperse Park visitors around the Park to relieve congestion in the Valley. Hubbard recorded that "a history center fit nicely into this ambitious program.

"About this time a small peaked-roof house on the old 'Soapsuds Row' close to the new Yosemite Lodge was threatened with destruction because it was in the path of the new road to Yosemite Falls. A little research showed that it had served as the office of the army superintendent at, of all places, Camp A. E. Wood, less than a mile from Wawona." Serendipity! It was the first of nine structures relo-

---

2. Brainchild of NPS Director Conrad L. Wirth, the background and details of Mission 66 are described in his book *Parks, Politics, and the People* (Norman: University of Oklahoma Press, 1980).

3. Hubbard first worked in Yosemite as a 19-year-old museum aide in 1937, attended the Field School in 1940, and returned in 1956 as chief naturalist, a position he filled with zeal and leadership for a decade.

4. Three years before he was elected president, in 1952, ex-general Eisenhower had visited Yosemite and undoubtedly saw the covered bridge when he passed it en route to the Mariposa Grove of Big Trees.

Jeremiah Hodgdon's homestead cabin, built at Aspen Valley in 1879, was the only two-story cabin in Yosemite. Here it is shown after being moved to the Pioneer History Center at Wawona. The Crane Flat ranger patrol cabin is in the background. (Courtesy YRL.)

cated to the History Center. Because of its size and its construction of logs, the two-story Aspen Valley cabin was photographed, each log numbered, disassembled, and trucked to Wawona before being treated with a preservative and painstakingly reassembled. Rarely were log cabins more than one story, so this one, built by Jeremiah Hodgdon in 1879, was unique. "How was it furnished?" Hubbard queried historian Margaret Schlichtmann, author of *The Big Oak Flat Road to Yosemite*.

"Send a truck!" was her answer, and that began a beneficial collaboration with her and her husband, Emil. Two naturalists traveled to the Schlichtmann's San Leandro home and "returned with everything needed to furnish the cabin authentically," Doug wrote, "and then some. Furthermore, the couple stayed at the Wawona Hotel for two weeks every summer. First they cleaned and polished the cabin's furnishings, then Margaret played Mrs. Hodgdon, sitting in a rocker on the front porch and telling stories to the visitors—the Park's first living history."

Later, "Living history demonstrators baked bread and made coffee on the old wood stove from the ranger cabin moved from Crane Flat,[5] which they shared with visitors attracted by the aromas."[6]

Another transplanted pioneer structure moved was a small one-room cabin built near Big Meadow by Half Dome's first conqueror, George Anderson.

5. That transplanted cabin was one of three identical ones built in 1915. College-boy ranger Jean Witter, its first inhabitant, carved his name and fraternity affiliation in it in 1916. This historical graffiti is rarely noticed. In 1923 he was one of three cousins who founded Dean Witter & Co.
6. The always popular Visitor Center's "living history program" has waxed and waned depending on the annual funding. Volunteers such as veteran blacksmith Jerry Coe return summer after summer to create living history.

Hubbard called the author and said, "Ask Jim Cuneo how it was furnished. He's an old-timer ."

"Gunny sacks and maybe a blanket on a make-shift bed," Jim said.

"What about kitchen equipment?" was my next question.

"A wood stove; frying pan and a saucepan or two," was Jim's ready reply.

"Dishes?"

"Maybe a plate, but he probably ate straight out of the pan," Jim answered. "I do."

Instead of furnishing it so crudely, however, the one-room structure was outfitted as a schoolhouse. "The old jail, from the Yosemite Valley, a tiny structure of rough granite blocks and soft mortar gave Gordo some headaches. It had a foot or so of sand above its ceiling, a fire proofing technique dating back to its original use as a powder house." Eventually the jail was cut in half, shored up with heavy vertical timbers, and trucked to Wawona on a bed of old tires.

From its grand opening in 1961, "Doug's Berry Farm" has been a significant visitor attraction, with horse-drawn stages carrying passengers through the covered bridge, the only one in a national park. A ninth structure, the pioneer tongue-and-grove kitchen, from Bridget and John Degnan's home in the Valley, was moved in the 1980s. Its chief feature is Bridget's large, built-in bake oven.

Hubbard was known to the public, not because he was the chief park naturalist or the moving spirit behind the history center, but because he wrote several well-illustrated Yosemite books. *Come With Me and We'll Go Exploring* featured Carl Sharsmith, the pied piper to the Park. It was the first book about the man who was a living legend long before the 1950s. Ranger-naturalists are far more likely to attract public recognition than is the law enforcement staff, since the former lead nature walks and give talks to hundreds of visitors year after year. No one of them was better known than Dr. Sharsmith. Somehow, even his eccentricities seemed endearing. His intimate knowledge of alpine botany and passion for all things natural was shared in a loving, non-pedantic way. But even his

Carl Sharsmith was the pied piper of Yosemite for 64 years. (Courtesy YRL.)

seemingly endless patience had limits—as his side-kick Will Neely related.[7]

"It was after the 657th time some visitor, after a whole stream of them had asked 'Say, ranger, where can I catch a fish?' The old-timer voice came on, drawlingly, tobacco spittingly 'Wal if'n I was yew. . . .'"

"Yes?"

"Wal yew know where the store is, don't you?"

"Yes, but. . . ."

"Yew jes' go up to thet store, walk inside to the far wall and yew'll see all of them rows of canned sardines. Catch 'em thar!"

Carl's initial encounter with the ebullient, impetuous William L. Neely, in 1949, was not much more auspicious. The newlywed Will and his wife were sliding down Mt. Lyell's glacier in moccasins, carrying a bouquet of "pretty blue flowers" when

7. See Neely's article on Sharsmith in *Yosemite Nature Notes*, vol. 46, no. 2, 1977.

Will Neely, the Field School class of 1950. At the left is Arthur H. "Art" Nelson. (Courtesy YRL.)

they met Dr. Sharsmith, ice axe in hand and a pipe clinched between his teeth, trailed by 22 Field Schoolers, all wearing stout footwear. They gasped almost collectively while Carl patiently explained that the pretty flowers were Sky Pilot, *Polemonium*, rare, and never to be picked. Actually Will, 26, had a degree in botany and a deep appreciation of plants, but nothing was sacred on his honeymoon.

Charismatic, volatile, nature-intoxicated Will redeemed himself in the 1950 Field School. But no matter how knowledgeable and competent Will became, he remained a non-conformist.

"I was assigned to Tuolumne Meadows in 1952 because I proved myself incapable of standing behind the information desk all day long. I was supposed to give the geology talk at the Valley Museum twice a day, all of us grouped around the plaster relief models of the Valley. I took the group out to see the real thing instead of the plaster. Chief Park Naturalist Donald McHenry [Hubbard's predecessor] caught me returning with my 75 visitors and called me into his office.

"'Will,' he said, 'It looks like you are an incorrigible field man.' The next summer I was sent to Tuolumne."

Neely reveled in the freedom and beauty of Tuolumne Meadows, where he and Sharsmith became close friends. Soon they transformed the nightly campground campfire into an acclaimed crowd pleaser with a combination of nature lore, songs, banter, and a roaring fire that kept the chill of the 8,600-foot altitude at a distance. For a few years they were an institution, the vital force that introduced people to a natural world they learned to revere and to help preserve. At the end of the 1950s, when Will was stationed at the new Bridalveil Campground off the road to Glacier Point and Carl was studying meadows in Sequoia-Kings Canyon national parks, Will couldn't resist spending some days off at Tuolumne, even conducting an all-day hike to Gaylor Lakes. "Two new rangers came along . . . they have little of the spark for interpretation, other than along strictly National Park lines," he confided to his journal on July 4, 1959. That night he attended the campfire. "I was greatly troubled by the program, It lacked spirit. I was surprised at how people stuck it out. Dick Jackson brought a pitiful amount of wood, sang a few songs, off key, talked like a stuffy ranger, ignored the children, laid down the law. None of the old spark. I got cold in the second row. Then Dave's talk was uncertain, tense, and over the heads of the children who got restless. It all seemed to be rather dull. A talk later tonight with Dave revealed that the office had given Dick Jackson specific instructions to 'modify the Neely-Sharsmith influence'—very disturbing, but understandable in the light that no one in the office is a naturalist. . ."

One of the main differences between Will and Carl was the latter's aversion to writing. He could talk all day long, Will said, "But writing is an agony." In contrast, Will was a prolific and rather philosophic journalist despite the demands of a tent-full of children (six between 1951 and 1959) and a loving, kindred-spirit wife. He added lively,

Movie producers paid rangers' salaries on their days off to provide security, and to ensure that Park resources were not unduly disturbed. In the summer of 1955, during the making of "The Long, Long, Trailer," the photogenic rangers posed with the stars. Left to right: Bob McIntyre, "Bud" Heller, Lucille Ball, Desi Arnaz, Odin "Sig" Johnson, and Art Holmes.

literate articles to the monthly *Yosemite Nature Notes.*

Early in their friendship, Will mused in his journal: "Perhaps someday I will carry on the Tuolumne traditions when Carl is gone, but I can never do it with the same magic manner that he does. He seems as enduring and as timeless as the granite, however, and he is as perennial as the grasses in Tuolumne's Meadows. I can not imagine a time when Carl will not be there. . . ." That was in 1952. Carl's magic prevailed 42 years more, through the summer of 1994, his last season in Yosemite. A few weeks after he left Tuolumne Meadows, Carl died at 91. In contrast, Will Neely, whose turbulent life style and drinking shortened his tenure, died in 1983 at age 63.[8]

Visits from VIPs were announced by requests for accommodations and an escort. In the 1950s when, on the whole, peace and prosperity prevailed in most of the world, with the notable excep-

8. Fellow ranger-naturalist Allan Shields, now a publisher, has edited and published three books of Neely's journals. The third, *A Yosemite Naturalist's Odyssey* (Mariposa, CA: Jerseydale Ranch Press, 1994) was a valuable source for this book. In 1996 Shields also edited *Climb Every Mountain*, a book devoted to memories of Carl. *Mountain Sage*, a biography of Dr. Carl Sharsmith, was first published in 1988 by the Yosemite Association, and reprinted by its author, Elizabeth Stone O'Neill, in 1996.

tion of the Korean War, an unusual number of foreign dignitaries visited Yosemite. In 1959, no fewer than 327 of them from 22 countries received special attention, ranging from fruit bowls in their rooms to guided tours or extra security.[9] Both the ranger staff of 21 permanent and 50-plus seasonals, and the employees of the Yosemite Park and Curry Company, were involved in providing special treatment.

In the early days, ranger escorts, (often Homer Hoyt), were selected on the basis of personality and knowledge of the Park. Looks helped too. In 1950 it didn't hurt that seasonal ranger Merlin Miller resembled a younger version of silver-maned Superintendent John Preston. "He relieved me of patrol duty," Miller recalled, "to escort a governor, a general, a chief of police, a prime minister, and even a president of the United States."[10]

Of these VIPs, Miller was least enthusiastic about the prime minister of Pakistan, who was disdainful of sites that usually induced awe. "What are you stopping here for?" the P.M. said, dismissing the close-up vista of Bridalveil Fall. "There's nothing to see."

In June 1954 Emperor Haile Selassie stayed overnight in one of the Ahwahnee Hotel's separate cottages. Ken Ashley and Merlin Miller guarded him that night, one at the back and one at the front of the cottage. Occasionally they had a glimpse of the Emperor pacing back and forth in black pajamas and a long string tie.

It was 4:30 a.m. before the lights finally went off. The rangers felt sorry for him and his personal bodyguard, whose eyes were red-rimmed from lack of sleep. They persuaded the bodyguard, a Captain in the Ethiopian Army, to get some sleep, but after an hour or two, the conscientious man was back.

"Next morning," Miller remembers, "the Emperor tried to give me a $100 bill for guarding him. "I refused, and couldn't help wondering if his poor bodyguard earned anywhere near that much per month."

When King Albert, Queen Elizabeth, and Crown Prince Leopold of Belgium visited Yosemite in October 1919, they traveled by special train from Merced to El Portal, and from there into the Valley by auto stage. Almost 40 years later, Leopold's son, King Baudouin, arrived by jet in Merced with his retinue of 30 and rode the rest of the way by limousine. Both his father and grandfather had regaled him with memories of their visit—staying at Camp Curry, riding horseback up to Glacier Point under the tutelage of ranger "you call me Billy and I'll call you King" Nelson, and Prince Leopold's overnight pack trip with Billy during which John Bingaman, then a guide for the Curry Company, taught him to flip pancakes in the air.

In May 1959 royalty merited the superintendent—who addressed the VIP properly as "Your Highness"—a Cadillac, and a Curry bus that carried six Belgian officials and seven representatives from the U.S. State Department, plus various lesser aides. The 24-hour visit was noted for its brevity, the number of activities, and kingly delays. At Castle Air Force Base, King Baudouin was so fascinated by the jets, tankers, and giant cargo planes that he delayed his departure for 40 minutes in order to inspect them. The next day, at Glacier Point, lunch was delayed while he made a solitary pilgrimage to the awe inspiring height, camera in hand.

John Stratton, management assistant to Preston, remembers the trip to the Mariposa Grove as the time when a delay was needed, but not made. "Superintendent Preston, driving the King in an open car led the way and I followed, driving a sedan with the court members. As we approached the Park South entrance, Preston pulled over to make a stop. The men in my car, all along in years and suffering from too much breakfast coffee, were poised to disembark and hurry to the restroom. Instead, Baudouin, a younger man, stood up in the car and motioned the superintendent to proceed without a stop. There was some muttering by the occupants of my car, and when we finally stopped at the Grove they bailed out quickly and headed for the trees. I'm sure they were greatly relieved."[11]

9. The various countries were listed in the 1958 Superintendent's Annual Report.
10. The president was John F. Kennedy, whose visit in 1961 is outside the scope of this book, but who required unprecedented precautions and security.

After three years service, lateral transfers were encouraged. That led to wider experience and better opportunities for promotion. A number of Yosemite's most able and ambitious men took advantage of this program by moving out and up. Lon Garrison and Dix Freeland predated this movement, and eventually became superintendents in prominent parks. Jimmy Lloyd, Billy Merrill, and Duane Jacobs followed later.

By the close of the decade, more women rangers had been hired, but they weren't common nor were they serving in all parks. Few minorities applied or were hired by the Park Service.

In Yosemite, retirements were part of the 1950s, making way for new blood and fresh ideas. During that decade Art Gallison left after 37 years, Gus Eastman after 25, Frank Ewing after 34, (but a total of 43 years as a government employee), Carl Danner after 24, John Bingaman after nearly 35, and Homer Hoyt after 36.

A handful of younger men neither sought nor accepted transfer, preferring to stay in Yosemite—particularly Herb Ewing, who followed the family tradition and remained firmly and happily in place until he retired in 1977 after 31 years.

Charles R. "Chuck" Scarborough was the opposite of Ewing. By the time he was transferred to Yosemite as assistant chief ranger under Sedergren he had already served in two national parks and was obviously well on his way up. Tragically, his tenure was cut short by an act of nature on the first day of summer 1954.[12] He was leading six provision-laden mules to the Merced Lake ranger station so that it could open for the season, and they were traversing the switchbacks below Nevada Fall. Galvanized by what sounded to him like a cannon

During his 40 year NPS career Jack Morehead served in Yosemite on three separate occasions: first as a ranger, then as chief ranger, and finally as superintendent. (Courtesy YRL.)

Escorting VIPs was only a small part of ranger duties. Most of the time, Stratton said, routine jobs kept them at desks or in the field, "grinding it out." There was more and more professionalism, reports, and red tape. Specialization was replacing the traditional seat-of-the-pants can-do ranger tradition.

---

11. Quote from Stratton's letter of March 18, 1996 to the author.
12. Scarborough turned 49 eleven days before his death.

exploding, Herb Ewing, bringing up the rear of the pack string, barely had time to dismount and flatten himself against a boulder before a barrage of rocks swept over him and ricocheted on down to the base of Clark Point.[13]

As soon as the rockslide subsided, Herb, ashen but unhurt, quieted his terrified horse and the mules near him. He called anxiously to Scarborough but there was no answering hail, and Herb's thudding heart jumped into his mouth. A lone ascending hiker readily agreed to take the animals back to a wide place in the trail where they could be tied. Herb immediately climbed over the slide to check on his boss.

He spotted Chuck's horse lying immobile on the switchback below, and then saw Chuck's body crumpled on the steep, rocky slope 75 to 100 feet below the trail. Sickened, Herb climbed down and felt fruitlessly for a pulse. By 12:45 p.m. he was on the emergency phone at Nevada Fall to advise Chief Ranger Sedergren of the accident. Somehow he managed to give a "clear and concise report" Sedergren said.[14] Later, after his examination of the battered body, Dr. Strum said that death had been instantaneous when the falling rocks had swept Scarborough and his horse off the trail.

Even though he had been in the Park only 14 months, he and his wife, Ann, with their two daughters, a teenager and an infant, were a popular part of the community.[15] The shocked sentiment of "It could have been me!"—the disbelief, the grief and mourning, were widespread and long lasting in Yosemite and other places where Scarborough had served.

Two other Yosemite rangers had died while on duty, but of natural causes. As described earlier,

"Jack" Gaylor died in 1921 while sitting in front of a campfire at Merced Lake Ranger Station. He was 65. Chief Townsley was 61 when he suffered his fatal heart attack while fishing. No Yosemite ranger, before or since Scarborough, has been killed while on duty.[16] No other event in the 1950s had greater impact on the ranger staff or the community.

A week after Scarborough's death, brand new college graduate Jack Morehead was deposited by bus in front of the Administration Building. He was 22, a Colorado native, and for the next 40 years, including military service, was with the Park Service.[17]

"There I was—new job, new place, all my worldly possessions in about three bags at my feet—totally lost and overwhelmed."

His spirits rose when Ken Ashley "actually helped me carry my bags over to the Rangers Club, and helped me get settled in. I was awed that a real Ranger would take the time and effort to help."

That afternoon he had an interview with the chief ranger. After learning that the recruit was from Estes Park, Colorado, "Sedergren asked me if I was a mountain climber. I didn't want to brag, or get myself into trouble by overstating my skills (even though I had done a lot of climbing, including an early ascent of Shiprock), so I told him I had done 'some climbing.' 'Do you know what a carabinier and piton are?' When I answered yes, he put me on the search and rescue team. What an entrance exam!"

Later, Morehead was in trouble with the Chief for, of all things, a climb. Lost Arrow had first been ascended in 1946 by noted climber John Salathe. Jack and Wayne Merry were determined to be the

---

13. Details of the tragedy were contained in Oscar Sedergren's official report, written June 24, 1954. The heavily traveled trail has always been, and still is, one of the safest in the Park. Oscar said that Scarborough was at the rear, but Herb's widow, Ruth Ewing, who checked this account for accuracy, said Herb told her that Chuck was leading, as was the custom for a superior.
14. Besides the deep fatal head wound, Scarborough sustained multiple lacerations, bruises, and fractures.
15. Knowing how fast bad news spreads, Sedergren asked his wife to confer with the assistant superintendent's wife on how best to tell Ann Scarborough the terrible news.
16. Decades later, two essential road crew employees, Sam Smallwood and Barry Hance, died in separate accidents while clearing snow from the Tioga Road.
17. While attending Colorado A & M, Morehead had worked seasonally in both Rocky Mountain and Glacier national parks, making a career of more than 40 years. At the author's "pretty please" solicitation, Jack Morehead took time out from kayaking on Morro Bay, near his retirement home, to write several colorful reminiscences, all of which have been helpful.

Soon after John Preston arrived as superintendent in 1952, he called all his staff together so that he could get acquainted with them. Those not wearing uniforms were on their day off. Tom Tucker said that "much good came from the meeting." Top row, left to right: John Mahoney, John Preston, John Bingaman, Oscar Sedergren, Art Holmes, Homer Robinson, Orthello "Wally" Wallis, and Duane Jacobs. Middle row: Harry During, Tom Tucker, John Mullady, Odin S. "Sig" Johnson, Herb Ewing, and Glenn Gallison. Bottom row: Walt Gammill, Harthon "Spud" Bill, Homer Hoyt, Ken Ashley, Fred Martischang, Marshall "Buck" Evans, and Dick McLaren. (Courtesy YRL.)

first rangers to make the dangerous ascent. "Since I was permanent and Merry was still seasonal, I claimed to be the first permanent ranger to ever climb it." While Wayne and I were sitting on top of the Arrow, feeling proud and triumphant, we discussed how high it was, and how long it would take for something to fall, etc. One of us (probably me) threw an empty can off and we timed it as it fell. Incredibly and unfortunately, Chief Sedergren happened to be watching us with binoculars at that precise moment. When we got back, we didn't get

congratulated for the climb, we got a reaming for littering."

Another time Morehead tangled with Sedergren was during his first summer of work, while he was living in a frame tent in the middle of Camp 15.[18] One night he was partly awakened by a female voice saying something about being lost, dead tired, and going to sleep on the spare cot. "Next morning, I woke up hoping it was a dream but, sure enough, there on the cot was a young lady.

"Well, since that sort of cohabitation was really frowned on in those days, I tried to sneak her out of

---

18. Upper River, as Camp 15 was renamed, suffered in the January 1997 flood and was not reopened.

the tent without anyone noticing—a mistake when your tent is surrounded by campers. It turned out that this particular girl had gotten separated from her friends at the Curry dance, had gotten lost, and crashed in my tent. A rather major effort was being made through the night by the rangers on duty to find her. Chief Sedergren really had a field day with me over that particular incident."

Had anyone predicted that the red-faced young ranger would serve as Yosemite's chief ranger, as he did from 1971 to 1974, or as superintendent from 1986 to 1989, both men would have hooted.

As a seasonal, Morehead was a GS-4, paid $3,175 a year, and his ambition was to become a GS-9 before he retired. As chief ranger he was a GS-13 and as superintendent a GS-15.

From the first, Morehead was critical of the conditions in Yosemite Valley. "I vividly remember how crowded, congested, and dirty the Valley was during my first summer. Even with the vastly smaller number of visitors, the Valley was in much worse condition than in the '90s. Everybody used wood campfires for their cooking, so smoke or smog filled the east end of the Valley."

His early experiences in Yosemite coincided with its visitation exceeding one million for the first time in history. The post-war generation of the 1950s was producing the babies that would balloon that figure to over four million in the 1990s. That influx had not been anticipated, nor was the Park's budget within light years of meeting the needs for services as basic as sanitary facilities. People could and did camp for weeks at no charge. Yosemite conditions were deplorable, according to Morehead, "You could drive anywhere and camp in absolutely any spot you could find to squeeze into—there were no designated sites, or limits on campers. People tried to preserve their 'space' by stringing cord or rope from tree to tree around their site and hanging sheets, towels, blankets, etc. on the ropes to create privacy. Campgrounds looked like huge laundries."

Morehead's temporary home, Camp 15, was in the process of being "Meinckeized,"—that is, redesigned with large designated campsites, parking spots, and definite roads. (A Park Service engineer named Edward P. Meincke was responsible for this innovation, which was eventually adopted for all the Park's major campgrounds.)

Morehead felt that the noise pollution and traffic congestion caused by the Firefall was "obnoxious." The traditional shouted communications between Camp Curry and Glacier Point, from where the embers were pushed, were intrusive enough, but afterward a soprano belted out "Indian Love Call," or "America the Beautiful," and people began the ritual of calling out "Elmer!" The din lasted for at least 15 minutes, completely disrupting the evening serenity.

Coincident with "Elmer," was the auto problem. "There was a huge traffic jam as cars, many of them parked illegally, tried to get back to wherever they came from." More noise and smog resulted. In a word, Morehead commented, "It was horrible. In those days, none of us thought the Firefall could ever be stopped. I'm glad we were wrong."

The last Firefall was in January of 1969. A few years earlier the Camp Curry dance hall, a long-time scene of dancing, drinking, and occasional disorderly conduct, closed under Park Service pressure. Nights now are peaceful and starry, though some campers persist in calling for the legendary "Elmer!" And many people still miss the Firefall.

Night shifts, called MOP (Midnight Operation Patrol) or GAP (Government Area Patrol), were disliked, but rotated among staff. "Some of us new single guys got it a lot more than others," Morehead observed. "There was no radio dispatch at night then so we had to stay near a phone, or rely on the telephone operator to let us know if a call came in that needed attention. We usually walked around the Utility Area Office complex every hour to check things out. Occasionally we would do a short patrol around the Valley by vehicle."

Especially on weekends that meant waking people parked or camping indiscriminately on the road edges and escorting them into an already crowded campground. After 10 p.m. rangers sent them to a parking area or allowed them to stay parked off the road until daylight, when they had to move into campgrounds. Another summer routine was breaking up beach parties that lasted past midnight. "This was made particularly difficult," Morehead admitted, "for some of us single rangers often knew the participants quite well. In fact, many times while off duty, we were among the participants told to put out the fire and go home![19]

During the 1950s there were two one-week sessions conducted by FBI special agents from the San Francisco office. Half of the rangers attended each session, thereby allowing the day-by-day operations to continue. **March 1950, front row, left to right: Norm Herkenham, Tom Tucker, Tom Sovulewski, and Fred Martischang. Back row: Gus Eastman, Bob McIntyre, John Bingaman, Homer Robinson, Glenn Gallison, John Townsley, and Art Holmes.** (John Bingaman collection.)

"My first Yosemite supervisor, Wally Steward, was wonderful—he taught me more than I could ever recall—Ken Ashley and Tom Tucker 'ran' the Valley. They were among the best supervisors I have worked with throughout my entire career. Glenn Gallison and I ended up doing a lot of rescue work together and I really thought he was wonderful. Dick McLaren, Frank Betts, and John Townsley were close friends. In the 1957 and '58 time period, Dick Stenmark and Wayne Merry were my closest buddies and climbing partners. I also recall working closely with Del Armstrong and John Henneberger on special operations, snow surveys, or SARs (Search and Rescue).

"As a beginning ranger, I got rotated around a lot on different assignments. While your duty location during the main part of the summer was pretty well fixed, during the off season you were expected to fill in wherever needed. I worked the entrance station at Arch Rock frequently. It was a super treat to pull duty at Badger Pass. This was working, so there were certainly no complaints. It also was great experience. I have often thought it would be wonderful if all rangers could be exposed to the same variety of work situations, jobs and experiences."

Other rangers were always quick to help. An

19. Morehead's bachelor days lasted only until April 1958, when he married Patricia Crabb, who worked for the Curry Company, in the Yosemite Chapel.

example of that has always stuck with me. One day on patrol, I got a call over the radio about a stranded person yelling for help. He was stuck on the slabs at the base of Half Dome, above Mirror Lake. I left my patrol car and, with street shoes and a piece of rope I carried in the car, walked out to assess the situation. In those days, we didn't have the individual hand-held radios the Ranger have now, so once I left the patrol car I was out of radio contact. I had, of course, called in the situation, so others knew where I was, and what I was about. When I got to the base of the slabs, I saw the stranded person, and it looked like I could get to him, even with no climbing equipment and street shoes. I did reach him, and got him down using the short rope I had brought, but it took quite a bit longer than I had expected. Since I hadn't called back in, the other rangers on duty assumed that something might have gone wrong. Now one of the rangers who really *didn't* like climbing was Tom Tucker. However, when I was just nearing the Mirror Lake parking lot with my 'rescued' visitor, here came Tom up the trail, fully prepared to help me out of what he suspected could be a technical rescue situation. He had ropes, pitons, hammers, carabiniers, and, best of all, he was wearing two hard hats, one for me. I always thought this was an absolutely classic example of the way rangers then supported each other, even when it was personally uncomfortable, or perhaps downright dangerous. There were so few of us, it was a necessity, but it sure left a lasting impression.

"Of course I was in awe of Chief Sedergren," Morehead added, "and in 1957, Frank Kowski was to me the epitome of the ranger's ranger. And John Preston was absolutely the grandest Superintendent ever."

Morehead was a member of the first class of the NPS Training Center Program held, in Yosemite in 1957. Need for a field training center had been obvious for years, and "Kowski's College," a Mission 66 program run by Frank Kowski and his assistant Bob McIntyre, was the answer. Its scope was broad, its goals laudatory, discussion leaders were experts from other parks and Washington D.C., and it carried on and expanded the precepts of Mather and Albright. Morehead felt enriched by the 12 weeks of training. "It was such a success," he said, "it was soon moved to Grand Canyon where it's still operating as the Horace M. Albright training Center.[20]

His own future as both Yosemite Chief Ranger, Superintendent, and finally Regional Director of the vast Alaska Region from 1991 to 1993, only increased his admiration and respect for the working rangers.

His long career mirrored the transition between traditional can-do rangers of the years from 1900 to 1960, included in this book, and the age of specialization that now prevails.

Lateral transfers, which mean that people like Morehead can keep moving and advancing are a mixed blessing. There is less and less time to truly acquaint men and women with a new place, inasmuch as transfers are so frequent. Yosemite had six superintendents in the first 50 years—1916 to 1966—but since Preston departed in 1965 up until mid-1998, eight men and one woman have served as head honcho for periods varying from 13 months to five and a half years. That is why this history ends with the close of the 1960s, for after that the brief tenures of rangers and superintendents were often too short for them to make the kind of individual impact that Lewis or Thomson did.

Jack Morehead summed up the '60s and the earlier years in his 1995 reflections by saying, "What I admired most of all about the rangers in that period was their ability to competently do absolutely anything! They were masters at most things, and if they weren't, they were totally fearless in trying. No specialization then; that probably was the end of the 'general ranger' period. We did fire fighting, wildlife management, people management, accident investigation, first aid, horse packing, skiing, interpretation, etc., all of it on a regular, continuing basis. A really competent, self-sufficient group."

Those stalwart men protected paradise, but so do the newer, higher educated breed of more spe-

---

20. The Yosemite sessions used what is now the Research Library, upstairs in the Yosemite Museum, as a classroom, the Rangers Club as a dorm, and various areas of the Park for field experience. June Banner was the popular secretary.

Bob McIntyre and Frank Kowski, in front of the Yosemite Museum about 1957 or 1958. (Courtesy Laura Meyer. McIntyre.)

cialized men and women. Whether on horseback or at the computer, rangers are still the guardians of Yosemite.

Pre-Mission 66 Lament

(Sung to an unknown tune)

The Parks are Overcrowded
The rangers are too few
The campgrounds are a mess
Whatever shall we do?

Ranger, please show them out,
Ranger, please throw them out,
Show them the way to go home.

The Secretary pondered,
Then gave a joyful shout

We'll build a dam in every park
And flood the tourists out!"

Ranger, please show them out,
Ranger, please throw them out,
Show them the way to go home.

Ferdinand

At an elevation of of 9,945 feet, Tioga Pass has to be about as near to heaven as a motorist can drive. To Ferdinand Castillo, its faithful and occasionally fierce guardian from 1954 through 1992, it was heaven! He arrived behind the snowplow in the spring and left, reluctantly, when the first heavy winter snow closed the road. In between, he greeted visitors going through Tioga Pass, sometimes referred to as "Ferdinand Pass," collected entrance fees, answered questions, and gave out verbal and printed information with warmth and a flair for the personal touch. "Hello, how are you? Going to the valley? Wonderful. Where are you from?" Half the time, he could name a prominent sports figure from the visitor's home state. If the driver was obviously foreign, Ferd could manage a greeting in several languages. If he recognized someone he knew, he or she received a royal welcome. To the author, "That new book of yours is the best I've ever read! Hurry and write some more." If he recognized a VIP, they received a chatty welcome there, and perhaps, a fruitbowl or bottle of wine at their destination. Ferdinand acted as a early warning system, alerting hotel managers and/or the superintendent to the impending guest. When he recognized ex-general Matthew Ridgeway, whom Sgt. Castillo had served under in Korea, he shot out of the kiosk to talk to him while traffic backed up half a mile.

All this garrulousness was not from an irishman, but a Mexican-Indian-American who spent 12 of his first 16 years in a Ukiah orphanage run by the Dominican sisters. Their grounding prepared him for a Catholic high school in San Francisco, and the University of San Francisco from which he graduated with a B.S. just in time to serve as a Marine in some of the bloodiest fighting in the South Pacific during World War II. He put in another stint for the Marines in the Korean conflict.

Between wars he taught and coached swimming at a San Francisco high school, and added to his reputation for verve by swimming in the famous Bay daily, no matter what the season or weather. After that, swimming both ways across Tenaya Lake was nothing but a warm up.

His career as Yosemite ranger began in 1954, and Tioga Pass quickly became a home, haven, and heaven both physically and spiritually. He reveled in his solitary climbs of sky-piercing peaks, cherished wildlife, wildflower blooms, wrote free verse, and enjoyed the gloomy, rock-walled cabin adjacent to the pass for it was his alone.

Traffic was light in the 1950s, but increased after the opening of the last 21-mile section of the Tioga Road that replaced the old wandering stage road.

Any visitor who stopped on a wildflower was told firmly to "stay on the trail!" A skateboard rider who veered off the roadway earned a shouted "Get off the grass!' He lined the road's shoulder with small rocks, and began a butterfly "cemetery" with remnants he lifted off car grills. Some people considered him eccentric, frequent visitors became his friends, and a handful complained that he was arbitrary, but few forgot him. When he traveled with a friend to other places, she said "No matter whether we were in a restaurant in Fresno, San Francisco, or Los Angeles, someone would come up to say 'Aren't you Ferdinand? You made my trip to Yosemite special.'"

But changes were affecting Yosemite and his security. As traffic proliferated, so did paperwork. His cabin was needed for an office, and Frerdinand had to move to the ranger camp at Tuolumne Meadows. That dispossession was an emotional trauma and a physical hardship because he didn't drive and seven miles uphill was too far to walk. Two people were needed to handle the ever-increasing throngs, so he had to share the small kiosk, often with a young inexperienced woman seasonal. Ferdinand resented that. The next blow was the introduction of machines to keep track of fees and traffic count. He was unprepared for anything remotely high tech.

Ferd was 75 in 1992, but his vigor and enthusiasm were still obvious, and so, according to Yosemite brass, was his stubborn insistence on greeting visitors individually, which sometimes slowed traffic to a standstill. Therefore in 1993 he was transferred to the isolated and little used entrance station serving Hetch Hetchy, where maybe 100 or 105 cars a day contrasted with Tioga's 2,000. To Ferd, Mather entrance station was exile, Siberia, hell. He was desolate and bitter. His legion of friends, including actor-environmentalist Robert Redford, protested in vain to the Park Service.

Ferdinand's spirit was broken, even his corny jokes were half-hearted, and his health failed. He died three days before Christmas 1993. But he returned to Tioga Pass once more, on August 20, 1994, when his ashes were scattered from a plane. Ferdinand Castillo was home, this time forever.

Ferdinand. (Courtesy YRL.)

Civilian Superintendents of Yosemite National Park

Washington B. Lewis	1916–1928
Charles G. Thomson	1929–1937
Laurence C. Merriam	1937–1941
Frank A. Kittredge	1941–1947
Carl P. Russell	1947–1952
John C. Preston	1952–1965

Biographies

It is virtually impossible to list everyone who worked as a ranger in Yosemite from 1898 to and through 1960. There are well over 500 names on the hiring list, and most of them only put in a season or two. I have tried to include all the permanent rangers who worked three or more years, and I did include some long-term seasonals who made, for one reason or another, significant contributions to the park and its visitors. A handful of outstanding seasonals, such as Clyde Quick, Dick Rogers, Don Pimental, Glenn Coy, Vern Nichols, Bob Crippen, Carl Sharsmith, and Will Neely were given permanent status so that they could be in the retirement system. Not all of them are on my list, because rangers' tenures after 1960 were not long. Lateral transfers were in effect, and it was uncommon for rangers to stay long enough in one park to have a lasting impact.

My main sources for factual information were: the hiring cards preserved in the Yosemite Research Library; miscellaneous letters and records at the research library or in my personal research files; the fine memories and recollections of Phyllis Freeland Broyles, Charolette Ewing Wilson, and Marian Woessner; and, of course, John Bingaman's book *Guardians of the Yosemite*, which contained his listing of rangers, most of whom he knew personally. His list is unalphabetized but more detailed than mine, and reflects a lot of work. To the best of his ability, the rangers were listed in the order in which they were hired—chronologically. In contrast, my list is alphabetical. A few names on his list suffered from printer's errors, the funniest being Homuth, Early U., which should have been Homuth, Earl U. I wonder what errors will be in my listing. Plenty, I bet!

Adair, Charles F., 1914–1935

Born in Bear Valley, Mariposa County, in 1874, the same year the first stage roads were opened to Yosemite Valley, Charlie worked as a miner in the Mother Lode and Arizona before becoming a Yosemite ranger. His specialty was insect control.

Trapped inside fire lines on the Alder Creek fire of the 1930s, he escaped death, but his health was so affected he had to retire in 1935, and died in 1936.

Legacy: Nine-acre Adair Lake, near Mt. Clark, where he planted golden trout, and two sequoia trees that he transplanted into the Park Service housing area.

Albright, Horace M., 1928–1929

Horace was an exceptional man with a phenomenal memory and abiding loyalties to his family, especially his wife, Grace, to his alma mater, the University of California at Berkeley, and to the NPS. His favorite parks were Yellowstone and Yosemite, in that order, and he was Yosemite's acting superintendent for several months in 1928–29. Even after he left the NPS, in 1933, he continued as a consultant, advisor, and friend until his death in 1984 at the age of 94.

Legacy: The NPS, of which he was confounder and second director, and the fond memories of legions of admirers. After Mather died, plaques were erected in Yosemite saying "There will never come an end to the good that he had done." This is also true of Horace Albright.

Albright, Robert M., 1938–1939.

Horace's only son, Bob, had absolutely no interest in becoming a ranger, but to please his father he spent a summer at Mesa Verde and two more in Yosemite while he was several years under age. Horace, usually a stickler for rules, pulled strings with NPS Director Cammerer and Yosemite Superintendent Merriam to hire Bob as a seasonal ranger. His dad paid his salary, although Bob didn't know it. His sister, Marian, would have loved the outdoor experience, but gentle, bookish Bob hated it. The season of 1939 was his last in uniform.

Albright, Stanley T., 1956–1962

HMA's nephew Stan Albright continued the family involvement with the NPS. Both his first and last jobs have been in Yosemite. Between 1958 and 1962, he was a buck ranger coping with crowds. After a career of rising through the ranks to directorships of regions and operations, he returned to Yosemite in mid-1997 as its 16th civilian superintendent.

Anderson, Clifford L., 1935–1947

His career as a Park Service ranger began in Yellowstone when he was 21. He served in Yosemite both before and after WW II.

Anderson, Ralph H., 1929–1953

Ralph Anderson was in Yosemite as a ranger, photographer, and information specialist until 1953, when he transferred to Washington D.C.. He died on an inspection trip for the Service in 1964. His wife, Millie, was a school teacher in Yosemite, and they had a daughter, Barbara Jean (B. J.).

Legacy: A splendid collection of photographs that he took in the Park, which are preserved in the Yosemite Research Library and are often reproduced in publications—such as this book.

Armstrong, Delmer M. "Del," 1956–1962

Del's specialty was biology. He worked as a biologist in Yosemite for several years, moving up from a G-7 to a GS-11. His wife, Donna, and he were well-liked and active in the community.

Ashley, Kenneth R., 1947–1959

Ken was an observant Yosemite ranger for over a decade. He was known for his keen sense of humor and affable personality. Now retired, he operates a mountain nursery in Colorado. His wife Ethel, then and now, was a great help in every way. They had two children, Jan and Dave.

Legacy: Many entertaining narratives for this book.

Beatty, Clifton C., (seasonal) 1942–1950

He taught high school in Merced, but he was a Yosemite ranger summers. During WW II he worked at Hetch Hetchy, and later at Crane Flat, Tuolumne Meadows, and Devils Postpile. At the Postpile he did everything from giving talks to guiding people to the fantastic rock formations, cleaning latrines and, at times, driving fearful visitors back up the steep, winding access road. (His intrepid wife, Esther, had to follow in their car to bring him back.) He liked it there, she remembered, "because he was his own boss as the only ranger." Nevertheless, his favorite place was Tuolumne Meadows because there were so many hikes to take campers on.

Beatty, Matthew E., 1932–1944

Ed Beatty was a park naturalist for 12 years in Yosemite. In 1940, he served as assistant park naturalist under Bert Harwell and was responsible for the planning and writing of four special issues of *Yosemite Nature Notes.*

Legacy: The original editions of *Bears in Yosemite, Birds in Yosemite,* and *A Brief Story of the Geology of Yosemite Valley.*

Betts, Frank J., 1956–1964

Frank Betts, like Dick McLaren and Del Armstrong, was a sparkplug, a fresh and enthusiastic spirit who was ardent and appreciative of the Yosemite experience, summer and winter. So was his wife, Kathy.

Bill, Harthon "Spud," 1952–1955

His brief tenure as Yosemite's assistant superintendent was marked by his ability to put Superintendent Preston's orders into effect with diplomacy and an understanding of employees' needs and problems. That skill led him to higher positions elsewhere.

Bingaman, John W., 1921–1956

Born in 1896 on an Ohio farm, John had ambitions that took him to California by 1916 when he was 20. He married Californian Martha Buyck, injured his health making tanks for WW I, and was classified 4-F. In 1918 he and Martha traveled to Yosemite to regain his health. He stayed 38 years, more than 34 of them as a ranger.

Legacy: Bingaman Lake, which he named after stocking it with trout, and three little books on park history: *Pathways; The Ahwahneches, A Story of the Yosemite Indians;* and *Guardians of the Yosemite,* first published in 1961. The latter was the original inspiration for this history.

Boothe, Clyde D., 1915–1927

All five of the Boothe brothers from Mariposa County were tall, husky achievers, two in business, two with the State Forest Service, and Clyde with the National Park Service in Yosemite. Before he quit to join a tractor manufacturing business, he served as assistant to Chief Ranger Townsley. It was said that Boothe always got his man when chasing criminals in the park, and not many trout escaped his well-cast hook.

Legacy: Beautiful but mosquito-plagued Boothe Lake, the first site of what is now known as Vogelsang High Sierra Camp.

Brockman, C. Frank, 1941–1946

Brockman was chief park naturalist for five years, during which his historical research and writing were important and enduring.

Legacy: Three special issues of *Yosemite Nature Notes* and his *YNN* articles on Yosemite's administrative officers to 1946.

Brown, Lester, (seasonal) 1915–1918

He began work in 1912 as a porter and handyman at Camp Lost Arrow. From 1915 until he joined the armed service in WW I, he worked as a clerk and teamster in winter and Park Ranger at $75 per month in summer. Lewis and Townsley assured him by letter that he would be welcomed back, but "I never went back, I wasn't blessed with a college education, so figured they would keep me on the outposts."

Legacy: Brown's retrospective 1964 letter giving details about early NPS activities in Yosemite and comments on Chief Ranger Prien (now in the Yosemite Research Library).

Brown, Otto M., 1927–1946

Native Californian Brown went to work in Yosemite before his 21st birthday as a wildlife ranger and, except for three years of army service during WW II, remained until 1946. One of the highlights of those years was being the camp cook for first lady Eleanor Roosevelt on her 1934 Yosemite trip.

Legacy: Unlike most Yosemite rangers, he didn't take advantage of naming a lake for himself, but called one Ardeth for his wife, and another Avonelle for his daughter. Both lakes are in the northern part of the park near Jack Main Canyon.

Broyles, Rothwell P. "Rod," 1948–1964

Rod was a seasonal ranger under John Bingaman at Mather in 1948, where he had a trial by fire on the 10,000-acre Rancheria fire near Hetch Hetchy. A protégé of Dixon Freeland, Rod married Phyllis Freeland, and began his career in Shenandoah and Yosemite, going on to eleven other parks. His last position was as superintendent of Pinnacles National Monument before he took early retirement to help care for his ailing father-in-law. The three Broyles progeny are Paul, Bea, and Elizabeth.

Legacy: Paul (born in Yosemite) proudly followed his father into the Park Service, serving first as a ranger. His present (1998) job is as Fire Management and Training Officer at the National Interagency Fire Center in Boise.

Bryant, Harold C., 1920–1930

Although Bryant was a seasonal in Yosemite, he helped originate the natural history work and the Yosemite Field School of Natural History, where many people received intensive and innovative outdoor training. A number of them were, or became, ranger-naturalists. After Bryant changed to permanent, his meritorious career continued in Washington, D.C., and finally as superintendent of Grand Canyon National Park.

Legacy: The now-defunct Yosemite Field School, and co-organizer with C. M. Goethe and Dr. Loye H. Miller of the nature walks and campfire talks, still a popular part of interpretive programs.

Bryant, Wayne, 1948–1956

Harold Bryant's youngest son, Wayne, also had a distinguished NPS career, starting as a seasonal in Bryce National Park and including Yosemite, where he had spent his youthful summers. During WW II he was on active duty in the Pacific area for two years.

Bull, Charles C., 1914–1916

Harvard graduate Bull interrupted his career in mining for two years in Yosemite. His promotion to chief ranger on January 1, 1916, was touted; but he resigned after only four months for mining, his first love.

Castillo, Ferdinand, (seasonal) 1954–1993

Born in Ukiah, California in 1917, Ferdinand was a deprived child until taken in by the Dominican Sisters and put through school, followed by a university education. After service in WW II and Korea he discovered Tuolumne Meadows and its surroundings and became a seasonal ranger, having found his spiritual home. He served the NPS every year until his death, in 1993.

Legacy: Myriad supporters are leading a movement to name a shoulder of Mt. Dana, Tioga Pass's 13,000-foot neighbor, "Ferdinand's Point"—with no success so far. Ferdinand himself enjoyed calling it "Lying Head Peak."

Clark, Lewis C., (seasonal) 1941–1943

In his first service in Yosemite, Clark was a ranger. Oddly when he returned in 1952, he worked successively as a laborer, cook's helper, and cook, and in 1953 as a fire control aid. All of his experience and background were used for guide books that he and his wife, Ginny, wrote and published on Yosemite, Sequoia, and Death Valley, where he had worked as a seasonal ranger. Ginny had an extensive publishing background and was indispensable to their writing and, eventually, to their own publishing firm.

Legacy: *Yosemite Trails*, first published in 1978, an interesting guide illustrated with pictures and maps

Clark, Samuel L., 1924–1929; 1939–1963

Sam, born in Arizona in 1899, spent all but 10 years of his Park Service career in Yosemite, with time out for service in WW II. He had many adventures in various areas of the park and was known for his good looks and his attention to detail. He met his German actress wife, Trudel, in a Colorado POW camp, where she was an entertainer and he was an officer. He returned to Yosemite with her and her two children, Rolf and Lucie Richter. After several fist fights at the Yosemite School, Rolf said "I lost that accent real soon!" Sam could be a bit flamboyant, a trait that intensified after his 1963 retirement.

Cole, James E., 1932–1940

Assistant Park Naturalist under Bert Harwell, Cole and his wife, Jessie, lived across the street from the elementary school, making it easy for his daughters, Joyce and Phyllis, to sleep late. He transferred from Yosemite to Joshua Tree National Monument as superintendent.

Legacy: "Cone-bearing Trees of Yosemite National Park," a special issue of *Yosemite Nature Notes,* originally published in 1939.

Danner, Lucian Carl, 1924–1949

At 39, with only a ninth grade education but a wealth of practical knowledge, Danner began his 25-year ranger career. He was admired for his initiative and original ideas for solving tough problems. Eliza, his wife, often assisted him. She also taught at the Yosemite Elementary during 1928–29. For years, Carl and his horse covered the Tuolumne Meadows District, partly as a district ranger. He handled rescues and plane crashes, earning praise and official commendations plus the respect of his fellow rangers. He was known to go that extra step for his friends. It was Carl who successfully tracked the Thompson sisters in 1948.

Doty, Helen C., 1950–1973

Although not a ranger, Helen was the rangers' sometimes fiery friend who spent 23 years in Yosemite as secretary to four successive superintendents. She began the annual popular Park Service Reunion in 1980 and organized it yearly, receiving the prestigious Yosemite Award herself in 1990 and again after her death, in 1996.

During, Harry R., 1928–1955

Harry was a ranger's ranger—capable, hardworking, dependable, good-looking, and affable. Except for the war years, when he served Uncle Sam in a different uniform, he dedicated 27 years to Yosemite before going to Rocky Mountain NP as chief ranger. His stint in charge of campgrounds in Yosemite Valley won Townsley's praise. He and his wife, Mary, had three children: Stuart, Mary, and Kent. Harry died in 1996.

Eastman, Gustave M., 1925–1950

Gus was almost 40, in 1925, when he signed on as a ranger. Before he retired, in 1950, he served in all six of Yosemite's districts. He was known for his good judgement and his emphasis on law and order. The highlight of his career was being the first district ranger at Wawona after it was added to the Park in 1932. He had to introduce rules and regulations to a hostile and independent community. His next big job (1935–1938) was overseeing the labor force that raised Hetch Hetchy Dam to its present height.

After his wife, Ada, died suddenly, he retired to Mariposa, remarried, out-lived his second wife, and died in 1977 at age 92.

In his first or second year of service he had to reprimand a motorist for pulling in front of waiting cars. The motorist wrote Chief Ranger Townsley, complaining about the ranger who treated him in a "contumacious manner." His fellow rangers never let him forget that.

Emmert, John M. "Jack," 1915–1933

At 27, Jack was chief electrician for Yosemite, and was made assistant superintendent there in 1931 under Thomson. Two years later he left to become superintendent of Crater Lake National Park.

Ernst, Emil, 1933–1957

Historian Carl P. Russell lauded Ernst as "a skilled forester and a valued friend of conservation." Emil was the author of articles on climatology, zoology, history, and other subjects. Unfortunately, his biography of Yosemite pioneer James Hutchings was never finished.

Evans, Marshal B. "Buck," 1940–1962

Born in Selma, California in 1907, he was a ranger in Sequoia before coming to Yosemite, where he served with distinction for 22 years. He transferred to Crater Lake NP as chief ranger in 1961. He and his wife, Armella, had three children. In Yosemite, daughter Jeannie was recognized as a champion skier.

Ewing, Frank B., 1916–1950

While Frank served as a ranger only from 1916 until 1918, he remained with the NPS in Yosemite for 34 years, as roads-and-trails foreman and finally as chief of operations. His most notable years spanned the time he was in charge of roads and trails, succeeding his illustrious father-in-law, Gabriel Sovulewski. In 1950 he retired to his ranch near Mariposa, now owned by his daughter Char-lotte. Historian Carl P. Russell wrote of Frank, "The section of the John Muir Trail in Yosemite was born and matured under Ewing's personal supervision."

Legacy: Trails and roads in the Park and the Ewing Wing of the John C. Fremont Hospital in Mariposa. He married Grace Sovulewski, who grew up in Yosemite, and they had two children, Herb and Charlotte.

Ewing, Herbert B., 1946–1976

Grandson of Sovulewski, son of Frank Ewing and raised in Yosemite, Herb was destined to be a ranger. Those two men took him all over the park, and he absorbed their history as well as the amazing geography. Thus Herb knew more about Yosemite than any ranger in his generation. After retiring, Herb was forced to live outside Yosemite, in Groveland's Pine Mountain Lake community. He died there in 1990. Ruth, Herb's wife, chronicled her transformation from a city girl to a competent woodsperson in a magazine article, which is quoted in Chapter 8. Their only child, Bob, did not follow the family tradition.

Fladmark, Elmer, 1958–1964

Elmer was another outstanding chief ranger, succeeding Oscar Sedergren. According to Tom Tucker, he was "an all-around good man." In 1958, after spending 18 months at Joshua Tree National Monument, where he was miserable, he transferred to Yosemite as chief ranger. He loved Yosemite and he loved to hike. In 1964 he was transferred to Grand Canyon as assistant superintendent, and unfortunately died two years later of cancer. His wife, Margaret, and their son, Bruce, survived him.

Freeland, Beatrice B.,

A music teacher, Bea had married Dixon Freeland a year before he began working in Yosemite. There, she shared his duties as a checking station ranger at the Bridalveil station on the original Wawona Road near the base of the famous fall. The couple had two children, Phyllis and Dixon B. Bea died in May 1998 at the age of 99. She was a remarkable lady.

Freeland, Dixon B., 1949–1953

He followed his father into the NPS in 1949, serving first in Yosemite as a ranger. After working in several other parks he became a superintendent and retired in 1983. Two of his children represent the third generation of Freelands in the National Parks: daughter Serra F. Sampsell is a maintenance worker at Harpers Ferry and married to a ranger; son Dixon David Freeland is a ranger.

Freeland, Edward Dixon, 1923–1929

Dixon, as he preferred being called, began his NPS career as a young ranger in Yosemite from 1923 until 1929. He was a member of the first five-man snow survey team that snowshoed into the high country carrying their food and gear, and headed Valley Patrol (motorcycle, horse, and car) for two years. His leadership abilities and poise with notables were so obvious that NPS Director Mather transferred him to Carlsbad Caverns National Park as chief ranger in 1929. After that he served as superintendent at five National Parks during an eminent 38-year career. He died in 1986.

Gallison, Arthur L., 1915–1953

Art represented the third generation of the Gallison-Turner family in Mariposa County when he was born there in 1896. At age 16 he went to work in the Park, and three years later became a ranger. After a year away during WW I he received an appointment as storekeeper and property clerk. That was 1919, and he remained, with promotions, in that line of work until he retired in 1953. His wife, Ruby Pearson, had been one of Mother Curry's girls at Camp Curry. The Gallisons had three children: Dorothy, Glenn—who became a ranger—and Robert.

Legacy: Gallison Lake near Tuolumne Meadows. In 1916 Art, a famed fisherman, was the first to plant trout in this lake.

Gallison, Glenn D., 1947–1957

Like his dad, Glenn was a champion fisherman. He joined the Park Service in 1947 as a ranger. In 1956 he became a ranger-naturalist, then moved to Olympic National Park, where he was the chief naturalist. Altogether he served the NPS for 38 years. He and his nurse wife, Beth, had four sons.

Gammill, Walter H., 1952–1970

Walter had been a ranger for 21 years before transferring to Yosemite. For several years he was the hard-working district ranger at Tuolumne Meadows. In 1960 he became district ranger at Wawona. He and his wife, Frances, had two children, Walter Jr. and Anita. She married a seasonal ranger, Bob Petersen, in the Yosemite Chapel.

Garrison, Lemuel "Lon," 1935–1939

Garrison's book, *The Making of a Ranger, 40 years with the National Parks*, is the basis for some of the longest and most amusing quotes in this narrative. His onward and upward career took him and his popular wife, Inger, to many places and positions before his retirement in 1973 and death in 1984 at age 80. Lon and Inger had a son, Lars, and a daughter, Karen. Their youngest son, Erik, who was born at Yosemite, died near the Grand Canyon at age 13.

Legacy: *The Making of a Ranger, 40 Years with the National Parks.*

Gaylor, Andrew J. "Jack," 1907–1921

Before he became a ranger, in September 1907, Gaylor spent two seasons packing for the Cavalry. He had been a packer earlier in such spots as Wyoming, Alabama, Cuba, and Manila. His Yosemite life was tamer but nonetheless adventurous; he died at Merced Lake in 1921 (see Chapter 5).

Legacy: No fewer than three Gaylor Lakes near Tioga Pass are named for Jack.

Givens, Frank R., 1930–1944

Yosemite was the first stop in a career that led Givens to a post as superintendent of the Virgin Islands, whence he retired in 1967. That he must have been a good skier was attested by a verse Bert Harwell wrote in the Givens' guest book:

Frank and I went out to ski
The snow was fine and dandy
Frank skied down upon his skis
And I slid on my fanny.

Godfrey, William C., 1927–1929

His Yosemite stay was brief, but his tenure at Crater Lake, where he was transferred as chief ranger in May of 1929, was even briefer. There he died of exposure on an official trip the following November.

Legacy: Bill contributed pieces on the Mariposa Grove, which he also illustrated, to *Yosemite Nature Notes* .

Godfrey, Elizabeth H. "Babs," 1929–1945

Bill's widow, Babs, and their infant son, Billy, returned to Yosemite Valley, where she worked for 15 years as the museum secretary and became a historian. In 1945 she transferred to Region Four.

Legacy: Her articles in *Yosemite Nature Notes* on subjects such as Yosemite Indians, artists, and pioneers are still consulted. She was the author of a special issue on the Indians, in 1941.

Haines, Oliver L., 1914

Haines, a 22-year-old student at Cal-Berkeley, was one of the college boy rangers. He lived in an abandoned cavalry cabin at the site of the former Camp A.E. Wood. That was the first of many such accommodations he had since he served in the U.S. Cavalry during WW I. He continued in the service and eventually became a general.

Legacy: A letter written from his cabin in 1914, telling a little about his job (see Chapter 2).

Hall, Ansel F., 1920–1923

Not long after Ansel Hall arrived in Yosemite, he had an accident while on motorcycle patrol and suffered a broken leg. Since Chief Ranger Townsley needed every one of his ten rangers, he assigned Hall to the information desk, a job he could handle in a wheelchair. Whenever he had time, Hall researched and wrote about Yosemite. He was the first park naturalist of Yosemite. As chief naturalist of the NPS, with an office in Berkeley, he painstakingly built a large-scale relief model of Yosemite Valley. He used a jigsaw, cardboard, modeling clay, and 25 pounds of brads. It merited an article in the *Christian Science Monitor* at the time, and floor space in the museum ever since.

Legacy: Compiled and edited two books: a 98-page *Guide to Yosemite* (1920) and the *Handbook of Yosemite National Park* (1921).

Hallock, Louis W., 1944–1949

Lou served in two NPS units before coming to Yosemite, where his performance as a ranger shone. He was promoted to chief ranger in three major parks before becoming a superintendent, retiring from Lassen in 1967.

Hansen, John J., 1940–1944.

Irreverent Johnny worked for the Curry Company and the Yosemite post office after his stint as a ranger. He left a widow, Pat, and two adult children when he died in the late 1980s.

Hartesveldt, Richard J., (seasonal) 1950–1959

Dick researched and wrote the first textbook on the need for fire in the life of the giant sequoias. Although it took 20 years for the NPS to accept the importance of fire's role, Hartesveldt's findings were the cornerstone of modern fire-control practices. Dick was a Ph.D. and taught at San Jose State.

Legacy: *Fire and Ecology of the Giant Sequoias,* a landmark book, published in 1965.

Harwell, Charles A. "Bert," 1929–1940

Bert was locally famous for his bird imitations, whistling, and versifying, all of which made him the Pied Piper of Yosemite. He directed the early days of the Yosemite Field School of Natural History. His wife, Emma, taught school in Berkeley, but their children, Ruberta and Everett, were often with him in Yosemite.

Legacy: He encouraged local Indians to continue their tribal customs and ancient crafts, and he began the Junior Ranger program, which continues today.

Heller, Elwyn M. "Bud," (seasonal) 1928–1963

Bud was one of the faithful long-term seasonals Yosemite attracts. He retired in early 1963 at age 60.

Henneberger, John, 1951–1956

John was transferred to Yosemite because of his mountaineering experience, although he had to be rescued himself on his first Yosemite climb. He redeemed himself on many other difficult rescues, some of which are recorded in Chapters 7 and 10.

Legacy: Even in the 1950s he was working on his monumental manuscript about the history of rangers in all national parks. A copy of it is available in the Yosemite Research Library. Now retired, John is working on several NPS historical projects.

Herkenham, Norman B., 1948–1955

Norm attended the 1941 Yosemite Field School prior to joining the Navy for four years. In 1948 he returned to Yosemite and became assistant park naturalist in 1950.

Herschler, J. Barton, 1929–1938

A park ranger in Yosemite, Herschler transferred to Rocky Mountain National Park as chief ranger in 1938. He retired as superintendent of Saguaro National Monument in 1958.

Hilton, Elton, 1925–1946

He was the Park's engineer during the period of the greatest development of roads and trails. His wife, Viola, was a homemaker, and their only child, Winifred, attended all eight grades of the Yosemite school.

Hodges, Clare Marie, (seasonal) 1918

On her first visit to Yosemite, age 14, she met the venerable Galen Clark. In 1918, she returned as the only school teacher and talked herself into a summer job as the park's first woman ranger (see Chapter 8).

Legacy: Not only was Clare Hodges the first woman ranger in Yosemite but the first woman ranger in the NPS.

Holmes, Arthur G., 1928–1930, 1935–1942, 1946–1956

Art's ranger life revolved around Yosemite, although he worked in other parks during his 36 years with the National Park Service. He was a handsome fellow who liked the gals and vice versa. He was married three times and had three children. Anita and Bill maintain his small cabin in Foresta, and their mother, Art's second wife, Dot, still spends part of her summers there. Art was 92 when he died in 1997 (see Chapter 5).

Legacy: Photographs and journals dealing with outpost life in the 1920s and 1930s, now held in the Yosemite Research Library.

Homuth, Earl U., 1945–1959.

Yosemite was his last Park Service position before he retired. His first name was misspelled 'Early' in Bingaman's book.

Hoyt, Homer B., 1923–1959

In his 36 years with the Park Service, Homer never left Yosemite, which he loved and served selflessly (see Chapter 5).

Legacy: A mass of interesting photographs of the park and its people, now in the Yosemite Research Library, and his cryptic but insightful patrol diary covering the years 1923 to 1928.

Hubbard, Douglass H, 1937, 1952–1966

Doug was a young and lowly museum aide when he first worked in Yosemite, in 1937. He was back in the Park briefly in 1940 to attend the Field School. In 1952 he returned to Yosemite to stay for 14 years. He was promoted to Chief Park Naturalist in 1959. He and his classy wife, Fran, had four children, David, Hoppy, Joan, and Janet, all of whom attended Yosemite Elementary.

Legacy: The Pioneer History Center at Wawona, sometimes called "Doug's Berry Farm," was Hubbard's baby, a place of preserved history and an enduring legacy.

Irwin, Oscar F., 1929–1935

Bingaman wrote that Irwin was 38 when he joined the service. He resigned six years later because of poor health.

Jacobs, Duane D. "Jake," 1932–1942, 1946–1953

The hiatus in Jake's Yosemite career was caused by a year as acting superintendent of Joshua Tree National Monument followed by three more with Uncle Sam's Navy. When he returned to Yosemite he was made assistant chief ranger under Sedergren. Jake was a steady achiever with an early interest in rescue work (see Chapter 7). After he left Yosemite for the second time he continued to achieve in high positions. He died in 1977. His wife, Althea, and only child, Nola June, survive.

Jake's legacy in my mind was his fairness and friendliness even to a child. I was nine when he impressed me with the low-key way he enforced the rules about pets and weapons. The "pet" was a leashed cat, the "weapon" my ineffectual slingshot that had come with my family and the cat from a highway job on the Sonora Pass road to a construction camp at Tuolumne Meadows. My lifelong love affair with Yosemite and respect for its guardians began with that paradise and with Jake's introduction to conservation.

Johnson, Odin S. "Sig," 1931–1941, 1942–1967

A quiet man, Sig was sometimes the butt of Scandinavian jokes, but his only reaction was a grin. He witnessed Chief Townsley's death and acted as one of the pallbearers. His wife was Sue and their children Ingrid, Julia, and Eric.

King, Sam, 1931–1948.

Sam was a high achiever from the time he joined the National Park Service at Hot Springs National Park, through his years at Yosemite and as superintendent of various parks and monuments before his retirement in 1966. He had a devoted wife, Norma, who outlived him. They had no children.

Kittredge, Frank A., 1941–1947

Kittredge had had careers with the Bureau of Public Roads and both the NPS regional and Washington offices before becoming a superintendent, first at Grand Canyon and then at Yosemite. A few months after he arrived, WW II began. Administration was complicated by a barebones budget and lack of manpower, since many rangers enlisted. Pseudo-patriotic interests, increased poaching and trespassing, and the fear of sabotage at Hetch Hetchy were everyday problems. In addition, the Navy took over the Ahwahnee Hotel, and military units trained in the Park. All this posed injury to the priceless environment. Kittredge was recognized in the Park for his protective diplomacy. Despite the fact that no liquor sales were allowed in the Park at that time, and he was a strict teetotaler, he was forced to allow beer to be sold to servicemen in a fenced area adjoining the store. Behind his back, it was known as "Frank's Place."

Lawson, Eric, (seasonal) 1914

He was one of the seven "college boy" rangers.

Leavitt, Ernest P., 1910–1931

After years of clerical work, partly for the army, he was promoted to assistant superintendent in 1916, under W. B. Lewis. Leavitt was the first non-military man to hold that position. Later he was superintendent at both Hawaii and Crater Lake national parks. He married Ann Canova of Coulterville. His sister, Amy, married Fred Alexander, longtime postmaster of Yosemite.

Legacy: A single well-proportioned sequoia tree, still standing along the driveway to Residence #1 at the site of the long-gone assistant superintendent's house.

Leidig, Charles T., 1898–1907, 1914–1916

Leidig, son of pioneering hotelkeepers, was the first white boy born in Yosemite Valley. His worth as a forest ranger was disputed, and was ultimately ended by army commander Benson (see Chapter 1). Inexplicably, he was rehired for the summers of 1913 and 1914. Art Gallison, who was an expert with the rod himself, said Leidig was the "best fisherman I ever saw."

Leonard, Archie C., 1898–1917

Like Leidig, Leonard was appointed special forest agent, soon called forest ranger, in 1898. During summers he guided and scouted for the Cavalry, and in the winter absence of troops he and Leidig patrolled and maintained law and order. It was a thankless job for which they were poorly paid and worked seven days a week, sometimes dawn to dark (see Chapter 2). A taciturn, capable man, he worked hard. Susie, his wife, was part Native American. They had several children.

Lewis, Washington Bartlett "Dusty," 1916–1928

"Dusty" excelled in everything he attempted, and he did a splendid job as Yosemite's first civilian superintendent. With scant funds he organized the Park and oversaw its early and greatest development. Heart attacks ended his promising career in 1928, and his life two years later. He was only 46 when he died. He was survived by his wife, Bernice, and young son, Carle (see Chapter 3).

Legacy: Lewis Creek, which flows into the Merced River from Gallison Lake and Bernice Lake, and Mt. Lewis in the high country near Tioga Pass.

Lloyd, James V., 1916–1932

Jimmie, as he was known, was adept at photography and, of all things, chiropractic. He was one of the earliest civilian rangers and became a management assistant to Superintendent Lewis. The administration was so short on funds that Lloyd had to buy his own camera, but he often sold photos to newspapers to make extra money. Not only was he the park photographer, but he excelled at public relations and became liaison man with the Mariposa County officials. His retentive memory was an asset then and later. After he and his wife, Ethel, were transferred from Yosemite, he was superintendent at several locations. Altogether he served the government a total of 52 years, 49 of them with the NPS, an unequaled record.

Legacy: Photographs. Lots of photographs!

Lowery, Vernon, 1929–1931, 1934–1942

Not much has been unearthed about this man who spent some time at Hetch Hetchy overseeing the dam workers. He left the Park Service in 1942, probably for service in World War II.

Mahoney, John M., 1947–1959

With the exception of 18 months as superintendent of Muir Woods, Mahoney spent 11 years in Yosemite. His specialty was forestry; he succeeded Emil Ernst as chief forester in Yosemite. He had a grin that wouldn't stop.

Mahoney, William Patrick Jr., (seasonal) 1936–1939

While attending Notre Dame, Mahoney worked in Yosemite during summer vacations. His wife's great uncle was James D. Phelan, mayor of San Francisco, who was an important force in seeing that Hetch Hetchy Valley became a dam site for San Francisco. Ironically, Hetch Hetchy was Mahoney's favorite place in the Park, and he enjoyed keeping the workers on the straight and narrow during the additional work on the dam from 1936 to 1938.

Legacy: His unpublished memoirs, which enhance this book (see Chapter 6).

Martischang, Fredrick M. "Marty," 1946–1958

One of Marty's more traumatic experiences in Yosemite was being flooded out of Arch Rock when his wife, Olive, was pregnant with their first child. They sat in their car, blocked by a rock slide a mile up the road. "I prayed a lot," he remembered. Ranger Bob Sharp and his wife were similarly marooned. Another sad experience for Marty was having to tell campers that their 10-year-old son had slipped and fallen to his death over Yosemite Falls. His proudest moment came when he was asked to return for special duty helping to guard President John F. Kennedy in 1962. In 1965, Olive, by then mother of three children, Mike, Lisa and Steve, died of a brain tumor. That, naturally, was the saddest event of his life.

McComas, Stanley, 1948–1951

Stationed in Yosemite for only three years, Stan, a popular ranger, moved up in NPS ranks after he left Yosemite.

McHenry, Donald E., 1947–1956

Don headed the naturalist division for 11 years before retiring early. In 1950 his wife, Bona Mae, became the first kindergarten teacher at the Yosemite school. They had two sons, Bruce and Keith; the latter died as a teenager in 1955 from a severe sunburn received while skiing shirtless.

McIntyre, Robert N., 1942–1950, 1953–1959

Wherever he was stationed, Bob's service was notable; Yosemite was no exception. During WW II he saw action as a naval officer in both the Pacific and the Atlantic. After returning to Yosemite, in 1946, he became a naturalist. His had a successful career and won many honors, such as a citation from the Secretary of the Interior. He and his wife, Maymie, had two children, Bob Jr. and Laura.

Legacy: Under Frank Kowski, Bob helped found and direct the first park ranger training school. It was well received and attended while offered in Yosemite. It was then was moved to a permanent site at the Grand Canyon, where it was renamed the Horace M. Albright Training Center.

McLaren, Richard C., 1952–1961

Dick was a member of a solid NPS family. His father, Fred, was a ranger as were two brothers, Doug and Bert. Dick was the only one to serve in Yosemite. He was a "hands-on" ranger, capable and willing to do anything he asked others to do. He and his wife, Lady Dee, had two daughters, Kathy and Pam. Dick was assistant chief ranger at Grand Canyon when he retired, in 1980. He died in 1991.

McLaughlin, James L., 1954–1961

He spent a lot of time as district ranger for the Arch Rock area with headquarters in El Portal. It was McLaughlin who had to keep the peace when Foresta inholders were served condemnation papers. He retired in 1980 and died in 1995.

McNabb, George R., 1915–1930

Before his time as a park ranger, George was with the cavalry. Primarily he was a carpenter, a job he returned to after a few years as ranger. He died in 1930.

Mernin, Gerald E., Jr., (seasonal) 1957–1960
It was only natural that Jerry Jr. would serve in his boyhood haunt at least as a seasonal.

Mernin, Gerald E., Sr., 1929–1947
Gerry was a big Irishman who became a Yosemite district ranger in 1946 after working all over the Park. A few months with the highway patrol and two years of wartime service had delayed his promotion. Before he had time to truly savor the new responsibilities, he was transferred to the Blue Ridge Parkway as chief ranger.

Merriam, Laurence C., 1937–1941
Merriam succeeded C. G.Thomson, who died in office, to become the third civilian superintendent. He arrived in Yosemite in June 1937, and his baptism was the December 1937 flood. His wife, Catherine, and two sons, Larry and John, had to evacuate Residence #1, after their back porch was carried off by the raging Yosemite Creek. The teenagers loved the experience, but Merriam shouldered responsibility for the flood during and afterwards. It did more property damage than subsequent floods because nothing had been done in the way of prevention. In August of 1941, Merriam was appointed director of Region 2 in Nebraska.

Merrill, Wilfred "Billy," 1927–1937, 1942–1949
"Two Gun Billy" was known for his display of revolvers and rigid enforcement of rules. He was a great outdoorsman, and after his retirement, in 1958, he wrote successfully for outdoor magazines. His wife, Margaret, authored *Bears in my Kitchen.*

Meyer, Leo, 1914
He was among the seven "college boy" rangers.

Michael, Enid, 1921–1942
Enid was a character, and could be abrasive, but her passionate interest in nature and wildlife produced fine work. She was 38 when she was hired, 59 when she quit after her husband's death. She wrote voluminously for the *Stockton Record* and *Yosemite Nature Notes.* Her specialty was botany and birds. She and her husband, Assistant Postmas-

ter Charlie Michael, took many pictures and filmed wildlife.

Legacy: Although altered over the years since she began it, the wildflower garden, now part of the Indian Village, was developed under her direction, having been designed by Ansel Hall.

Miller, Merlin, (seasonal) 1945–1970
Merlin turned out to be Sedergren's speed cop. He and his wife, Betty, spent 25 happy summers in Camp 6, part of the time with their children, Ronald, Suzanne, and Carolyn, who was born in Yosemite.

Legacy: The adventures he relived for this book (see Chapter 6).

Moe, Lester M., 1940-1942, 1945-1966
After three years at Glacier National Park, Les came to Yosemite as a ranger. After service in WW II he worked in Yosemite except for a brief interval in soggy Rainier National Park, where he, his wife, Nelle, and children Nancy, Maynard and Allen, suffered from health problems and homesickness. Once back in Yosemite, he transferred to the engineering department. Frank Ewing was building the trails, but some of them were laid out by Les. Nancy had one of the few lasting Yosemite romances, for she married Bob Eckart, also a graduate of Mariposa Elementary School.

Legacy: A series of panoramic photographs Moe took from fire lookouts located in state and national parks. They were used at lookouts to pinpoint fires, and some are still in use.

Moody, Warren "Jack," (seasonal) 1927–1937
Moody was a teacher by vocation but an outdoorsman by avocation. He was an excellent and conscientious ranger who admired Townsley as a "superb rider" and Freeland as a "natural leader."

Legacy: An autobiographical book called *Yosemite Ranger on Horseback,* published in 1990, and quoted in Chapter 6 of this book.

Morehead, John M. "Jack," 1954–1955, 1971–1974, 1986–1989
Colorado native Jack Morehead spent over 40 years, including time in the military, as a government employee, most of that with the NPS. Despite mishaps and misadventure in Yosemite, he

achieved high position there—as chief ranger and later as superintendent. He married Patricia Crabb and they had a daughter, Shawn, and son, Mark.

Legacy: Jack's memories enliven Chapter 10.

Morse, Walter B., 1922–1932

The "silver dollar" ranger stayed only 10 years, but his motorcycle wreck was talked about for years longer than that (see Chapter 5).

Mullady, John T., 1947–1956

Johnny was a typical "buck ranger" (bucking for promotion along with many others). He was a stickler for rules and also a bit of a dandy who carried 21 freshly ironed shirts on a three-week back-country trip with the Sierra Club. The promotion came when he was selected to be chief ranger of Organ Pipe Cactus National Monument in Arizona. His father was an NPS attorney.

Murdock, Nelson, 1954–1960

After six years with the Forest Service and 15 with the NPS, Nels spent six as assistant chief ranger in Yosemite, mostly under Oscar Sedergren. His next job was as chief ranger at Yellowstone.

Myers, William A., (seasonal) 1930–1932

While a 90-day wonder at Tuolumne Meadows during vacations from Stanford, Bill wrote entertaining columns for his hometown newspaper. In 1933, his father gathered them together with work of his own into a book that was published in Michigan.

Legacy: The rare *Back Trails* is quoted extensively in Chapter 5. Bill's characterizations of Carl Sharsmith and Henry Skelton are marvelous. So is his detailed account of a ranger's day.

Neely, William L., (seasonal) 1951–1975

Will's love for Yosemite was mirrored in his journals (see Chapter 10).

Legacy: Will's published journals, particularly *A Yosemite Naturalist's Odyssey*, edited and published by Alan Shields, Jerseydale Ranch Press, 1994.

Neilson, Keith, 1955–1962

Neilson was assistant superintendent under Preston. He was an able man, with 30 years of NPS background in administration budget and accounting. In Yosemite he played an important part in implementing Mission 66.

Nelson, Dan, 1955–1961

Bingaman wrote that Nelson was Yosemite's fire chief and assistant chief ranger before transferring to Glacier NP as chief ranger.

Nelson, William H. "Billy," 1917–1936, 1943–1945

Billy served in every job Yosemite offered, even acting chief ranger during Townsley's 1934 absence. For seven years he was in charge of the campgrounds in the Valley, which he checked from his white Arabian, "Sheik." Because he was capable and colorful, he was chosen to escort the King of Belgium in 1919. He began their trip in his own inimitable way, saying, "The Chief told me what I was to say to you, but I've forgotten, so you call me Billy and I'll call you King." In July 1934, Billy was one of the rangers who accompanied Eleanor Roosevelt on a camping trip to Young Lakes. It was he who supplied her with a hot water bottle. When the First Lady returned to Yosemite in 1940, Townsley, who chauffeured her from San Francisco, took her to see Billy in retirement. Billy was 63 when he retired in 1936, but seven years later he donned his uniform again to help out during WW II. He was survived by his wife, Carolyn, when he died in 1952.

Legacy: Nelson Lake, a 16-acre lake six miles from Tuolumne Meadows, at elevation 9,636.

Packard, J. W. B., 1946–1951

After three years as a seasonal, Byrne became a permanent ranger in Yosemite, and in 1951 transferred to Crater Lake.

Parker, Harry C., 1940–1942, 1946–1952

Harry's initial exposure to Yosemite and its wildlife was as a member of the 1936 Field School of Natural History. He was 30 and already director of a Massachusetts natural history center. In 1940 he joined the NPS. After a few months in Olympic NP in 1940 he transferred to Yosemite as a naturalist, made an immediate hit with the staff and public, and met Katherine "Kit" Johnson, another Field Schooler. They were married at the base of El Capitan in October 1942. A month later, Harry left for service in WW II. When he returned after four years in the Aleutians, he assumed a managerial position with the Yosemite Natural History Association and its periodical *Yosemite Nature Notes.* Harry excelled in everything he did—lecturing, writing, editing, and interpreting. Unfortunately, he died in 1961 at the height of his career. Survivors were his wife, Kit, a son, Harry Mac, and a daughter, Betsy.

Legacy: *Mammals of Yosemite,* first published in 1952.

Parsegan, Edward L., 1950–1956

John Bingaman liked to tell of the time he told Ed to saddle up and ride to a fire. When Martha looked out a bit later and saw that Parsegan had the saddle on backward, she ran out of the station hollering "Ed! Ed!" just as he was trying to figure out how to get on the horse. Martha resaddled the animal, and presumably Ed learned. However, he continued to annoy fellow patrol rangers by wrapping freshly caught fish in his sleeping bag to keep them safe from bears, which, naturally, attracted them instead. He had many other such exciting experiences, although not marked by ineptitude. One was the 1955 flood, which forced him and John Henneberger to evacuate Arch Rock entrance station (see Chapter 9).

Pearson, Grant, 1939–1942

Pearson loved Mt. McKinley, where he later became superintendent. Nevertheless, he asked to go to Yosemite to get experience with crowds. Townsley saw that he got that and then some.

Legacy: A rare and entertaining autobiography, entitled *My Life of High Adventure,* which is quoted in Chapter 5. His impressions of the Chief are still humorous.

Presnall, Clifford C., 1929–1933

A ranger-naturalist under Bert Harwell, Cliff enjoyed exploring and camping in Yosemite. His wife, Ruby, compiled, lettered, and made good sketches for a pamphlet she titled *Songs of Camp and Trail.* Talk about rare editions! Cliff's writing was limited to three articles in *Yosemite Nature Notes.* He moved to Zion NP in 1933.

Preston, John C., 1952–1965

From his beginning with the NPS in 1926, John

was a comer. By November of 1952, when he transferred to Yosemite as superintendent, he had had a wealth of experience in four national parks, two as superintendent, and in Washington, D.C. That background served him well during the implementation of Mission 66, the battles with the preservationists over the building of the new Tioga road, and the increasing encroachment of commercialism. His 13-year tenure in Yosemite was challenging and rewarding. He and his gracious wife, Elizabeth ("Betty"), earned their retirement but even then kept moving. During his retirement John served many times as hearing officer for hearings on wilderness establishment. He died in 1989, she in 1997.

Prien, Oliver R., 1913–1916

Prien's tenure was short. See chapter 3 for background on the controversial first chief ranger in Yosemite, who served in that position less than a year before being asked to resign.

Quick, Clyde, (seasonal) 1944–1973

Quick was such an excellent and long-tenured seasonal that he deserves inclusion in this list. His wife, Arthayda, was another important asset to the NPS (see Chapter 8). Clyde died in July 1986, a day before his 75th birthday.

Reed, Ernest R., 1918–1939

Ernie was 40 when he joined the NPS in Yosemite after working with the Fred Harvey eating houses for years. That he enjoyed his own cooking was obvious from his corpulence and that of his wife, Jessie. Bingaman said they "lived to eat." Ernie's earliest job in the park was running the old Bridalveil checking station. During winters, however, he often utilized his culinary skills to act as cook in the Rangers Club. After the All-Year Highway opened, in 1926, he was in charge of the Arch Rock entrance station. A jovial greeter, he did the landscaping around the station as well. He died of a heart attack in Lewis Memorial Hospital in 1939, survived only by Jessie, a host of friends, and well-wishers.

Reymann, John, (seasonal) 1931–1931

Much to everyone's surprise, Will and Midge's

Peck's-bad-boy son John grew up to be a ranger, although not for long.

Legacy: Information given to Ansel Hall, and tape recordings of his growing up in Yosemite Valley, made for the author. He died in May 1998, age 84.

Reymann, William M., 1927–1938

A native of Mariposa County, where his parents and grandparents pioneered. As a young man, Bill was associated with mines in Nevada. He began work in Yosemite as a powerhouse operator about 1918 but became a ranger in 1927. Bill was an ardent ranger-naturalist with a great interest in wildlife. He and his wife, Flora "Midge" Haigh, a nurse and also a native of the county, befriended local Indians. He died on New Year's Day in 1938, of complications following major surgery. He was only 54.

Legacy: With help from machinist Al Kottner and blacksmith Fred Bruschi, Reymann created the first mobile bear trap with a large piece of culvert pipe mounted on the axle and frame of a quad (four-wheel-drive) truck with hard rubber wheels. Modified versions of the trap are still in use today.

Rich, Charles B., 1919–1927

During his eight Yosemite years, Rich was a law enforcer working undercover, and caught several criminals. While the All-Year-Highway was under construction, largely by convicts, Rich tracked and arrested a few who tried to escape. In 1927 he resigned to join the Secret Service in Washington, D.C., but returned to Yosemite at least twice, guarding president Franklin D. Roosevelt in 1938 and his wife in 1940.

Riegelhuth, John "Jack," 1940–1945

Jack began work in the park at the ripe old age of 23, and survived some tricky climbing. Much later, his brother Dick was the longtime chief of natural resources in Yosemite.

Robinson, Homer W., 1940–1953

An assistant chief ranger, Robinson was in charge of fire suppression. In addition, he was a good all-round ranger who was always interested in helping young rangers. His wife, Grace, and he had two children, Homer "Pete" and Patricia.

Legacy: *The History of Business Concessions in Yosemite National Park,* a small landmark booklet published by YNN in June 1948. It is still used and prized by historians for its accuracy and detail.

Russell, Carl P., 1923–1929, 1947–1952

During his first time in Yosemite, Carl succeeded Ansel Hall as chief park naturalist, a job he enjoyed in a place he loved. He directed the preparation of exhibits for the then new Yosemite Museum as well as acquiring historical artifacts and memorabilia for the archives. He directed all naturalist activities such as walks, talks, and slide shows. He researched and wrote numerous articles and began the first edition of *One Hundred Years in Yosemite,* which was published in 1932. He expressed reservations against the exploitation of bears at the feeding platforms each night when it was popular with visitors. He urged non-molestation of the bears, not exploitation, and certainly not slaughter, as some people advocate after every incident—usually provoked by humans. He was a whirlwind. Socially, he and his wife, Betty, and son, Dick, were active in the Yosemite community. (A daughter died young.) When Russell returned in 1947 it was as superintendent, a complex job while Yosemite boomed, visitation accelerated, and Harold Ickes was a hands-on Secretary of the Interior. Russell retired late in 1952 to write two books on the western fur trade.

Legacy: *One Hundred Years in Yosemite,* now in its seventh edition, revised and updated, and still a bible of Yosemite history.

Sault, Herbert R., 1922–1926

Bert was a short-term ranger who packed a lot of experiences and high old times into his tenure. When he was in the valley he stayed at the Rangers Club, rooming with Jimmie Lloyd. Single government employees had dinner together. "That was my downfall," Bert remembered, for he met school teacher Helen Mickel. They were married in 1926 and left Yosemite. Later they had one child, Shirley, who worked in the Park off and on and met her husband there. Bert's children by his first marriage have always been Yosemite devotees. Juanita, "Salty," worked at the hospital, where she met a doctor whom she later married. Jack was a lineman and lumberjack, and Bill was a student at Yosemite Elementary School.

Legacy: A number of tape recordings Bert made recounting some of his humorous experiences in the Park. Some are quoted in this book.

Scarborough, Charles R. "Chuck," 1953–1953

Chuck worked as assistant chief ranger for a little over a year before being tragically killed in a rock slide (see Chapter 10).

Sedergren, Oscar A., 1944–1958

Sedergren had a hard act to follow as Yosemite's chief ranger, since his predecessors were Townsley and Wegner. Before long, Sedergren too gained local respect for his leadership and judgement. These qualities had earned his rise from his first NPS job on a trail crew in Sequoia in 1920 through 23 years at Mt. Rainier NP, five of those as its chief ranger. After his Yosemite tenure he was assistant superintendent of Olympic NP. Two years after he retired in 1965, he was awarded the Meritorious Service Award by the Department of the Interior for his 43 years of dedicated service. His wife, Flo, immersed herself in the community, and their daughter, Sandy, said that "Growing up in Yosemite was a fairy-tale existence."

Sharp, Robert H., 1949–1951, 1959–1961

His first service in Yosemite was cut short by poor health, but he came back as the park forester in 1959.

Sharsmith, Carl W., (seasonal) 1931–1994

Dr. Sharsmith, known widely as Carl, was a legend in his lifetime. Three books were written about him even before he died at age 91 in 1994, and another one since. Countless articles were written about his talents, enthusiasms, knowledge, humor, eccentricities, and frugality. Although he hated writing, he had more than 50 articles and reports published, the bulk of them in *Yosemite Nature Notes*. He was a ranger-naturalist, usually stationed at Tuolumne Meadows where he was a pied piper of nature. His longevity of 61 seasons (he missed a few summers) exceeds the 51 years of Jimmie Lloyd, but as a seasonal rather than a permanent ranger. For most of these years he was a professor of botany.

Legacy: A splendid herbarium he put together at San Jose State College, plants named for him, and in the fond memories of thousands who experienced his love of nature. Naturally, he is part of this book.

Skakel, James C., 1936–1942

Formerly with the Border Patrol, Skakel was a loner, happiest when stationed at an outpost like Buck Camp. Details of life in Yosemite were tape-recorded for this book by his son, Bob (see Chapter 8). Eleanor Roosevelt complimented Skakel on his fine horsemanship, which praise he often proudly retold and never forgot.

Skelton, Henry A., 1898, 1915–1932

Skelton was one of the special forest agents in 1898, and was appointed as an NPS ranger in 1915. He did a great deal of mounted patrol work, often alone for days at a time. Later he was named district ranger at Tuolumne Meadows. In 1931, 90-day-wonder Bill Myers mentioned him in a newspaper column: "Henry . . . is one of the best men to work for in the whole outfit. Tuolumne Meadows is now the envy of everybody in the Park, for with Henry as 'head man,' and the natural beauty and seclusion of the country itself, one couldn't ask for a better place to work."

Legacy: Two lakes, one of 10 acres and the other of four, about six miles from Tuolumne Meadows.

Solinsky, Elbert A. "Al," 1915–1929

Solinsky negotiated the timber and land exchanges that saved valuable forest from being logged. In the 1920s, he and Bert Sault measured 685 miles of trails by pushing a bicycle tire equipped with an odometer over them. They put up trail signs the next year. Solinsky became an assistant superintendent in Yosemite before transferring to Crater Lake NP as superintendent. Donna, Barbara, and Jane were his daughters, Dean the only son.

Sovulewski, Gabriel, 1895–1997, 1906–1936

Sovulewski never lost his Polish accent, but he Americanized himself in every other way. After he arrived in the USA in 1888, when he was 22, he joined the US Army, and that brought him to Yosemite for three seasons beginning in 1895. He returned in 1906 to supervise NPS winter operations and before long was named supervisor. His dedication, service, integrity, and hard work, especially in trail building and maintenance, impressed everyone. So integral to Yosemite was he that he, and later his American-born wife, Rose Rider, were allowed to be buried in the small Yosemite Cemetery. They had seven children: Grace, Gabe, Mildred, Bob, Tom, Lawrence, and Joe.

Sovulewski, Thomas, 1949–1950

Tom grew up in Yosemite, and as early as 1922 was a messenger boy for the NPS. Before serving briefly as a ranger, he was a laborer and truck driver. He was also a legendary fisherman.

Sprinkel, Russell, 1929–1941

Sprinkel wasn't a ranger, but as chief clerk in the Yosemite Office, he "kept the rangers honest."

Sproul, Allan, 1914

Sproul was one of the "college boy rangers" in 1914 even though he was barely out of high school when he reported for work. His account of that memorable summer in the Mariposa Grove appeared in the April 1952 *Yosemite Nature Notes,* and is the basis of Chapter 2. Sproul's career in banking was illustrious, and his brother Robert Gordon Sproul was another achiever as president of UC Berkeley from 1930 to 1958.

Legacy: The reminiscences in *Yosemite Nature Notes.*

Stratton, John W., 1957–1961

Since he was a management assistant, John didn't have much experience in the field, but his tale of helping to escort Belgium's King Baudouin to the Mariposa Grove as related in Chapter 10 is delightful.

Thomson, Charles Goff "Colonel," 1929–1937

The ex-Colonel was 46 and superintendent of Crater Lake NP when he was transferred to Yosemite to take ailing Dusty Lewis's place as superintendent. During his active administration, he directed the acquisitions of the Wawona Basin and the Carl Inn tract, the construction of both the Wawona and Glacier Point roads, the supervision of the Civilian Conservation Corps (CCC), and a mul-

tiplicity of other projects. His intelligence, leadership qualities, and sound judgement were respected. A heart attack in March 1937 killed him. His wife, Hazel, and sons Pete and Jeff survived. Pete had a couple of books published later, and the "Colonel" was the author of two novels about the Philippines.

Townsley, Forest S., 1913–1943

An entire chapter of this history is devoted to dynamic, hard-driving, long-time Chief Ranger Forest S. Townsley (see Chapter 4).

Legacy: Twenty-acre Townsley Lake, near Vogelsang High Sierra Camp, was the scene of some of his happiest hours and the place of his sudden death on August 11, 1943.

Townsley, John A., 1950–1959

John was 16 when his father died. He and his mother had to leave Yosemite, where he had lived all his life, but he came back the very next year as a seasonal fire guard, and again in 1947. His next assignment in the Park was as a seasonal ranger from 1950 to 1955, his college years. Ray Warren, who worked under John, spoke of his admiration for him. "He really was sensitive to the environment. 'I don't want a sign of humans in this area when we get through cutting wood' he would tell his crew." One of their jobs in the pre-electricity days of the 1950s was cutting 20 to 25 cords of firewood. "He would challenge us to see who could chop decaying trees the fastest and cleanest, and he always won." After a short time in Hawaii NP, he returned again to Yosemite as a permanent ranger until 1959, when he was sent to Oregon Caves National Monument as a management assistant. After that he was superintendent of five NPS units before becoming head man at Yellowstone NP. It seemed inevitable that he would be transferred eventually to Yosemite as superintendent, but cancer ended his life in 1982. His wife, Elaine Ferris, was working in Yosemite when they met. She, daughter Gail, and sons David and Forest survived him.

Tucker, Thomas R., 1946–1962

Tom added a year to his age, 17, so he could be hired on a trail crew in 1940. Six years later he became a ranger. Everyone liked Tom. He was conscientious, hard-working, and dependable, possessing both common sense and a sense of humor. The only person in the park who intimidated him was Chief Ranger Sedergren, who was chary with praise. In fact, the way Sedergren made Tom district ranger of the Mather district illustrates that. While the Tuckers and Sedergrens were standing in a wedding reception line outside the Rangers Club, Sedergren casually asked Tom, "When can you report to Mather Ranger Station?" Tom was obviously flabbergasted. The chief ranger continued, "You're the new district ranger there. You didn't think I would appoint anyone else, did you?"

In 1962, Tom reluctantly left Yosemite to be superintendent of Cabrillo and Channel Islands National Monument. The allergies of his wife, Evelyn, dictated the move. Their three children, Eva Linda, Tom Jr., and Jim moved also, but Jim returned in 1974 as a ranger.

Legacy: Stories in this book from telephone interviews, tape recordings, and letters.

Uhte, Robert F., 1948–1951

Son of Doris Hallock, ranger Lou Hallock's wife, Uhte (pronounced You-tay) spent two summers as a seasonal and another as a permanent in Yosemite, and then was transferred to the San Francisco regional office.

Legacy: During his summers in Yosemite, Bob researched and wrote an article on Yosemite's pioneer cabins. It was published in the May 1951 *Sierra Club Bulletin,* and later was reproduced as a separate item that is now of ever-increasing value.

Van Bibber, Philip Thomas "Tom," 1947–1951

While stationed at Yosemite Creek on the old Tioga road, Tom was both campground and patrol ranger. After that he worked in maintenance in the Valley until 1963. "There's more money in maintenance," he stated. "I could get married, build a home near Mariposa, and go home weekends."

He married Beverly Heyne, and they had two daughters and a son.

Legacy: A daily log he kept while at Yosemite Creek in 1949 and 1950, excerpts of which appear in Chapters 7 and 8.

Wallis, Orthello L., 1950–1954

Sometimes called "Mr. Fish" because of his intense interest in the history and management of

trout, Wallis was an outstanding man and wrote well. Not only was he on active duty with the Marines in WW II but was wounded on Okinawa. After the war he obtained his Masters degree in fish and game management before returning to Yosemite.

Legacy: Co-authorship of *Fishes of Yosemite National Park,* a special issue first published in 1944. His research and writing of a comprehensive manuscript entitled "Yosemite Trout Investigation, 1951–1953," is held in the Yosemite Research Library.

Walquist, Clarence "Spud," (seasonal) 1948–1948

"Spud" was a particularly competent seasonal. Rod Broyles remembers that "Spud" had lots of savvy, was always pleasant, and was interested in seeing that park visitors were enjoying themselves. He was one of the original Sons of the Pioneers singing group.

Wegner, John H., 1916–1944

Wegner, born in Merced in 1884, worked in the Old Village store before he signed on as a ranger, one of the earliest to work for Yosemite NP. His expertise was in fire control, and he was active in setting up a fire prevention plan. In 1928 he became permanent and was promoted to assistant chief ranger. After Townsley's death Wegner was acting chief ranger for six months before transferring to Sequoia NP as chief ranger. His wife, Rose Thornton, was also from Merced. The couple had one child, a son, who had his name Frances changed to John like his father's.

Legacy: Wegner Lake near Hetch Hetchy, a lengthy interview on park history, and pioneer fire prevention.

Westfall, Archie, 1931–1933

Although he was a ranger only briefly, Mariposa native Arch Westfall was well-known as a packer and corralman. Bill Myers, the 90-day-wonder with a pen, described him in a July 1931 news column: "Then there's Arch Westfall, six foot three, and locally known as 'Highpockets.' Arch is a real cowboy, even if for the time being he has degenerated into a ranger. He has been following the rodeos for a good many years, and has carried off plenty of prizes in roping and bronc-busting."

Witter, Jean C., 1914–1916

He was one of the seven "college boy rangers" in 1914, but he returned for the next two summers. Thanks to oral interviews conducted by the University of California at Berkeley, some details of his first two summers at Crane Flat are printed in this book.

Legacy: He carved his name, fraternity affiliation, and the date 1916 above the door in the Crane Flat patrol cabin, which is now on display at the Pioneer History Center at Wawona. His greater legacy is Dean Witter & Company, which he and his cousins Dean and Guy founded in 1924.

Wosky, John B., 1935–1952

Wosky put in 17 active years as assistant superintendent under Thomson, Merriam, and briefly Kittredge before moving to Crater Lake NP as full superintendent. He had a wife, Naomi, and daughter, Joan, who attended Yosemite Elementary School.

Wright, George M., 1927–1929

Wright did wildlife work in Berkeley for the NPS, then was made head of the Park Service's wildlife program in Washington, D.C. Unfortunately the fine work he was doing was terminated when he was killed in a car wreck at age 32. In Yosemite, he was assistant park naturalist with a keen interest in wildlife.

Index

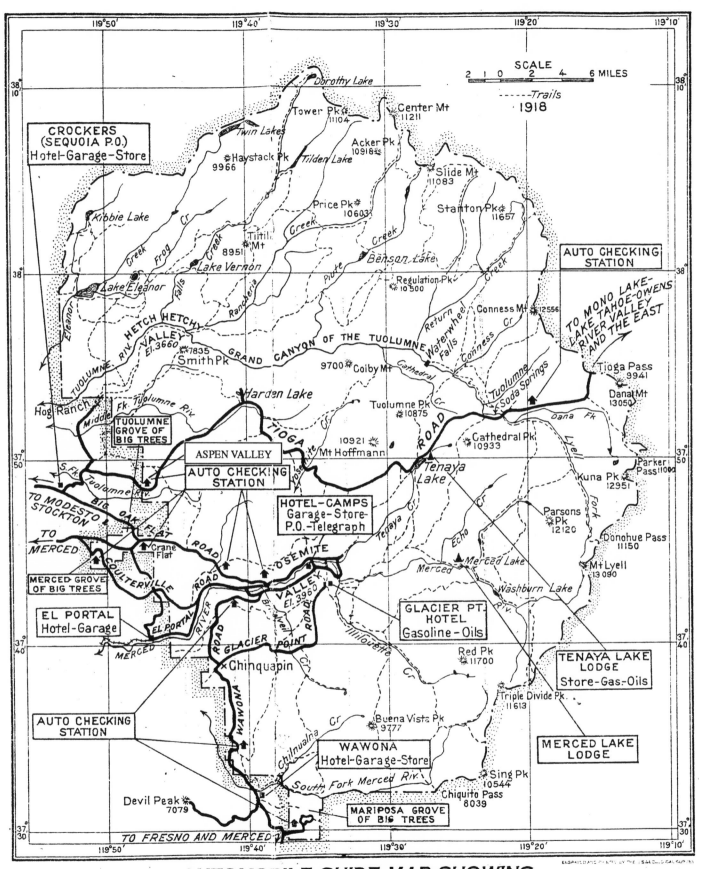

AUTOMOBILE GUIDE MAP SHOWING
ROADS IN THE YOSEMITE NATIONAL PARK
CALIFORNIA